AN ANCIENT EGYPTIAN

BOOK OF THE DEAD

AN ANCIENT EGYPTIAN
BOOK OF THE DEAD

The Papyrus of Sobekmose

Translation, Introduction,
and Commentary by

Paul F. O'Rourke

On the jacket: *(front)* Vignette from Chapter 136B of the papyrus (see fig. 29). The god Re is shown in a solar boat as a falcon head with a sun-disk; the boat rests on a sky-sign surmounting a field of stars; *(back)* A series of vignettes from Chapter 149 of the papyrus (see figs 30–35). They represent places inhabited by supernatural beings whom the deceased must pass by in the Netherworld. *Frontispiece*: Vignette from Chapter 126 of the papyrus (see fig. 40). The rectangular field is a lake of fire that the deceased must pass by in the Netherworld. The four baboons are its divine guardians.

This volume was organized by the staff of the Brooklyn Museum
PROJECT EDITOR: James Leggio, Head of Publications and Editorial Services
COLLECTION PHOTOGRAPHY: Sarah DeSantis, Museum Photographer and Manager of Publication Imaging; and Jonathan Dorado, Assistant Photographer
DIGITIZATION OF HISTORICAL IMAGES: Tracie Davis, former Digital Imaging Archivist
PHOTO RESEARCH: Alice Cork, Picture Researcher

The conservation of the *Book of the Dead of the Goldworker of Amun Sobekmose* was supported through a grant from the Leon Levy Foundation.

First published in the United Kingdom in 2016 by Thames & Hudson Ltd, 181A High Holborn, London WC1V 7QX

An Ancient Egyptian Book of the Dead: The Papyrus of Sobekmose © 2016 Brooklyn Museum
Text and illustrations © 2016 Brooklyn Museum
Layout and design © Thames & Hudson Ltd, London
Designed by Lisa Ifsits

Brooklyn Museum
200 Eastern Parkway
Brooklyn, NY 11238-6052
United States
www.brooklynmuseum.org

British Library Cataloguing-in-Publication Data
A catalogue record for this book is available from the British Library

ISBN 978-0-500-05188-7

Printed and bound in China by C & C Offset Printing Co. Ltd

To find out about all our publications, please visit **www.thamesandhudson.com**. There you can subscribe to our e-newsletter, browse or download our current catalogue, and buy any titles that are in print.

Contents

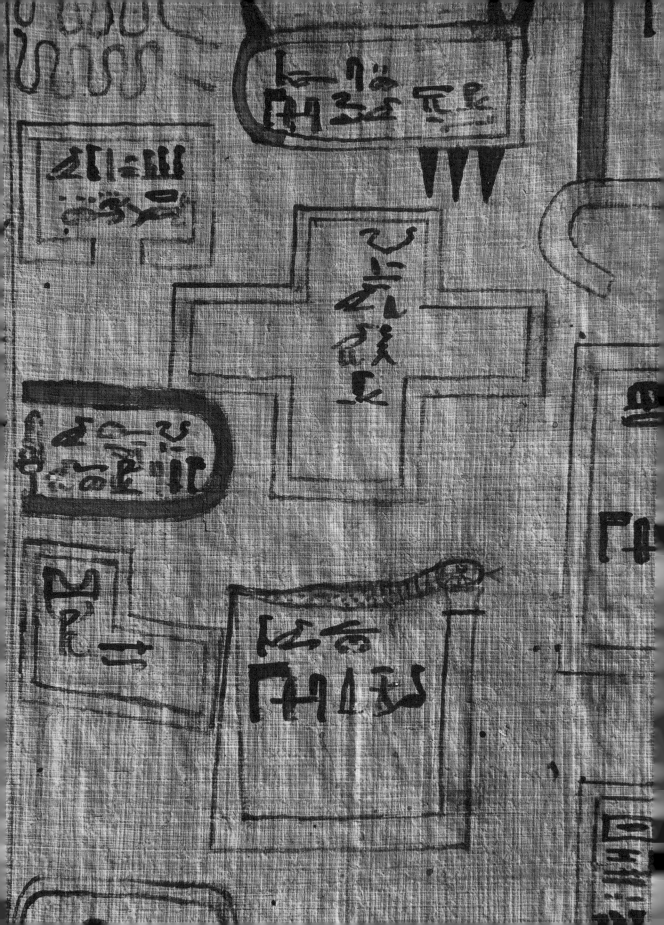

Foreword

Museums are places to look at beautiful objects, firsthand and in the flesh, so to speak. Yet as deeply fulfilling as that experience is, museums also do more. They inspire many visitors to meditate on what our individual lives may mean, in the greater scheme of things. Paul Gauguin memorably inscribed one of his most ambitious paintings with the words "Where Do We Come From? What Are We? Where Are We Going?" Museums, too, often invite us to ask questions about what we sometimes call, for lack of a better term, the human condition.

The ancient papyrus known as the *Book of the Dead of the Goldworker of Amun Sobekmose*, in the collection of the Brooklyn Museum, is a document of the human condition if ever there was one. Among the most important, earliest, and most extensive examples of the Book of the Dead genre, it served the departed goldworker Sobekmose as a guidebook in his journey beyond this world.

In this funerary document, the deceased speaks. Sobekmose appears before a postmortem tribunal and actively argues that he is honest and righteous—therefore fit to enter the next world and take his rightful place among the blessed dead and the gods who reside there. And in many of its almost one hundred chapters, he travels through a shadowy landscape bristling with dangers. Guided by the texts and images contained in his private Book of the Dead, he treks across a Netherworld that tests him at every turn.

Although not intended as a narrative, this ancient scroll nonetheless has a dramatic story to tell: how Sobekmose argues for his right to be reborn into the next world, and how he makes his way through it. The successful completion of his perilous journey affirms that he did indeed live

his life properly, within the Egyptian worldview, and ensures that he and his name will live on in perpetuity. The fulfillment of so basic a human wish can hardly fail to resonate with us across time. Three and a half millennia after his death, Sobekmose and his story can seem very much alive, as Museum visitors encounter his personal papyrus—meticulously conserved, and now splendidly on display in our Egyptian Galleries.

Through the enormous generosity of Shelby White and the Leon Levy Foundation, the Museum was able to conserve and restore this unusually extensive papyrus, and make it accessible to researchers and the public. Over the course of three years, scores of fragments mounted between many sheets of glass turned into a continuous, fully restored ancient manuscript that is now some twenty-five feet in length. While conservation was under way, the Museum commissioned its distinguished research associate Paul F. O'Rourke to make a full, accessible translation into English, introducing today's readers to how the ancient Egyptians thought about the mortal destiny of the individual. The present publication—a major step forward in the literary and scholarly quality, and the sheer readability, of Book of the Dead translations—plays out for us the elusive yet very personal beliefs about "Where Are We Going?" once held by a great civilization.

ANNE PASTERNAK
Shelby White and Leon Levy Director
Brooklyn Museum

Preface: Translating an Ancient Text

Offering a full translation of the *Book of the Dead of the Goldworker of Amun Sobekmose* into English is an ideal way to introduce modern readers to ancient Egyptian ways of thinking about human destiny. The translation can help us to make sense of what may often seem a remote and alien civilization. Moreover, virtually all of the existing translations of material from the Book of the Dead corpus published in English are only compilations of various texts drawn from a number of different sources, or are often available only in excerpt form. This publication is the first to present a continuous translation in English of a single extensive text that can speak to us from beginning to end in the order in which it was composed.

Since an endeavor like this is a daunting one, writers beginning with Aristotle have sometimes given advice on how to conduct a translation, such as this example:

> Whoever wishes to translate, and purposes to render each word literally, and at the same time to adhere slavishly to the order of the words and sentences of the original, will meet with much difficulty. This is not the right method. The translator should first try to grasp the sense of the subject thoroughly, and then state the theme with perfect clearness in the other language. This, however, cannot be done without changing the order of the words, putting many words for one word, or vice versa, so that the subject be perfectly intelligible in the language into which he translates.
>
> Moses Maimonides[1]

In addition, there are special difficulties in translating a religious text, as noted by the Egyptologist François Daumas: "For one who deciphers an Egyptian text for the first time, especially a religious text, some obscurities always remain, just as they do in those that have been translated many times over."[2]

The act of translation is made up of many steps, and each ancient text comes before its translators with its own set of challenges. We do not always know the exact meaning of certain words we encounter. And although we have come far in determining the rules of syntax that govern most sentences we read, we can still be brought up short by the relationship between clauses and sentences. Certain clause types have a wide range of applications—such as causal, temporal, or concessive—leaving the translator with several different avenues of interpretation. For example, "temporal" implies a relationship of simple before-and-after, while "causal" implies direct cause-and-effect—something essentially different. And in treating the utterances of the deceased in the Book of the Dead, existing translations show their greatest variety: some translators will understand a sentence as a declarative statement, others as a wish.

Moreover, ancient texts are rarely free of the errors and problems that arise during the process of copying by hand. Indeed, we cannot even assume that every text has been copied from a reliable exemplar. In addition, a religious text like an Egyptian Book of the Dead brings its own set of difficulties: the language of Books of the Dead abounds in oblique allusions and puzzling metaphors that often remain elusive despite the best efforts of its readers.

The translator's first task is to attempt to establish what the text *says*. Once that step is taken, far more challenging than it may at first appear, the next is to decide what the text *means*, a step that requires, among other things, a (re)examination of *how* the text says what it says. With this complex process in mind, it becomes clear that crafting a translation for a text like the Brooklyn Museum's papyrus *Book of the Dead of the Goldworker of Amun Sobekmose* is arduous and challenging—but highly rewarding.

The translation presented here is the end product of what I hope has been a careful adherence to the logic of these steps. Yet it is far from perfect because, contrary to what Maimonides claims in the quotation cited above, the translation of an ancient religious text can probably never be "perfectly intelligible." Each translation of a text can only be an attempt to "grasp the sense" of the original while staying true (to whatever degree one can) to its language and idioms. Note that Daumas, an eminent and accomplished master of grammar and Egyptian religious literature, used the verb "to decipher" (*déchiffrer*) above to describe his reading of a text, a word that clearly points to the inherent difficulties he saw in undertaking such a task. I have done my best to keep the language of the text foremost in mind when proposing an English rendering. One must be vigilant here, as a document like the Book of the Dead, a sacred text dealing with life and death, must be accorded a high degree of respect. At every moment, one must remain on guard against making the text say what it does not.

Where the textual readings in the *Book of the Dead of the Goldworker of Amun Sobekmose* do not agree with those found in relatively contemporaneous manuscripts, I have not assumed that these differences are due first and foremost to scribal error. I have made every effort to translate the text as it was written.

Of course there are a number of instances where, for example, the scribe has clearly committed the common error of metathesis (the transposition of two or three signs); there, I have translated according to what the scribe obviously intended and not what is actually present in the text. Much more worrisome are the many instances in which the text seems hopelessly garbled and simply makes no sense as it stands. In some such cases, I have given a tentative translation; in others, I have made notations or suggestions in the notes that accompany the translation. In further cases, where the papyrus is damaged and no text appears, I have not made a translation *per se* but have indicated in the notes what may have once been present.

When my friend the architect Jason Chai had finished the home he designed and built for his family, he was asked whether he had finally built his dream house. He replied, "This is today's dream house; that's all we can ever really do." It is in that spirit that the translation presented here is offered.

* * *

A project of this scope and nature often begins as a dream. In the mid-2000s, Toni Owen, Paper Conservator in the Brooklyn Museum at that time, and I began an ongoing discussion about finding a way to conserve the *Book of the Dead of the Goldworker of Amun Sobekmose* so that it could be considered for display in the Egyptian Galleries. Thanks to a generous grant from the Leon Levy Foundation in 2009, the Museum undertook a complete conservation and restoration of the papyrus to include it in a new installation that opened to the public in the spring of 2010, with the Sobekmose papyrus installed in stages as the conservation of different sections was finished. The conservation work was completed in 2011. I offer profound thanks to Shelby White, Trustee of the Leon Levy Foundation, for making all of this possible.

I thank Ken Moser, former Vice Director for Collections at the Brooklyn Museum, and the members of the Conservation Department immediately responsible for the conservation and restoration of the papyrus—Toni Owen, Rachel Danzing, Pavlos Kapetanakis, and Caitlin Jenkins—for their painstaking and determined work, which extended over a period of three years.

During the conservation work, I first undertook this translation in the hope that it could somehow be used in the installation. I had earlier obtained an excellent set of transparencies of the papyrus made before its treatment. The digital images made from those allowed me to begin my initial study of the manuscript. I thank Betty Leigh Hutchinson for producing this set of images, which greatly facilitated my study of the papyrus and my work on the translation.

By the time I had finished the translation, the sheer length of the working manuscript had made it quite clear that the full text could not be accommodated within the space of the gallery. Several selections from the translation were then made, which now appear on handsome panels above the papyrus in the gallery. I thank former Assistant Graphic Designer Tomoko Nakano for their design and creation.

After the installation of the object, a decision was made to prepare the full translation for possible publication. I suggested that I write a series of essays to accompany the translation, as the nature and content of ancient Egyptian religious texts can seem somewhat abstract and foreign, even to the motivated reader. Over time, these essays were consolidated into what now serves as the Introduction to this volume. I would like to thank James Leggio, Head of Publications and Editorial Services. James took a close interest in this project, and his suggestions about how to consolidate the introductory material most effectively made an obvious and immediate improvement to this section of the book. He also offered valuable suggestions about making the translation and its accompanying notes readily accessible to the reader. It has been his firm and patient guidance along the way that made the transformation of manuscript to book so seamless and enjoyable for me. He has also been a staunch advocate that this publication see the light of day.

I thank Sarah DeSantis, Museum Photographer and Manager of Publication Imaging, and Jonathan Dorado, Assistant Photographer, for the photographic plates and the detail images of the papyrus that grace the pages of this book. My thanks go as well to Deborah Wythe, Head of Digital Collections and Services, and Alice Cork, Picture Researcher, for the excellent ancillary images that illustrate the introductory material. Thanks go as well to Collections Manager Walter Andersons and his team of art handlers for quickly and safely making the papyrus available for photography on two separate occasions.

My colleagues in the department of Egyptian, Classical, and Ancient Near Eastern Art—Richard Fazzini, Curator Emeritus, former head of the department, and head of the Brooklyn Museum Mut Expedition in Egypt; Dr Edna R. Russmann, Curator Emeritus; Dr Edward Bleiberg, Curator and current department head; Dr Yekaterina Barbash, Associate Curator; and Kathy Zurek-Doule, Curatorial Assistant—deserve acknowledgment as well. In particular, I would like to thank Edward Bleiberg for his constant and steadfast encouragement as I brought this project from inception to conclusion. I also wish to thank Yekaterina Barbash for reading sections of the manuscript and for her helpful and thoughtful suggestions, from which I routinely benefit in all of my work. In addition, I thank Kathy Zurek-Doule for the immeasurable ways she helped me move through this project and through so many others before this one. She has an uncanny knack for guiding my way clearly through what seems an inextricable maze to me at times. All of the members of my department have always been pillars of endless support and sources of inspiration to me. Words are not enough to convey the magnitude of my thanks to them.

PAUL F. O'ROURKE
Research Associate, Egyptian Collection
Brooklyn Museum

Notes

1 Moses Maimonides, "Letter on Translation," addressed to Rabbi Samuel Ibn Tibbon (12th–13th century). Ibn Tibbon translated Maimonides' *Guide for the Perplexed* from Arabic into Hebrew; that edition first appeared in 1204, followed by a revised edition in 1213 complete with a glossary and Ibn Tibbon's marginal notes. During the translation project the two men appear to have corresponded regularly, although only one letter has survived. Robinson 2014 (see Reference List).

2 Daumas 1958, pp. 4–5.

Introduction

The ancient Egyptians believed that deceased persons found themselves in an afterlife filled with dangers. Some were familiar, such as snakes and scorpions, and others not so familiar, including animal-headed demons that wielded knives and blocked the gateways of the Netherworld, and dangerous areas such as the treacherous Ring of Fire. In order to navigate the realm of the dead safely and successfully, the deceased needed a range of protective and sustaining powers.

To meet this need, the Egyptians of the New Kingdom and later periods often included in a burial a papyrus roll inscribed with texts and in some cases images, a type of document now called a Book of the Dead.[1] A Book of the Dead was not reading matter as we understand the term; rather its texts formed a manual filled with knowledge to help the deceased move freely, and survive, in the next world. Such a papyrus roll in a burial gave the deceased a vital handbook of specialized information.

The *Book of the Dead of the Goldworker of Amun Sobekmose,* in the collection of the Brooklyn Museum, is one of the most important known examples from this genre, partly because of its early date (*c.* 1470 BCE) and its unusual place of origin, Saqqara, as the great majority of contemporary exemplars of the Book of the Dead come from Thebes. As a physical object, too, this particular Book of the Dead papyrus is an impressive treasure from antiquity. The roll is over twenty-five feet long and just under fourteen inches high, and includes a number of images that serve to illustrate the text. The papyrus contains ninety-eight individual chapters (or spells), nearly all of them from the Book of the Dead corpus. A rare example among surviving Books of the Dead, the Brooklyn papyrus is inscribed on both the recto and the verso (the front and the back of the scroll), and in two different types of handwriting, called cursive hieroglyphs and hieratic, respectively.* The placement of extensive texts on the verso is a feature hardly known from other Books of the Dead of the New Kingdom.[2] In both form and content, the Brooklyn papyrus is a unique document of ancient Egypt.

* In this book, specialized words are generally defined at first use. See the Glossary for a selection of technical terms, divine symbols, divine epithets, place names, and the names of gods.

The specialized knowledge in a Book of the Dead was secret and hidden, not to be shared freely, and the language is indeed often enigmatic, but unquestionably in many places evocative and very beautiful. These fascinating texts, concerning matters of life and death, offer a look into the mindset of the ancient Egyptians, highlighting their beliefs and anxieties about this world as well as the next. Let us begin by exploring the relationship between those two worlds.

The Worlds of the Living and the Dead

It is commonly believed that the ancient Egyptians were obsessed with death, and that for them, life itself was little more than a preparation for death. However, a great many texts from Egypt's long antiquity make it clear that this was simply not the case. Instead, such texts speak to us about how people lived their lives at that time and treat of things quite recognizable to the modern reader: for example, we have birth records, marriage contracts, deeds documenting the purchase and sale of property, lawsuits, and divorce agreements (fig. 1), as well as death certificates.[3] The joys and sorrows described in those texts—written in hieratic, demotic, Greek, Latin, and Coptic—resonate for us with the concerns of daily life.

As in most ancient societies, daily life in Egypt imposed physical hardship on all but the most wealthy and powerful. Most of the Egyptian populace lived in relative poverty and simplicity.[4] The non-elite lived largely on and from the soil, and played a major role in the agricultural activity that virtually defined Egyptian society and its economy for millennia (fig. 2). Despite the high percentage of the population that these people comprised, we know little about individual members of this social class before the Ptolemaic and Roman periods.[5] We are much better informed about the lives of the elite, who made up only a fraction of the populace.[6] We know names and have genealogies from which we can trace a family through a number of successive generations. From scenes and texts in tombs and on stelae and from inscriptions on statues, we also have information that has been used in the past in attempts to reconstruct the lives of Egyptian officials (fig. 3).[7] Based on the examination of human remains from Egypt, what can be said is that life was not only challenging, but also bleakly short (perhaps thirty-six years),[8] and families, elite and non-elite alike, had to be quite large to attempt to maintain the population at a stable number.[9]

Old Age. Within that circumscribed lifetime, the onset of old age arrived shockingly early for many. "Senior years" could come as well in the form of early retirement for some, as government administrators, and perhaps even priests, left their jobs so that their sons could assume their positions (fig. 4).[10] Regardless,

Fig. 1 Papyrus with a divorce agreement in Greek
This papyrus outlines the terms of a divorce between Aphrodisia and her husband Ptolemaios.
It specifies that the divorce is a mutual agreement and that Aphrodisia's dowry, bridal goods, and
the real estate purchased by her alone have been restored to her without complaint. Documents
like this one illustrate the legal rights and authority that women enjoyed in ancient Egypt.

Fig. 2 Farming near Bedrasheim, Egypt, *c.* 1966
The image of this modern farmer plowing his field using two donkeys offers a good example
of how traditional, non-industrial modes of farming long continued to be employed.

Fig. 3 Group statue of Nebsen and Nebet-ta
Nebsen was a Scribe of the Royal Treasury and his wife Nebet-ta was a Songstress of Isis, titles that
certainly place their holders within the highest rank of Egyptian society. Their dress, adornments,
and the exceptionally fine quality of their statue also serve to underscore their status.

Fig. 4 Relief of an aged courtier
Representations of the elderly in Egyptian art are more typically encountered in sculpture in the
round. This somewhat rare relief depicts an unnamed but clearly aged individual, as the deep lines
on the face and the swelling of the artery on the forearm convey.

one's later years were not romantically looked forward to as the golden years. As we are rather chillingly reminded:

> *Frailty has come to pass; old age has descended.*
> *The limbs grow heavy, feebleness renewed.*
> *Sleep is escape for him every day.*
> *Strength has come undone; the heart is weary.*
> *The mouth is silent; it cannot speak.*
> *The eyes are weak, the ears deaf.*
> *The heart sleeps, weary every day.*
> *The heart—it cannot remember yesterday.*
> *The bones are in pain all over.*
> *What is good becomes evil.*
> *All taste departs.*
> *What old age does to men is evil in every way.*
>
> Maxims of Ptahhotep (ll. 8–21), 3rd millennium BCE

This condition was endemic not just to Egypt. The curse of old age resonates similarly in many cultures. In the Greek elegiac and lyric traditions, the horrors of old age also resound darkly:

> *But when painful old age comes*
> *That renders a man ugly and ignoble*
> *Base thoughts wear him down; round his thoughts*
> *He does not delight in the rays of the sun as he looks upon them*
> *But (is) both an object of contempt for boys, and one of scorn for women.*
> *So the god has fashioned old age grievous.*
>
> Mimnermus, Poem 1, 7th century BCE[11]

Yet the onset of old age in Egypt was also the time to address important concerns and not merely dwell on its discomforts. The first concern was for the elders of the passing generation to transmit their knowledge to the next generation (typically, to their sons). As we learn further from Ptahhotep:

> *Bid your servant to become a staff of old age (for you).*
> *Instruct him in the matters of the judges,*
> *The wisdom from among the ancestors,*
> *The ones of old who listened to the gods.*
> *Then the like shall be done for you (and)*
> *The hardships of the common people dispelled (and)*

The Two Banks will toil for you ...
Instruct him in the words of old.
Then he shall provide an example for the children of the great ones (and)
The art of listening will enter into him (and) every heart made upright
(by) what he has said.

                     Maxims of Ptahhotep (ll. 28–40), 3rd millennium BCE

In the eyes of the Egyptians, the stability of society lay in the passing on of wisdom from one generation to the next. Only through that transmission could society continue to thrive and to flourish.

Preparation for the Afterlife. The second concern, and a more important one for the individual Egyptian, involved preparation for the afterlife. As we hear it so clearly stated in the *Tale of Sinuhe*:

> *... old age has begun for you. Virility is coming undone for you. Give your mind to the day of burial, to the passing to the state of the blessed dead, the night of the* sefetch-*oils set apart for you, the mummy bandages in the hands of Tayt, a funeral procession made for you on the day of burial, a mummy mask of gold, its head of lapis lazuli, heaven above you, you being placed in the funerary sledge, oxen to drag you, musicians before you. The* muu-dance[12] *will be performed at the door of your tomb. Funerary offerings will be invoked for you; slaughtering will be done at the niche of your false door, your pillars hewn of white stone in the midst of the children.*[13]

The Proper Burial. Additionally, it is of no small significance that burial must take place in the land of Egypt. Again the *Tale of Sinuhe* advises that

> *Your death shall not be in a foreign land; the Amau-people will not perform your initiation rites.*[14] *You will not be placed in the hide of a ram (when) your grave is made.*[15]
> *Old age assaults you. (When) you have reached old age, it is no small thing for your corpse to be buried.*[16] *You shall not be buried by foreigners.*[17]

The decree that the king sends to Sinuhe, ordering him to return home, outlines three essentials for a proper burial: mummification; the placement of the mummy in a tomb; and commemoration through offerings and rituals, such as a funerary procession complete with professional mourners (fig. 5). All of this activity was part of the process through which the deceased became a transfigured, immortal being known as an *akh*.

Fig. 5 Relief of mourning women
The procession that brings the deceased to his tomb in the necropolis is a commonly depicted tomb
scene, often found as part of the vignette for Chapter 1 of the Book of the Dead. In addition to the
family members accompanying the coffin, there are often large groups of women, and sometimes
men, forming part of the procession as well. They are thought to be mourners hired for the occasion,
professionals who were familiar with the ritual aspects of this part of the burial service.

It is of great importance to understand the *akh* not just as a transfigured spirit
but as an ancestral one too. With death came not only physical dissolution but
social disintegration as well.[18] At death, the deceased immediately ceased to be a
member of the community of the living. For the Egyptians, such disconnection
from the social world to which one belonged was unthinkable: to live in isolation
was to live in a world of dishonor and degradation.[19] As we can see from the passages quoted above from the *Tale of Sinuhe*, the one aspect of life in a foreign land
that the text openly disparages is the treatment of the dead by non-Egyptians. In
this section of the story, the king carefully outlines why it is of the utmost importance for Sinuhe to return to Egypt—to be buried, not in a pit somewhere in the
wilds wrapped in a ram skin, but properly, in a tomb in an Egyptian necropolis.

Just as he had functioned as a meaningful member of Egyptian society while
alive, so the Egyptian official hoped to serve when dead. Egyptian tombs were
conceptually similar to Egyptian houses. They often had discrete chambers in
which differentiated activities were to be carried out. They had public spaces—
among them, chambers that lay at ground level that the living could visit and

Site	Function	Architectural form
1 Upper Level	Aspect of solar cult, sun worship	Superstructure in the shape of a chapel or pyramid or a facade recess with a stelophorous statue
2 Middle Level	Site for worship and ceremonial cults, social monuments to the tomb occupant	Courtyard and horizontal inner tomb chambers such as transverse and longitudinal hall and shrine
3 Lower Level	Aspect of Osirian cult, realization of landscapes of the next world, and resting places of the body	Subterranean burial complex with shafts and corridors, antechambers and side rooms, and a burial chamber containing the sarcophagus

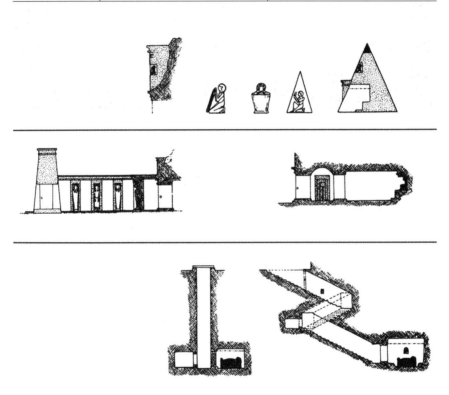

Fig. 6 The three levels of a New Kingdom tomb
These schematic drawings give a clear view of the accessible upper chambers of a Theban tomb
and the inaccessible lower areas of the tomb. Once the burial had been completed, the subterranean
parts of the tomb would have been sealed by filling the access shafts with stone and rubble.

Fig. 7 Aerial view of the pyramids at Giza
At the upper right is the area of the Great Pyramid of King Khufu and the smaller structures around it. Their arrangement shows how carefully royal burials were laid out. To the immediate right (the front) of the king's pyramid, three smaller satellite pyramids in a row are visible; these are the burial sites of his queens. To their right (i.e., in front of them), and also to the left (the back) of the king's pyramid, are the numerous tombs of the court officials. The gridded pattern of their layout parallels that of Egyptian towns.

in which they could gather during festival times. And the tombs had private, secret spaces, as well, that lay beneath the surface of the ground, with no means of access except for the deceased (fig. 6).[20] Not only was a tomb a house for the dead: it was located in a necropolis, a carefully arranged network of dwellings that somewhat resembled a town in its layout. A necropolis of Egyptian officials was often laid out in the vicinity of or around the tomb of a much more powerful member of society, such as the king. Thus, the royal pyramid and the satellite tombs of royal officials surrounding it not only recalled the layout of a town but formed an image of the royal administration—one built of stone, the material for structures intended to be permanent, such as temples—with the king at head and center and his subordinates arranged carefully in his presence, as can be seen clearly in the Old Kingdom royal cemeteries at Giza (fig. 7).[21] For these reasons, burial in a tomb in a necropolis, a "city of the dead," was understood as a powerful way for the deceased to become socially integrated once again.

In the *Tale of Sinuhe*, the king is the one who graciously and generously provides for Sinuhe's preparations for the next life. That is because Sinuhe has no
Egyptian sons to help provide for him. The sons he has were born of non-Egyptian
women. When he left to return to Egypt, Sinuhe passed on his possessions and
positions of power to his sons, who were to remain in the foreign land that was,
in fact, their proper homeland.[22]

A Son's Role. In the Egyptian world, the father initiated his son into the social
community,[23] as the instructions in the *Maxims of Ptahhotep* tell us. The son
received his father's wisdom, and his administrative or priestly titles and positions. With death, the nexus between father and son was temporarily broken.
It was mended, however, through a simple reversal of the normal social roles: it
now fell to the son to initiate his father into the social community of the *akhs*, the
transfigured ancestral spirits. The son was to perform certain funerary rituals:
not those of the days of death and burial, which were undertaken by the *lector-*
priest, but those to be carried out daily after the burial. He was responsible as
well for the memorial chapel of his father. The son was also expected to endow
his deceased father with life by intervening on his behalf, restoring and main-
taining his place and status in society,[24] and simply by pronouncing his name.
The Egyptian word *ren* ("name") was virtually interchangeable with the term *ka*
(a complex, technical term that means "persona," "quintessence," "life force,"
and "identity," among other things).[25] The utterance of the name of the deceased
not only invoked his memory but was a creative act, as the name was understood
to be an independent manifestation of the nature and character of that which
was named.[26] Thus, invoking someone's name was the act of memorializing, that
is, keeping his name and his presence alive, hence the common occurrence of a
man's name or names on stelae, statues, and tomb walls (fig. 8).

The son did so primarily by inheriting and assuming the bureaucratic,
priestly, and social roles that were once his father's. The son's presence on earth,
endowed with his father's knowledge, and often with his father's administrative
or priestly titles as well, was in itself a natural and daily memorializing of his
father's prior existence on earth. We can also see another attempt at familial
memorializing in the practice of naming a child after his grandfather.

Additionally, by performing other memorializing acts, the son could also
ensure his father's continued presence on earth. A common type of memorial
sculpture known from Egypt is the temple statue, usually a representation of
a deceased priest (fig. 9). The statue was set up in the temple to guarantee the
continued presence of the deceased in the social group in which he had once
functioned. Such statues were placed in the areas of the temple to which the
public at large did not have access. They were located on the route traveled by

Fig. 8 Relief of Itwesh
The inscription accompanying this relief offers two different names for the deceased, a phenomenon attested only in the Old Kingdom. The first, his "great" name, Semenkhuptah, was the name given at birth; such names typically contain a royal or divine name, here that of the god Ptah. The second, or "good" name, Itwesh, was apparently either given at birth or acquired later. It is thought to be the name by which an individual was more commonly known or called.

Fig. 9 Temple Statue of Pawerem, Priest of Bastet
The inscriptions on the statue inform us that Pawerem held a minor priestly title in the clergy of the goddess Bastet, probably in her sanctuary in Bubastis, a city in the eastern Delta. The figure inside the *naos*, or box-shaped shrine, that Pawerem holds before him is an image of the goddess Bastet. The position of his arms recalls the Egyptian hieroglyph ⊔ (*ka*), a word that means something like "quintessence," "life force," or "identity," but the pose was also understood as a gesture of protection. Thus, the composition of the statue may reflect the reciprocal relationship thought to exist between man and god.

the divine image in certain cult rituals. By the placement of the statues in such locations, the deceased owner of the statue was able to participate in divine temple rituals in much the same way he did in life. A short text found on many of these sculptures says, "His son made/did this for his father." Such a statement points up the act of memorializing expected of a son; it also serves to remind us of the nexus between one generation and the next and that between the dead and the living.

Similarly, the genealogies found on temple statues, whether short or lengthy, were not simply part of an administrative or priestly family's arsenal of bragging rights; they served to underscore the strong sense of tradition that the Egyptians held, and to reiterate the reciprocity of responsibilities between and even among the generations. They also point to the important role that certain families played in the social stability of a given locale.

Memory in Stone and Words. Some of what has been stated above, however, represents an idealized wish. Many of the preparations for eternity that were initiated did not last beyond a few generations.

> *A generation passes, another remains*
> *Since the time of those of the beginning.*
> *The gods who came into being before rest in their pyramids,*
> *The nobles and akhu too are buried in their pyramids.*
> *(But) those who built houses,*
> *Their places do not exist,*
> *What has become of them?*
> *I have heard the words of Imhotep and Hardedef,*
> *Whose sayings are recited in (their) entirety.*
> *What of their places?*
> *Their walls are ruined, their places do not exist,*
> *Like that which never happened.*
>
> Harper's Song,[27] 13th century BCE

But within the framework of that bleak picture, note the allusion to permanence: "the words of Imhotep and Hardedef, whose sayings are recited in (their) entirety."[28]

The act of memorializing in Egypt seems to have necessitated a written form, an idea that goes back to the first appearance of writing in Egypt.[29] The Egyptians were clearly aware of the fact that what was built of stone could crumble and pass away, and would likely do so. But that which was conceived of in the mind and heart and put down in writing had real potential to last forever, an idea that would reverberate millennia later in the words of Horace, one of Rome's greatest poets, referring to his own artistic work:

> *I have built a monument more lasting than bronze,*
> *Taller than the regal mass of the pyramids ...*
> *One which neither the sequence of years without number*
> *Nor the flight of time can make fall to ruin ...*
>
> Horace, *Carminum Liber* III.30. 1–2, 4–5[30]

The Purpose of the Book of the Dead

The great number of examples of Books of the Dead from ancient Egypt now known in public and private collections around the world seems to highlight the importance that such objects played in Egyptian funerary belief.[31] But what exact purpose, we may ask, did they actually serve?

Simply put, their purpose was the re-creation of the deceased.

With death came the disintegration of the body and the loosening of what bound its constituents together. The biological connective elements of earthly life—blood and breath—no longer exercised their normal function.[32] Mummification of the dead in Egypt was not seen simply as an attempt to preserve the corpse. It was seen as a process through which the now disintegrated body was reconstituted—an act of re-creation.[33]

The mere act of embalming the corpse, however, was not enough to achieve full re-creation. Through the funerary rituals, consisting of both words and gestures carried out by the *lector*-priest in the embalming house, the deceased was now to be transformed into an *akh*, an immortal, transfigured, ancestral being.[34] The *akh* came into being after death through the seventy-day process of mummification and the recitation of mortuary liturgies by the *lector*-priest, that is, through a complex process that involved both act and speech.[35]

The Egyptians believed that the transformed being called an *akh* was capable of a meaningful existence in the afterlife. But existence in the next world was thought to be only somewhat like existence in this life. It was similar in that food, drink, clothing, and other material comforts were believed necessary for one to function properly in the afterlife; hence, the materially endowed tombs known from Egypt and the presence of texts, as well as pictures, in the public spaces of the tomb were all intended to help the deceased obtain these necessities. In addition to the need for providing for material concerns, however, it also seems that the deceased would have to work in the next life as well, or perhaps more correctly, would have to provide labor for the work gangs in the Netherworld (fig. 10), as the presence of inscribed funerary statuettes called *shabtis*, intended to perform tasks for the deceased, makes clear.[36] And at the same time, the deceased needed a way to cope with the dangers posed by, for example, demons that blocked his way forward through essential passageways (fig. 11). Thus, in order to navigate the realm of the dead safely and successfully, the deceased needed a range of protective and sustaining powers as well.

The Book of the Dead was believed to equip its owner with a wide range of prerogatives to deal with the requirements and threats just outlined. The individual chapters of the Book of the Dead offered the know-how to move about freely in the next world, to gain the necessary food and drink, and even to have others do required work. They also gave their owners information about an environment that was often hostile and whose inhabitants could be treacherous. Certain texts gave their owner the specialized knowledge required to pass through guarded gates and to navigate around or past dangerous settings, such as the Ring of

26

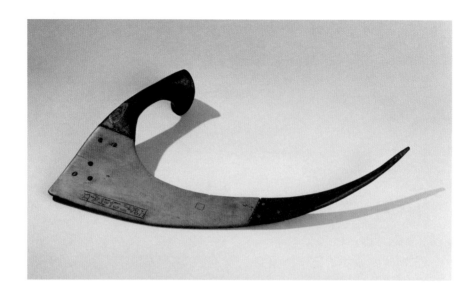

Fig. 10 Ceremonial sickle of the Cultivator of Amun Amunemhat
Since the title of the owner of this sickle, Amunemhat, was "Cultivator of (the god) Amun,"
the inclusion of this object in his tomb may have been thought to connect him with his
earthly life and responsibilities. An alternative theory is that the sickle was to serve him in
the Netherworld as a symbolic object; scenes depicted in tombs often show the deceased
at work, reaping grain in the fields of the blessed.

Fig. 11 Relief with Netherworld deities
This relief shows the gatekeepers of the fourth and sixth secret gateways of the House of Osiris
in the Field of Reeds, a place in the Netherworld. The texts accompanying the relief give the
names of the gatekeepers, knowledge that allows the deceased to pass them by and enter through
the gates they guard. The relief's text and images come from Chapter 145 of the Book of the Dead.

Fire.[37] They thus offer the modern reader a glimpse into the mind of the ancient Egyptians, detailing beliefs about this life as well as the next.

Reading through these texts, we encounter several recurrent themes. The first is that the deceased claims ready access to everything needed for survival as an *akh*: food, water, and beer in abundance. The second is the insistence that the dead are fully functioning beings who can walk, breathe air, speak, and give aid to others, including the gods. There are also claims to be able, with some help, to overcome virtually any adversity and to be under the special protection of one or any number of deities. Another assertion made is that the orientation and the expectations of the world just entered are no different from those of the world of the living: the dead continue to eat food, not feces, and to walk with their heads above their feet, not upside down. For the deceased, the Book of the Dead was a tool of powerful magic.

Although, to be sure, certain spells, such as Chapter 17, were intended to convey very specialized information about deities and place names, we must understand that not all of the chapters of the Book of the Dead were intended to impart "information" as we think of that term. As we learn from the Sobekmose papyrus, its overall purpose was not just to *inform* the deceased about the Netherworld but also to *affirm* his very right to exist and function there. Many of the texts are couched in the first person and, thus, are statements coming from the mouth of the deceased himself. Often the deceased is seen to be stating to the denizens of the Netherworld exactly what he intends to do. He does not ask, nor does he make requests. Instead, he speaks and then acts accordingly.

Once again, the synthesis of speaking and acting can be seen as a force that endows the individual with power and authority. That was the intention that the makers and owners of Books of the Dead had in mind when including such an object in an assemblage of funerary objects.

Background and Earlier Traditions

The individual texts collectively known as the Book of the Dead form part of the long-standing tradition of ancient Egyptian funerary literature. The evidence that we have from Predynastic burials shows that the practice of burying the dead with material goods was intended to both sustain and protect them. It probably does not require too great a leap of the imagination to suggest accompanying the act of interment was some form of liturgy recited aloud for the benefit of the deceased. Even though the later practice of writing allowed such recitations to be inscribed in more permanent form on a tomb wall, coffin, papyrus, or other funerary object, the Egyptians did not abandon their oral traditions.

The earliest written forms of Egyptian funerary texts are simple statements found on tomb walls, stelae, and statues from the Early Dynastic Period and the early Old Kingdom. The information that they provide focuses on achieving a continued existence in the hereafter. They tell us little if anything, however, about how that world was envisioned at the time.

The Pyramid Texts. We encounter the first extensive collection of funerary texts in the pyramid of King Unas, the last king of the Fifth Dynasty (fig. 12). All of these texts are written on the walls of the subterranean (i.e., inaccessible) chambers of the pyramid and on the king's sarcophagus as well.[38] They include spells against snakes; rituals for funerary meals; texts to aid the transformation of the king into a star and into animal forms; offering spells; and texts intended to help the deceased king ascend to and cross the sky. The successors of Unas in the Sixth Dynasty, as well as several queens from that period, continued this practice, again confining the texts to the subterranean rooms of the pyramid complex. Hence, this collection of funerary texts was named the Pyramid Texts by their finder, Gaston Maspero, in 1881.[39]

The number of individual spells (or chapters) in the Pyramid Texts runs to several hundred.[40] The texts are presented in a sophisticated and highly developed literary form. They cannot have been the inventions of the late Fifth Dynasty, but are more likely a written form of texts drawn from an oral tradition that had a very long history and development.

The purpose served by the inclusion of these texts in the royal tomb has attracted much interest over time and has generated more than a few theories. What is to be noted first and foremost is that they were carved onto the walls of the tomb and parts of the king's sarcophagus. Thus, their intended permanence cannot go unnoticed. Some scholars have suggested that they were placed in the subterranean chambers in this permanent form for the direct use of the king. Attractive as this theory may sound, it raises more questions than it answers: why in some texts does the deceased king speak directly while in others he is addressed and proclaimed in the third person? Why, for example, does the "voice" in the sarcophagus chamber address the deceased king whereas elsewhere it is directed to the realm of the gods? Some have pointed to this shift in voice and focus as evidence of the different types of rituals from which the Pyramid Texts as a whole were drawn. Whatever the case may be, the presence of written texts does seem to suggest a desire for a permanent, albeit artificial, voice.[41] Their presence also offers the added advantage of guarding against a failure by the cult priests to recite the texts when needed. A critically important feature of texts of cult ritual is their correct and proper recitation, and the presence of texts carved in stone may have been thought to fulfill this requirement permanently.

Fig. 12 Pyramid Texts in the tomb of King Unas
Painstaking work often went into the decoration of a royal tomb. The scribes decorating the interior
of the pyramid of King Unas used its ample wall spaces to inscribe what have come to be known as
the Pyramid Texts. A close inspection of the hieroglyphs shows a range of colors in the signs, the result
of their being carved in raised relief and then meticulously painted.

Another theory is that by locating such texts on the walls of the subterranean chambers, the dead king was now wrapped in an envelope of permanent recitations and protection. In certain Egyptian creation myths, immanent manifestations of the creator-god were projected at the moment of creation to the four cardinal directions—west, east, south, north—where they served as guardian gods.[42] Through this activity, the cosmos as the Egyptians knew it was defined and prescribed. The presence of the manifestations of the creator-god served both to define the limits of created existence and to guard against the encroachment of the forces of chaos that lay just beyond. It is possible that Egyptians thought of the subterranean rooms of the royal tomb as a model of the space of creation, bounded by four walls representing the cardinal points. The texts surrounding the deceased king thus afforded him the same type of protection and definition that benefited the creator-god at the beginning of the cosmos.

The permanent recording of written texts offering protection and regeneration also falls squarely in line with the power that the Egyptians accorded the spoken word. Within the space defined by walls covered in texts, the deceased king may have been seen as perpetually divinized, able to endure permanently, and move about freely, with all threats to his new and, hopefully, continuing existence held at bay.

The Coffin Texts. The next set of funerary texts we encounter is called the Coffin Texts, so named because they were found on the flat surfaces of wooden coffins of private individuals from a number of communities in Egypt during the Middle Kingdom (fig. 13).[43] This corpus contains some Pyramid Texts, thus continuing that tradition, but has been enriched by the addition of new texts as well (largely connected with the embalming ritual).[44] Unlike the Pyramid Texts of the Old Kingdom that were carved in hieroglyphs on stone, the new texts were written in red and black ink in cursive hieroglyphs or hieratic, most often on the interior walls of the coffin.

The Coffin Texts form an expanded corpus with more than eleven hundred individual spells. Its texts do not, however, form a series to be recited in a ritual. Their arrangement within the coffins as a group suggests they were seen more like a store of knowledge.[45] Additionally, the choice of cursive hieroglyphs, a specialized form of writing, hints at the special nature of these texts. Their placement mostly within the coffin, in close proximity to the deceased, throws light on the nature of their artificial voice. Perhaps, like the Pyramid Texts, they were intended to extend cultic recitation beyond the normal constraints of time and space: the deceased was now forever within the range of the "voice" of the funerary priest(s).[46] Their location also suggests that they were secret texts that were intentionally hidden.

Fig. 13 Coffin Texts from the inner coffin of Gua
The Coffin Text spells can be seen clearly written in the columns at the head end of this inner coffin.
The general layout of the texts, the use of both red and black ink, and the sign shapes are similar
to those of the recto text of the *Book of the Dead of the Goldworker of Amun Sobekmose* and clearly
reflect the strong ties between the Coffin Text and Book of the Dead traditions.

The Coffin Texts continued the emphasis on transformation and provisioning
found in the Pyramid Texts. Moreover, the new texts drawn from the embalming
ritual were perhaps thought to be made more efficacious by transferring them to
the coffin itself.[47] The texts have the enigmatic and allusive language of hidden
texts, and the knowledge they lay claim to is that of power and magic. And their
placement within the coffin once again appears to have wrapped the deceased in
a layer of protective text intended to be permanent.

The Emergence of the Book of the Dead

Beginning in the late Middle Kingdom, funerary texts as a whole began to
undergo a process of innovation. A new text type, which we now call a Book of
the Dead, was formed through a curtailment of old material and the addition
of much that was new. (The new texts largely focus on the Netherworld and its
inhabitants.) That said, the Book of the Dead tradition remained strongly linked
to that of its predecessor, the Coffin Texts.

The medium on which the new text type was written was at first a linen
shroud placed over the deceased; a roll of papyrus soon came to be the preferred

medium. The somewhat misleading term Book of the Dead appears to have been coined by Richard Lepsius, the founder of German Egyptology, in the early 1840s.[48] (The Egyptian name for one type of such a funerary text was the "Book of Going Forth by Day."[49])

The word *book* in the term Book of the Dead is also something of a misnomer. For us, a book with a known title is recognizable: all of its constituent elements are present for us to read through, from the beginning to the end. A Book of the Dead, however, did not comprise that kind of reading experience; like the Coffin Texts, its texts formed a manual filled with knowledge that was believed would help the deceased function in, navigate through, and survive in the next world. Thus, the papyrus rolls buried with the deceased were powerful tools intended to provide a receptacle of specialized knowledge, the mere possession of which could make one a more efficacious *akh*. (Indeed, another innovation of the Book of the Dead comes from the fact that most of its spells seem to take for granted that the deceased is already elevated to the status of an *akh*.)

Although the Book of the Dead formed a part of a much larger and longer tradition, it also shows certain breaks with the earlier traditions. Some of the transformation spells, intended to aid in changing of the deceased into an *akh*,[50] that formed part of the corpus of Pyramid Texts and that of the Coffin Texts, for example, were now largely separated from the rest of the mortuary literature. The rejection of certain older material can also be seen in the severe curtailment of the use of Pyramid Texts. Additionally, although the Book of the Dead does draw on material found in the Coffin Texts, much of this material was eventually reworked and the number of total spells was reduced by almost eighty-five percent: whereas the Coffin Text corpus comprises more than eleven hundred individual texts, the collection of individual texts called the Book of the Dead is just shy of two hundred (though rarely did any single papyrus contain all of them).[51] Most important, the texts of the Book of the Dead corpus show an increased interest in the topography and nature of the Netherworld and its inhabitants.[52]

The earliest exemplars of the Book of the Dead were written on the wooden coffin of Queen Mentuhotep of the Thirteenth Dynasty.[53] The Book of the Dead texts on her coffin were written in hieratic lines, not in columns of cursive hieroglyphs used for the Coffin Texts on her coffin. By the end of the Second Intermediate Period, linen mummy shrouds had become a favored medium, and once again the writing used was cursive hieroglyphs; all of the shrouds with Book of the Dead texts from this period are royal. Linen continued in use until papyrus became standard for the Book of the Dead at some point during the reigns of Hatshepsut–Thutmose III.[54] Book of the Dead texts were also put on tomb walls and coffins dating to this period.[55]

Probably at some point in the joint reign of Hatshepsut and Thutmose III, Book of the Dead texts written in cursive hieroglyphs in columns became the standard text form. Such a text layout on papyrus ran contrary to the then-current practice of writing hieratic in horizontal lines laid out in square or rectangular columns for other texts on papyrus. Perhaps the Book of the Dead practice was intended to link the new tradition with that of the Coffin Texts whose texts were composed in such a way. Or it may be that the vertical columns of cursive hiero-glyphs conformed to the text layout found on the papyrus exemplars used by the scribes writing Coffin Texts in the Middle Kingdom, a text layout typically found on most Middle Kingdom papyri. Eventually, hieratic came to be (re)adopted for the writing of Books of the Dead in the Third Intermediate Period,[56] but cursive hieroglyphs persisted and continued to be used in the writing of certain texts, especially those that appeared in the single vignette found at the beginning of Books of the Dead from this time. While hieratic gave way to demotic in the Late Period for the writing of texts on papyrus, hieratic continued to be used in Books of the Dead for a long period of time, almost to the exclusion of demotic. In the Ptolemaic Period, as religious innovation became more widespread, the practice of writing Books of the Dead in cursive hieroglyphs in columns was revived,[57] even though hieratic Books of the Dead are known as well.[58]

As noted earlier, a complete set of texts that forms the text corpus called the Book of the Dead would have included nearly two hundred chapters and almost as many images. For the most part, Books of the Dead of the New Kingdom con-tained a small and somewhat limited number of individual texts, although some early Books of the Dead contain more than one hundred texts and were written on very lengthy papyrus rolls.[59] By the Late Period, lengthier Books of the Dead containing many of the known texts become more common.[60] But already by the Third Intermediate Period we find Books of the Dead consisting of a single spell on one sheet of papyrus (fig. 14).

The choice of which spells to include in an individual Book of the Dead lay open; factors like the social status of the deceased, the location of the cemetery in which the deceased would reside, and personal considerations of the owner may have played some role in the production of a Book of the Dead. More important, a careful study of individual papyri shows that real independence and freedom were exercised in the choice of which spells to include in an individual book.[61] However, since a number of texts commonly appear in set groups that we call "sequences," the decision to include one specific text led to the inevitable inclu-sion of others.[62] Some of these sequences are recognizable as clusters of spells that address the same concern: the restoration and protection of the physical properties of the deceased, for example,[63] or transformation into animal form to ensure greater mobility and freedom of movement.[64] Some of the sequences

Fig. 14   Papyrus with Chapter 166 of the Book of the Dead
This somewhat damaged papyrus is a self-contained document that has the text of Chapter 166 of
the Book of the Dead. First appearing in Books of the Dead of the Third Intermediate Period, the chapter
was here inscribed as a single text on a small sheet of papyrus that was then rolled up, tied, and worn
at the neck as an amulet. Such an object was believed to endow its owner with magical protection. The
creases or folds still visible in the photograph show that this papyrus had been rolled and tied that way.

Fig. 15   Inscribed mummy bandage
At some point in the Late Period, the Egyptians began to inscribe the linen bandages used in
mummification with individual chapters and scenes from the Book of the Dead corpus. This may
have been done for economic reasons, as inscribing the bandages themselves obviated the need for
a roll of papyrus. It may also have been done to bring these funerary texts into even closer contact
with the deceased's body.

seem linked by individual words or phrases.[65] Other sequences can be shown to appear as regular units, but what links the individual texts in such instances still eludes us.

* * *

From their actual findspots, when known, we can see that a Book of the Dead was a highly specialized piece of tomb equipment. It was not simply placed anywhere in the tomb like many of the other funerary provisions of the deceased. The early Books of the Dead of the kings were large sheets of linen placed directly on the torso of the deceased. Papyrus Books of the Dead have been found from the New Kingdom, parts of which were actually wrapped around the upper part of the body and head of the deceased. From the Third Intermediate Period onward, Books of the Dead were often placed between the thighs of the deceased, deep inside the mummy wrappings. Late Period texts have also been found on the abdomen and parallel to the spine; or placed beside the body; or located directly above the head.[66] Book of the Dead texts in the Late Period and later came to be written on the individual linen mummy wrappings themselves (fig. 15).

Such loci for Books of the Dead do not suggest accessibility as their main purpose. Rather, they imply that the physical contact between the object and the deceased played an important role (an idea already at work in the Coffin Text tradition). Papyrus Books of the Dead found wrapped inside the mummy bandages point strongly to another concern: secrecy. Specialized knowledge was secret and hidden, not to be shared freely. The notion of secrecy is further evidenced by statements found at the end of certain spells of the Book of the Dead. See, for example, the coda of Chapter 162: "This roll great of mystery, do not let any eye see it, (for) this (is) an abomination. Making hidden what one sees is truly effective millions of times." Additionally, the language used for these texts is allusive and enigmatic, and for a modern reader often quite elusive.

New Funerary Texts

The return to traditional religion after the disruption of the Amarna Period ushered in many innovations in Egyptian funerary religion. A major change in the Book of the Dead tradition was a broad increase in the use of illustration. The Books of the Dead of the early and middle Eighteenth Dynasty were rather sparing in their use of pictorial vignettes.[67] They were replaced by a new tradition of more lavishly illustrated Books of the Dead that in some cases show one or more vignettes for a spell. The use of a broad variety of colors in these vignettes increased as well. The illustrations found in some of the best Books of the Dead

Figs 16, 17   Vignettes from the *Book of the Dead of Neferrenpet*
The introduction of papyrus as the preferred medium for making Books of the Dead in the early
New Kingdom offered a new medium for Egyptian painters. The artists who drew or painted the
vignettes for these Books of the Dead created some of the finest Egyptian paintings and drawings
known from ancient Egypt.

of the Nineteenth and Twentieth Dynasties offer examples of the finest painting
from this period (figs 16, 17).

The illustration tradition that had developed and grown stronger during the
Ramesside Period eventually saw image begin to eclipse text in the funerary
papyri. An increasing number of these illustrations focused on the places and
beings found in the Netherworld; such illustrations, like the language of the
funerary texts, are often enigmatic and allusive. This increased use of images
seems to have been intended to intensify the reality of the words of the texts.
Voice and word were joined by image to offer increased effective power and protection for the dead. At Deir el-Medina (the village of the workmen who built and
decorated the royal tombs in the Valley of the Kings), the subterranean chambers
of the workmen's tombs—spaces that were normally undecorated—came to be
decorated with vignettes from the Book of the Dead. The deceased was no longer
surrounded by writing but rather by representations that effectively placed him
directly in the Netherworld (fig. 18).[68]

In the centuries following the Ramesside Period, such innovations continued.
The layout of a Book of the Dead underwent a noticeable change. Cursive hieroglyphs were abandoned as the medium of writing. The Book of the Dead was now
composed in hieratic lines laid out in columns. Along with that innovation came
another: the severe curtailment of illustration in Books of the Dead themselves.[69]
The new practice was to include a single vignette at the beginning of the papyrus
showing, almost invariably, the deceased in a posture of prayer before a seated
figure of Osiris or of Re-Horakhty.

Fig. 18 Tomb painting of Re as a cat killing Apophis
In this painting, the knife-wielding cat is a manifestation of the sun-god Re. The snake represents Apophis, the archenemy of the solar deity, who attempted each night to thwart the sun-god's journey through the night sky of the Netherworld. This well-known scene belongs to Chapter 17 of the Book of the Dead.

Fig. 19 Amduat papyrus
The funerary text genre called the Amduat was first introduced in the New Kingdom and was restricted to royal burials, although a few high-ranking officials of that time expropriated it for their tombs as well. The texts and vignettes of this book illustrate the twelve-hour nocturnal journey of the solar deity through the Netherworld. By the Third Intermediate Period, an abbreviated version of the Amduat came to be used by private persons. Such papyri depict only one or a few hours of the nightly solar journey. Here we see the representation of the twelfth hour of the night. On the extreme right, the sun-god is shown as a scarab, his manifestation as Khepri ("Coming into Being"); he is about to pass into the eastern horizon of the sky. Just below, Osiris is shown as a mummiform deity who will remain in the Netherworld along with the bodies of all of the deceased.

Fig. 20 Fragment from a Book of Breathing
Although much text has been lost at the top and bottom of this papyrus, the extant text indicates that it belonged to a late genre of funerary texts known as a Book of Breathing. Such a text was drawn largely from earlier material, much of it found in the Book of the Dead corpus. Its purpose, much like earlier texts from the Egyptian funerary traditions, was both to allow the deceased to move freely in the Netherworld and to protect him from the dangers found there.

In another innovation, tomb owners were now sometimes equipped with a second papyrus in addition to a Book of the Dead. One such papyrus containing an abbreviated version of a funerary text, the Amduat, or "That Which Is in the Netherworld," was known largely from the royal tombs of the New Kingdom (fig. 19).[70] The scenes and texts of the Amduat record the journey of the sun through the Netherworld during the twelve hours of the night. The Amduat papyri, however, used material only from the last four or, more typically, the last one or two hours of the night.

Occasionally included in the burial was a third papyrus called a "mythological" papyrus in modern parlance. It was a roll of lavishly decorated scenes connected with the Netherworld whose textual matter was reduced almost to the form of tags.

The inclusion of the second or third papyrus may be explained as follows: the reduction of the use of vignettes in a Book of the Dead at the beginning of the Third Intermediate Period may have been thought to create a void that needed filling. Both the Amduat and the "mythological" papyri were amply illustrated, with word playing a very subordinate role to that of image. Including different types of papyri in a burial, the text-oriented Book of the Dead, and an image-oriented papyrus like the Amduat or "mythological" papyrus, may have been thought to offer power and protection to the deceased that was also considered maximally effective.

The Late, Ptolemaic, and Roman Periods all witnessed further innovations in the tradition of funerary texts as well. During the Saite Period (664–525 BCE), the Book of the Dead corpus was subjected to a dramatic revision. The individual texts themselves were edited, reworked, and put into a single sequence, creating a new text form considered canonical and fixed; as such, it persisted in use well into the Ptolemaic Period.[71]

During the Ptolemaic Period, a widespread decline in the employment of a Book of the Dead as a funerary text took place. The number of manuscripts decreased noticeably; the use of highly abbreviated texts became quite common. Additionally, new funerary texts were developed, such as the Book for Traversing Eternity and the so-called Book of Breathing (fig. 20). These new works drew heavily from earlier material but showed extensive reworking, blending excerpted older material with that which was new. The resulting synthesis was no longer a Book of the Dead per se, but a funerary text that was still believed to bestow power and protection on the deceased. A number of these texts offered the additional advantage of being written in demotic, the script most widely used at that time and one that better reflected the spoken language of the time.

The decline that began in the Ptolemaic Period continued into the Roman Period. Books of the Dead written in demotic now appeared, though such a practice never became common. Painting funerary texts and images on large linen shrouds became prevalent in the late Ptolemaic and early Roman Periods (fig. 21), though examples of such objects often show how poorly understood the original meanings of word and image had become.

Other Texts in the Tomb Complex

Egyptian tombs often had different chambers for different purposes. At ground level, there were spaces that the living could visit and in which they could gather during festival times. There were also spaces only for the deceased.[72] Over time, the distinction between the accessible and inaccessible parts of the tomb became more pronounced. By the time of the New Kingdom, a private tomb was largely envisaged as tripartite: (1) the burial chamber, located below ground, accessible only by the deceased; (2) the chambers at ground level, whether open or closed, giving access to the living; (3) a pyramid-like structure, or simply a small pyramidion, often surmounting the tomb complex as a whole. In this way, the tomb complex can be seen as a model of the cosmos: the heavens above, the earth underneath, and the Netherworld below all (see fig. 6).

Such an arrangement may strike one as somewhat peculiar, but to the Egyptian way of thought, it not only made perfect sense—it was necessary to ensure a successful transition from this world to the next for the deceased. Several texts can be instructive here. For example, Book of the Dead Chapter 26, a chapter known already from the beginning of the New Kingdom, ends with an assertion that the deceased cannot be kept from the gates of the West so long as his *ba*, corpse, and name remain integrated, just as his spirit, body, and identity did while he was alive on earth. The reintegration of the constituent parts of the deceased, however, was not the same as it was on earth. In a number of Egyptian texts, the constituent parts of a divine being—*ba*, body, and attributes—are said to reside in different locales. A New Kingdom text is also of interest here: "O these gods (and) goddesses whose names have been pronounced, who dwell in the sky (but) eat upon the earth, whose *uraei* are upon their heads, whose *bas* are in Busiris, whose mummies are in the necropolis (and) whose names are not known...."[73] Like that of the gods, the natural state of the blessed dead was thought to inhabit several spheres of the cosmos simultaneously.[74] But we should understand that although the constituent parts of the deceased and the gods reside in different locales, they do so not permanently but within the solar cycle of day and night; and at specific moments within this cycle, they are reintegrated and reanimated. Thus, we can see the different purposes that the differentiated areas of the tomb may have served for the deceased.

Fig. 21 Linen funerary shroud
On this shroud, the deceased is shown twice, accompanied by the goddesses Nephthys on the right
and Isis on the left. He faces what appears to be a bound pillar, a representation of the god Osiris well
known from funerary representations dating to a thousand years earlier or more.

Tomb interiors in Egypt often show us lavish illustration and decoration on the walls of the accessible chambers. These illustrations appear to be reflections of the life of the tomb owner, showing him overseeing agricultural affairs, fishing and fowling with his family in the papyrus marshes, and receiving offerings from priests or family members. This pictorial decoration was routinely accompanied by texts written on doorposts, architraves, stelae, false doors, and even the walls of the tomb. These texts had a specific function. They were to be read by others who were to carry out their instructions for the benefit of the deceased. The recitation of some of these texts, particularly those found on tomb stelae, helped the deceased achieve the status of an *akh* (fig. 22).[75] Their high visibility and their location in the public parts of the tomb ensured that they could be read and recited by anyone who happened by and who could read.

The great majority of these texts appear to be somewhat generic in nature, as texts found in one tomb are quite often encountered in others, even if only in a somewhat similar form. Their apparent ubiquity and generic nature, however, do not diminish their value. Every feature of an Egyptian tomb, no matter how seemingly insignificant, served a function, and function informs meaning. For written texts, where they are found and the context in which they were recorded is part of their meaning.[76]

Since it was imperative that the content of these texts be actualized, their language is always plain and lucid, typical of the language of liturgies whose message must be conveyed clearly in order to be rendered effective. In some ways, these texts parallel the liturgical and ritual texts found in temple cults. But temple rituals had spatial and temporal boundaries in that they had predetermined times in the annual calendar and fixed places within the temple for their (re)enactment. The tomb texts were permanently accessible and thus were not prescribed by cultic time and space.[77] Their placement in the accessible areas of the tomb removed the boundaries associated with temple rituals.

Tomb texts of this type are often couched in the language and formulae of a wish.[78] They are strikingly similar in form and content to the greeting formulae familiar from addresses to the living, like those seen in letters (both real letters and the letters found in the papyri used in schools as models for students training to become scribes). The wishes are those one expects to find in a funerary context: pleas for aid in the recitation of transformation texts and requests for food offerings and water. A conspicuous feature of virtually every text in these parts of the tomb is the name of the tomb owner, his titles, and abbreviated or extended genealogies. There is absolute clarity about the identity of the intended recipient.

Among these texts is one of particular interest, the tomb "autobiography." Early in the Old Kingdom, texts that were extensions or developments of the titular and genealogical tags of the deceased become more common in the tomb.

The earliest examples from this genre laid out details about lineage or gave a "résumé" of the deceased as official or priest. Unlike the other texts found in the tomb, the autobiographical text is usually found only once in the tomb, on a stela or on a wall of the tomb itself. In it, the deceased claims to have helped the unfortunate: he has given them bread, beer, and clothing; he has helped them cross the Nile, possibly so that they can carry out proper funerary rites for their own family members. He is one praised by his father, beloved of his mother, and honored by his siblings. In short, while on earth, the deceased claims that he was a meaningfully integrated member of his family and society at large. A brief survey of a small number of these texts, however, reveals their similarities, leading one to conclude once again that these texts are formulaic, follow certain principles of convention, and are, thereby, devalued.

Later in the Old Kingdom, we encounter, within the idealized autobiographical framework, texts that speak to individual achievement and sometimes extensively so. This autobiographical tradition continues until it dies out in the

Fig. 22 Funerary stela of Senres
The short text on this stela consists, for the most part, of a request for invocation offerings to be given to the owner of the stela, phrased as "... every good and pure thing on which a god lives ..."

Fig. 23 Stela of Anherkhawi
In the lower register of this stela, the owner is shown kneeling in a position of adoration, his hands raised before the image of the god Re-Horakhty, shown in a solar boat in the upper register. The text on the stela is a prayer addressed to the god, essentially comprising what is known as a Hymn to the Setting Sun. Solar hymns are found in later New Kingdom Books of the Dead and form part of what has been designated as Chapter 15 of the Book of the Dead corpus.

post-Amarna New Kingdom, when it is replaced by a text type that stresses the personal relationship the deceased had with an individual god (fig. 23); this new genre of texts eventually made its way from the tomb to the temple statue set up by the son of the deceased in an act of commemoration. Despite the apparent differences between these two forms of autobiography, the intent of both is the same: to lay claim to merit and to state that what the deceased has asked for should be granted because he is the type of person who is deserving. Thus, we cannot dismiss these texts as mere conventions that are devoid of meaning.

The specific location of the autobiographical text within the tomb also helps inform its meaning. The text is found adjacent to texts that record the wishes of the deceased. The juxtaposition of these different text types likely indicates that they form a unity and were to be read as such. The first group of texts catalogues the wishes of the deceased; the second text, the autobiography, lists the reasons why the tomb owner should have his requests granted. In life, he gave help and aid to others who could not act for themselves; now he asks those present (the person or persons reading the texts) to grant him assistance in turn. Death brings with it many reversals of roles. The one who acted for others while on earth must now depend on others to act for him.

Therefore, we can see that these texts—although not properly funerary texts in the same way as the Book of the Dead—were intended to aid the deceased in a number of ways. They were there to help ensure the continuation of his cult so that his material needs in the hereafter would be met. More important, perhaps, they were there as vehicles of commemoration, texts designed to make sure that the deceased would be remembered, not forgotten, and to record as permanent the fact that he was once an effective member of both a family and a larger social unit, such as a *phyle* of priests attendant on a certain deity. Thus, he deserves from others the attention in death that he gave to others in life.

In sum, the texts that that we find in the accessible upper areas of the tomb, like the illustrations they accompany, memorialize the deceased as a former member of his community. The writing found in the burial chamber, usually limited to individual objects such as papyrus rolls, canopic chests, and the coffin itself, serves to aid the deceased as an *akh* in his new community, that of the dead, and in his journey through the Netherworld.

* * *

The *Book of the Dead of the Goldworker of Amun Sobekmose* is one exemplar from a tradition that survived for more than twenty-five centuries, from the Pyramid Texts, to the Coffin Texts, to the Book of the Dead and its later derivatives. But it was a tradition that underwent almost constant innovation and change. A study of these texts shows that the innovations were not made simply for the sake of change itself or in the name of progress. Rather, they reveal the propensity of the Egyptians for reexamining and reinterpreting their ways of thinking, and a willingness to innovate. The ancient Egyptians did not, however, effect change through a rejection of the old and the invention of the wholly new as the Greeks, for example, did. In their acts of reinterpretation, the Egyptians always showed a remarkable ability to effect change through *re*-creation. So often, when we encounter something that seems new in Egyptian thought, we find, sooner rather than later, that it actually is something old and something borrowed. For the Egyptians, it seems to ring true that there really was "nothing new under the sun." The burial of a young woman at some point in the Roman Period, discovered by Flinders Petrie at Hawara in the late 1880s, may offer a further illustration of the degree to which the ideas underlying Egyptian funerary practices endured. The deceased had been buried with a roll of papyrus. But the papyrus placed under her head was not a Book of the Dead, nor even a later derivative. Rather it was a roll on which was written the better part of Book 2 of the *Iliad*.[79] Whoever had included that object in the burial seems to have been familiar with the idea that written matter provided some form of power and protection for the dead. The placement and presence of that roll of papyrus in her burial speak volumes to the persistence of religious practices and their power to endure even when they are no longer properly understood.

Notes

Works cited here in abbreviated form can be found in full in the Reference List. Translations are the present author's, unless otherwise indicated.

1 For the practice of including inscribed texts in a burial prior to the New Kingdom, see the discussion in the section "Background and Earlier Traditions," below.
2 One notable exception is the *Book of the Dead of Mesemnetjer* (Louvre E.21324), which dates to the reign of Hatshepsut/Thutmose III. It has forty-three chapters on the recto and twenty-four on the verso; all are written in cursive hieroglyphs except for the final chapter of the verso, Chapter 133 (see Munro 1988, pp. 279–80), which is written in hieratic.
3 Except for the documents from the village of Deir el-Medina, where the men working in the Valley of the Kings lived, the evidence from pharaonic Egypt is scant

compared with that from Egypt under Ptolemaic and Roman rule. The term "pharaonic" Egypt does not denote the name of a specific period but is used to describe Egypt under the rule of pharaohs who predated the Ptolemaic and Roman Periods.
4 See Meskell 2002, p. 13.
5 The vast majority of archaeological materials documenting the pharaonic period comes from burials. The village of Deir el-Medina is one of our few sources for material relating to daily life. The documentation from there consists of several hundred papyri and several thousand ostraca written in hieratic; we have letters and documents from elsewhere, but they are very few in number. By comparison, the materials dating to the Ptolemaic, Roman, and Byzantine Periods come from a score of towns and villages. That documentation consists of hundreds

of thousands of papyri and ostraca written in demotic, Greek, Latin, Coptic and Arabic.
6 John Baines, in Shafer 1991, p. 132, suggests that the ruling and administrative class was roughly fifty thousand out of a population of between one and one and a half million, thus between three and five percent of the whole. The percentage may actually have been much smaller, since Baines's number certainly includes scribes, many of whom did not belong to the social class that left behind documentation such as decorated tombs and temple statues.
7 A note of caution: information gained from a funerary context may be somewhat or even completely misleading. Much of the information that one may attempt to recover from tomb scenes and tomb texts is highly conventional and idealized. See the section "Other Texts in the Tomb Complex" below.

8 Nunn 1996, p. 22, suggests an average life expectancy of thirty-six years for the pharaonic period. See also Baines, in Shafer 1991, p. 133.

9 Robins 1994–95, pp. 27–28, suggests that the infant mortality rate, including failed pregnancies, hovered rather consistently at seventy percent.

10 Meskell 2002, p. 91; McDowell 1999, p. 37.

11 Campbell 1967, p. 27.

12 A ritual funeral dance performed on the day of burial.

13 *Tale of Sinuhe*, B190-197. Blackman 1972, p. 32; Gardiner 1916, pp. 68–71. The phrase "in the midst of the children" refers to the satellite tombs in the cemetery built around the pyramid of the king. The children mentioned here are likely the royal children, among whom certain officials were granted burial. The same situation obtained later as well in the Valley of the Kings and the Valley of the Queens.

14 Literally, "The Amau-people will not initiate you." The Amau-people were the Asiatics with whom Sinuhe was then dwelling. The term "initiation rites" refers to funerary rites.

15 *Tale of Sinuhe,* B197-198. Blackman 1972, p. 32. The word used for "tomb" or "grave" here is *ḏr*, which indicates a primitive grave; Hannig 1997, 1012a.

16 For (*i*)ꜥ*b* (lit., "unite") in the sense of "bury," see Gardiner 1916, p. 59, n. at 159.

17 *Tale of Sinuhe,* B258-259. Blackman 1972, p. 37; Gardiner 1916, p. 98.

18 Assmann 2005, pp. 39–63.

19 *Ibid.*, p. 41.

20 For the substructures of the private tombs of the Eighteenth Dynasty, see Dodsen and Ikram 2008, pp. 225–28, 246.

21 On town layout so described, see Meskell 2002, p. 31.

22 *Tale of Sinuhe*, B238-240.

23 See Assmann 2005, pp. 47–52.

24 *Ibid.*, pp. 50ff.

25 On the meaning and importance of the terms "name" and *ka*, see Hornung 1983, pp. 482–86 and 475–80, respectively.

26 *Ibid.*, pp. 482ff.

27 The papyrus *pBritish Museum 10060*; see Fox 1977, pp. 393–423.

28 Imhotep and Hardedef were Egyptian sages famous for what they accomplished in their lifetimes. Imhotep was the supposed designer and builder of the Third Dynasty Step Pyramid complex of King Djoser at Saqqara; Hardedef—reputed to be the son of Khufu, the owner of the Great Pyramid—was the man to whom the first known example of the genre called Instructions, a type of wisdom text, was attributed. No writings of Imhotep have yet been found, and only the beginning of Hardedef's *Instructions* has survived, in a much later New Kingdom copy.

29 The Homeric hero, by contrast, seems to have felt that an *uninscribed* monument could memorialize his deeds. See, for example, *Iliad* 7.89–91; see also the discussion in Svenbro 1993, pp. 53 and 59, n. 47.

30 Horace is the name modern commentators use for Quintus Horatius Flaccus (65–8 BCE). The excerpt comes from the last of eighty-eight poems arranged in three books that were published in 23 BCE. They represent Horace's artistic output from what may have been more than a decade. Other books of his poetry had been previously published: two books of *Satires* in the late 30s BCE and the *Epodes* in 29 BCE.

31 There are over three thousand individual texts gathered or cited in the Totenbuch-Projekt, Bonn. See http://totenbuch.awk.nrw.de.

32 Assmann 2005, p. 26.

33 *Ibid.*, pp. 31ff.

34 On the *akh*, see Barbash 2011, pp. 36–40; Hornung 1983, pp. 494ff.; and Englund 1978, *passim*.

35 See Assmann 2005, pp. 33ff.

36 The placement of *shabti* (or *shawabti*) figures in the tomb was designed to help the deceased participate in any obligatory labor he may encounter, not to help him avoid it. See Assmann 2005, pp. 110ff.

37 See Chapter 136B.

38 The pyramid of Unas, last king of the Fifth Dynasty, contained 227 chapters out of a later total of 759. They were also found in the tombs of the kings and several queens of the Sixth Dynasty. The sophisticated nature of these texts in both form and content strongly suggests that their composition and development long predated their first appearance in this pyramid. See Allen, J.P., 2005 for a translation of the Pyramid Texts.

39 Maspero, an important French Egyptologist, was at this time the director-general of excavations and antiquities for the Egyptian government, a position he held from 1881 to 1886.

40 Some 759 individual texts are recorded in Sethe 1908–22.

41 Assmann 2005, pp. 239ff.

42 In one myth, there are sixty of these manifestations; in another, seventy-seven. For these myths, see Goyon 1985, *passim*.

43 The sites known include Kom el-Hisn, Saqqara, Dashur, Lisht, Herakleopolis, Beni Hasan, Bersheh, Qau, Meir, Akhmim, Asiut, Abydos, Dendera, Thebes, Gebelein, and Aswan. See Lesko 2001, pp. 287–88.

44 See Assmann 2005, pp. 249–50.

45 *Ibid.*, pp. 248–50.

46 *Ibid.*, pp. 248–49.

47 *Ibid.*, pp. 249ff. and *passim*.

48 See Lepsius 1842.

49 We must proceed with caution here, however, as Books of the Dead do not appear to bear the phrase "Going Forth by Day" as a title. The *Book of the Dead of the Goldworker of Amun Sobekmose*, for example, has that heading for only two of its recto texts, though the verso does have a number of texts titled "Going Forth by Day." The low number of such texts may possibly reflect the early date of the Brooklyn papyrus. For the first appearance of the term and its subsequent use, see Backes 2009, pp. 5–27.

50 There are many transformation texts in the Book of the Dead, but their purpose is different; they are intended to assure the deceased that he can take on different animal forms, which will afford him greater mobility, access to the company of the gods, and the assurance of a continuing existence.

51 The exemplars containing all or nearly all of the texts of the Book of the Dead are all from the Saite Period (664–525 BCE) or later.

52 Dorman 2014, p. 3, notes that this difference can be seen between the funerary literature of the Middle Kingdom and that of the New Kingdom in general.

53 Geisen 2004, pp. 3–10.

54 See Munro 2010, pp. 55, 59–61.

55 Book of the Dead texts inscribed on the walls of New Kingdom tombs are largely limited to the Theban necropolis. See Saleh 1984. Book of the Dead texts written on coffins first appear as early as the Thirteenth Dynasty and were limited to a few royal coffins. The texts written on New Kingdom coffins are invariably found in a highly abbreviated form; their occurrence is somewhat rare. See Munro 2010, pp. 55, 59–61.

56 Hieratic was used at the beginning of the Eighteenth Dynasty for the writing of several early Books of the Dead or sections thereof. See, for example, Munro 1995b, *passim*.

57 The overall appearance of these papyri is strikingly different from that of the New Kingdom Books of the Dead. The hieroglyphs look quite different and the layout of text and vignette is distinctive as well. Many of these exemplars come from Akhmim. See Mosher 2001, *passim*.

58 Many of the hieratic Books of the Dead come from Memphis and Thebes. There do seem to be some differences, however, in the composition and layout of the papyri originating from these two areas. In these late Books of the Dead, we are clearly seeing the effects and importance of localized traditions. See Mosher 1992, pp. 143–72.

59 The Nineteenth Dynasty *Book of the Dead of Ani*, now in the British Museum, is seventy-eight feet (nearly twenty-four meters) long. It is lavishly illustrated and contains more than seventy individual texts and/or vignettes. The Eighteenth Dynasty *Book of the Dead of Nu*, also in the British Museum, is approximately sixty-five feet (twenty meters) long and has one hundred thirty-six texts and a high number of vignettes. Another British Museum object, the *Book of the Dead of Nebseni*, also from the Eighteenth Dynasty, is seventy-eight feet (nearly twenty-four meters) in length. Even though the Brooklyn *Book of the Dead of the Goldworker of Amun Sobekmose,* is only approximately twenty-five feet (seven-and-a-half meters) long, it contains nearly the same number of texts as the *Book of the Dead of Nebseni*. This apparent discrepancy can be explained by the fact that the Brooklyn papyrus is written on both the recto and the verso (the two sides of the papyrus) and that the texts on the verso are written in lines of hieratic, a form of writing that allows an extensive amount of text to be written in a rather limited space.

60 Papyrus rolls from this period of more than forty feet (twelve meters) are frequently encountered.

61 See O'Rourke 2014, pp. 313–14.

62 Spell sequences became established more firmly and quickly with the passage of time. Books of the Dead from the Ramesside Period of the New Kingdom show a greater adherence to the use of set sequences.

63 For example, Chapters 23-24-25-26-28-27, for which see the translation of the recto texts in this volume.

64 For example, Chapters 83-84-85-77-86-82-87-81.

65 See, for example, Chapters 104-76 found at the beginning of the recto of the *Book of the Dead of the Goldworker of Amun Sobekmose,* which are linked by the single word "cicada."

66 See Martin and Ryholt 2006, especially pp. 273–74.

67 Some of the Books of the Dead of the later Eighteenth Dynasty are also amply illustrated, such as the *Book of the Dead of Nebseni*. Nebseni was a draftsman and may have been personally responsible for the illustrations of his Book of the Dead as well as its texts. See Lapp 2004, pp. 23–24.

68 Assmann 2005, p. 251.

69 A number of papyri from this period show that the tradition of illustration continues, as they have a number of beautiful vignettes that certainly earn them the right to be called illustrated papyri. An examination of any of these, however, like the *Book of the Dead of Gatseshen* in the Egyptian Museum, Cairo, will show that the vignettes play a very subordinate role to text, reminiscent of the situation that obtained in the first half or so of the Eighteenth Dynasty.

70 A few private officials of the early Eighteenth Dynasty who would have had access to these secret sacred books put them in their own tombs as well, such as the official Weser, owner of Theban Tomb 61 from the time of Thutmose III.

71 See Quack 2009, pp. 11–34.

72 For the substructures of the private tombs of the Eighteenth Dynasty, see Dodsen and Ikram 2008, pp. 225–28, 246.

73 See the papyrus *pChester Beatty* 9, vs.B. 175–77, in Gardiner 1935, p. 113 and pl. 61. This idea shows its growing prevalence in a number of other texts, some of which are later. See, for example, *pLeiden* I 344, in Zandee 1992, pp. 188–91; and *pBrooklyn 47.218.49*, col. x + 6$^{13\text{-}14}$, in O'Rourke 2015.

74 Assmann 1995, p. 133, no. 4; pp. 187–89; Assmann 2005, pp. 90ff.

75 See Assmann 2005, pp. 243–47.

76 *Ibid.*, p. 238.

77 *Ibid.*, pp. 249, 251–52.

78 *Ibid.*, pp. 252–59.

79 Turner 1980, pp. 76–77.

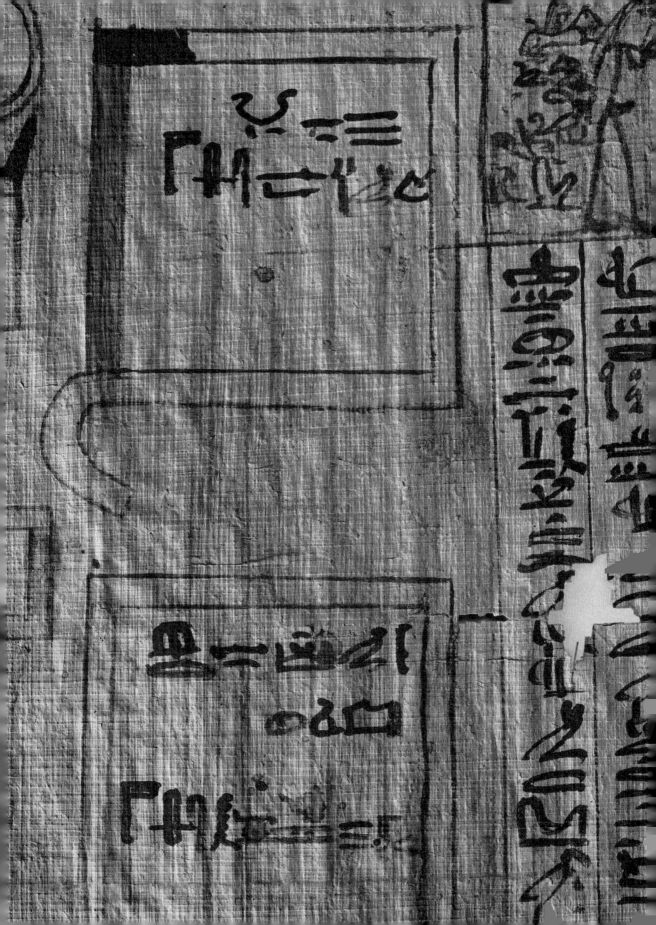

Book of the Dead
of the Goldworker of Amun
Sobekmose

Description
of the Papyrus

TITLE: *Book of the Dead of the Goldworker*
of Amun Sobekmose
(often cited as *pBrooklyn 37.1777E*)
PLACE FOUND: Saqqara, Egypt
PERIOD/DATE: New Kingdom, early Dynasty 18,
joint reign of Hatshepsut and Thutmose III
(*c.* 1479–1458 BCE) or possibly earlier
MEDIUM: Papyrus, ink, pigment
DIMENSIONS: 14 in. × 25 ft (35.6 cm × 7.7 m)
REPOSITORY: Brooklyn Museum
CREDIT LINE: Charles Edwin Wilbour Fund
ACCESSION NUMBER: 37.1777E
CONSERVATION: Through a grant from
the Leon Levy Foundation

* * *

The Papyrus Roll

Book of the Dead of the Goldworker of Amun Sobekmose (pBrooklyn 37.1777E) is an inscribed and decorated papyrus roll, now approximately twenty-five feet (seven-and-a-half meters) in length. Its height is just under fourteen inches (thirty-five-and-a-half centimeters).[1] Its fragmentary right edge indicates that the original beginning of the roll has been lost. How much text has disappeared cannot be established with certainty.[2] The present initial chapter of the papyrus, however, appears to be missing only a single column of text. If it was the original first chapter of the papyrus, it may have been preceded by a somewhat narrow blank sheet of papyrus, the means used at the time of its creation to protect the beginning and end of a papyrus roll.[3] The papyrus is inscribed on both the recto (front) and the verso (back),[4] a noteworthy feature for a papyrus of this type.

Texts

The papyrus is made up of ninety-eight different chapters (also called spells),[5] nearly all from the Book of the Dead corpus. The recto has fifty-six individual texts; the verso, forty-two. The papyrus therefore has close to half of the texts known from the corpus that had reached nearly two hundred in number by the Late Period. Only one New Kingdom Book of the Dead seems to have more individual chapters, the Book of the Dead of an official named Nu.[6] The placement of extensive texts on the verso of the Brooklyn papyrus is a rare feature, to the present translator's knowledge known from only one other Book of the Dead of the New Kingdom.[7]

The fifty-six texts on the recto are written in cursive hieroglyphs in columns that read from right to left. Each of its 535 columns of text is separated from the others by a single black guideline. The columns as a unit are also framed by a single black line above and below. As mentioned above, damage to the right edge of the papyrus indicates that an unidentifiable number of columns have been lost from the beginning of the papyrus. The layout and appearance of the final columns at the left end of the papyrus show that the texts here are complete and that the scribe had finished his work on the recto. The height of the columns runs about eleven-and-a-half inches (thirty centimeters), leaving a small margin above and below the columns. Beginning at the damaged right-hand edge of the texts of the recto, one can see two horizontal lines of text, one above and the other below the text field. Each comprises a sequence of offering formulae.[8] The beginning of each of these texts is also lost; again, it is unclear how much of the beginning of the papyrus may be missing.

The forty-two chapters of the verso are written in hieratic and arranged in twelve broad columns, showing a range from eighteen to twenty-seven lines. The position and layout of the first and last columns indicate that all of the verso texts have survived.[9]

A careful study of the texts of the Brooklyn papyrus leads to some interesting observations. First, a number of the individual chapters of the *Book of the Dead of the Goldworker of Amun Sobekmose* show little agreement with the same chapters known from Books of the Dead of the later Eighteenth Dynasty. The majority of these variant texts in the Brooklyn papyrus conform more closely to spells known from the Coffin Texts that date from hundreds of years earlier.[10] Second, the thematic material of the texts of the recto shows differences from that of the verso. The texts of the recto largely focus on the presence of the deceased in the Netherworld: (re)acquiring his physical powers, navigating his way past a number of obstacles, and successfully passing through judgment. The theme of "Going Forth by Day" is largely absent; in fact, the phrase occurs only twice.[11]

By contrast, eleven of the verso texts are in fact chapters for "Going Forth by Day," as their titles indicate.[12] Many of the other texts of the verso have clear solar or celestial references, showing a departure from the topography of the recto texts, which is clearly located in the Netherworld.

Numbering of the Texts

The numbering of the chapters in the *Book of the Dead of the Goldworker of Amun Sobekmose* may seem somewhat peculiar, as the chapter numbers appear to be out of sequence. This is because those Books of the Dead that were the first to be published in the mid-nineteenth century of our era date to the Saite Period. Those papyri had a fixed arrangement of chapters. The sequence numbers assigned to their chapters at that time are those still used today to identify chapters from the Book of the Dead corpus as a whole. Since Books of the Dead from earlier periods did not follow what was to become a new sequence, the numbering the modern reader encounters when reading an earlier funerary text, such as this one, may seem to be out of order. In addition, because of the very early date of the Brooklyn Museum papyrus, some of the chapters appear in atypical sequences or places in the papyrus when compared with other Eighteenth Dynasty Books of the Dead.

Vignettes

Four vignette fields illustrate the texts of the recto.

The first belongs to Chapter 136B, whose title is "Spell for Sailing in the Great Barque of Re to Pass by the Ring of Fire" (see fig. 29, in the recto translation). The god Re is shown in a solar boat as a falcon head with a sun-disk equipped with a *uraeus*. The boat rests on a sky-sign surmounting a field of stars. A similar vignette is found for this chapter in a number of Eighteenth Dynasty Books of the Dead from Thebes; more important, it is found as well in the Eighteenth Dynasty *Book of the Dead of Nebseni,* from Saqqara.[13]

The second sequence of vignettes belongs to Chapter 149, whose proper title, not seen in the Brooklyn papyrus, is "Spells for Knowing the Mounds of the House of Osiris in the Fields of Reeds" (see figs 30–35). It shows fourteen small vignettes, each separated from the others by a guideline. The vignettes that we see here are known from a number of Theban texts and again from the papyrus of Nebseni from Saqqara.[14] The placement of the vignettes in a sequence over the text is the normal means for illustrating this chapter.

The third vignette occupies the whole of the bordered area of the papyrus, taking up the space of what would be about thirteen or fourteen columns of text. It represents Chapter 150, a spell that has no text but consists of a vignette giving a completely pictorial representation of the fifteen mounds of the Field of Reeds (see figs 36–39).[15]

The fourth vignette belongs to Chapter 126 (figs 40, 41). It shows four baboons seated at the edge of a pool surrounded by six braziers. In roughly contemporaneous Books of the Dead, this vignette more typically shows only four braziers and a significantly smaller representation of the pool. In the Brooklyn papyrus, the text that immediately precedes this vignette is the final part of Chapter 125, and that which immediately follows is a text that has the title of Chapter 146 but a different, composite text.[16] Thus, the text of Chapter 126 was omitted, as was often the case, and the vignette was included to stand for the whole.

Following this final vignette, a number of texts, including the lengthy Chapters 145, 18, and 17, run uninterrupted for more than two hundred columns. The scribe ended his composition of the recto with Chapter 93, part of a sequence that continues immediately on the verso.

One detail worth noting is the single borderline that frames the text and vignettes. A two-line border (and sometimes a pair of two-line borders) is more common in texts of the Eighteenth Dynasty. The Book of the Dead of a man named Nebemteret shows an arrangement similar to that of the Brooklyn papyrus.[17]

Scripts and Writing Types

The texts of the recto are written in cursive hieroglyphs (figs 24, 26), a script used in the Coffin Text tradition. As noted above, there are very strong links between the Coffin Texts and the Book of the Dead, but there was not a seamless transition from the one tradition to the next. The earliest texts from the Book of the Dead corpus are found on the now-lost coffin of Queen Mentuhotep of the Thirteenth Dynasty. Her coffin shows a mixture of texts from the two traditions and two forms of writing: the Coffin Texts found there are written in cursive hieroglyphs while the Book of the Dead texts are written in lines of hieratic.[18] The early Books of the Dead on linen from the end of the Seventeenth and the beginning of the Eighteenth Dynasties were written in cursive hieroglyphs. Several Books of the Dead written on papyrus from the same period, however, show an admixture of writings in cursive hieroglyphs and hieratic[19] or simply in hieratic.[20] Cursive hieroglyphs did become the norm for Books of the Dead, possibly in the joint reign of Hatshepsut and Thutmose III in the early Eighteenth Dynasty, and continued in use for the duration of the New Kingdom (fig. 26).[21]

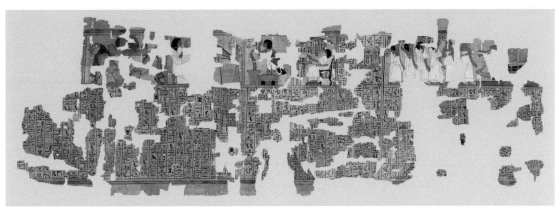

Fig. 24 Recto: cursive hieroglyphs
In the sixth column from the right, immediately following the rubrics or signs written red, are found
the title and name of the owner, Sobekmose, written in the Egyptian script known as cursive hieroglyphs;
these signs are highly stylized. Their form came to be somewhat standardized during the latter part of the
reign of Thutmose III (*c.* 1479–1425 BCE) or shortly after.

Fig. 25 Verso: hieratic script
Immediately following the rubrics or signs written in red in the second line of the present figure are found
the title and name of the owner, Sobekmose, written in the cursive Egyptian script know as hieratic.

Fig. 26 Cursive hieroglyphic writing from the *Book of the Dead of Neferrenpet*
The signs written in the columns below the vignettes offer a good look at the specialized writing used
in New Kingdom Books of the Dead.

Cursive hieroglyphs were also adopted as the writing system for other funerary texts in use during the New Kingdom and later.[22] For some New Kingdom Books of the Dead, a peculiar layout of the writing was employed as well. Called retrograde writing, the orientation of the writing of the signs looks as if the text reads from right to left, but in actuality it reads from left to right. This practice of retrograde writing is found only in Books of the Dead of the New Kingdom and was not universally employed. The *Book of the Dead of the Goldworker of Amun Sobekmose*, for example, was not written in the retrograde manner.

For the verso texts, the hieratic script was used (see fig. 25). It has often been stated in print that hieratic was not used at all in Books of the Dead until the Twenty-first Dynasty, when it became the script of choice for that genre. That statement needs correction.[23] All the same, the Brooklyn Museum text, with its twelve columns of hieratic lines used to write forty-two chapters, is extremely unusual, and distinguishes it as a very rare Book of the Dead exemplar. The early date of the papyrus may explain the extensive use of this type of writing.[24]

The texts of each of the chapters were written in a black ink made up of soot and water, for the most part. Most chapter headings were written in a red ink made from red ochre, a natural pigment derived from clay containing iron oxides. In a number of chapters, the coda was written in red ink as well. Additionally, in several chapters, individual words or phrases were written in red ink. The use of red ink in place of black generally served to highlight the beginnings and ends of individual texts and draw attention to words and phrases that had special significance within the body of a text. Texts or sections of texts so written are called rubrics.[25]

In the case of Chapter 136B in the Brooklyn papyrus, we see what appears to be a peculiar use of rubrics. The text header "To be recited" is written in red and seems to be scattered somewhat randomly through the writing of the chapter. Its presence here is best explained as follows: the scribe who made the exemplar from which the Brooklyn papyrus was copied used red ink to write a phrase at the top of each column of Chapter 136B in his papyrus, a practice known from certain texts on tomb walls; in turn, the scribe who drew up the Brooklyn Book of the Dead followed his model carefully and used red ink for every sign written in red in the original exemplar. As the spacing of the words in the Brooklyn papyrus was different, the scribe made a copy in which this rubricized phrase seems to occur somewhat randomly throughout the text.[26]

The different types of script lead to a question: Were the texts of the recto and verso in the Brooklyn papyrus originally individual and separate "books," perhaps derived from different sources? As noted above, the final chapters of the recto and the initial chapters of the verso are continuous parts of a larger sequence.[27] Therefore, the texts of the recto and verso actually do form a connected and integrated whole and, thus, were intended to be read consecutively.

Date

The precise date of production of this funerary papyrus is still open to question. A carbon-14 test (fig. 27) performed on a small, uninscribed fragment from the papyrus gave a general date range of 1620–1430 BCE and suggested a more specific date range of 1540–1450 BCE.[28] The extensive use of hieratic script on the verso and its paleography; the forms of the cursive hieroglyphs on the recto; and the overall appearance of the layout of the recto, with the text written in vertical columns and a scarcity of vignettes, all strongly point to a date probably in the early fifteenth century BCE, perhaps during the joint reign of Hatshepsut and Thutmose III (*c.* 1479–1458 BCE),[29] or possibly even earlier, thus conforming to the parameters suggested by the carbon-14 test.[30]

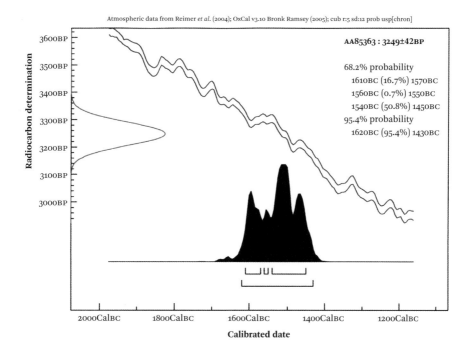

Atmospheric data from Reimer *et al.* (2004); OxCal v3.10 Bronk Ramsey (2005); cub r:5 sd:12 prob usp[chron]

AA85363 : 3249±42BP

68.2% probability
1610BC (16.7%) 1570BC
1560BC (0.7%) 1550BC
1540BC (50.8%) 1450BC
95.4% probability
1620BC (95.4%) 1430BC

Radiocarbon determination (y-axis): 3600BP, 3500BP, 3400BP, 3300BP, 3200BP, 3100BP, 3000BP

Calibrated date (x-axis): 2000CalBC, 1800CalBC, 1600CalBC, 1400CalBC, 1200CalBC

Calibrated date

Fig. 27 Carbon-14 test for *Book of the Dead of the Goldworker of Amun Sobekmose*
The graph and the accompanying statistics show that carbon-14 dating can suggest only a range of dates within which the original manufacture of the papyrus likely took place. The stylistic analysis of the papyrus vignettes, the handwriting of the text, and the overall appearance of the papyrus, taken in conjunction with the information provided by the carbon-14 test, have all been correlated to project and support the narrower timeframe here identified for the creation of the *Book of the Dead of the Goldworker of Amun Sobekmose.*

<h2 style="text-align:center">Provenance</h2>

As was the case with so many of the objects in this part of Brooklyn's Egyptian holdings, specific details about the time and place of the acquisition of the papyrus are scant. According to the earliest accession records, the provenance of the papyrus was said to have been "Sakkarah,"[31] one of the cemeteries west of the ancient city of Memphis in northern Egypt. Such a provenance also contributes to seeing the papyrus as something of a rarity, as the majority of the Books of the Dead known from this period have been found in the Theban region in Upper Egypt, particularly those dating from the early New Kingdom. A comparison of a number of the chapters in the Brooklyn papyrus with those found in the papyrus of Nebseni, known to have come from Saqqara, is quite revealing.[32] Several rare texts occur in both papyri; the division of Chapter 17 into three sections is found in both, and the division points used, as well as the order of the three sections, are exactly the same; and a number of textual variants not found in other papyri are common in both. Therefore, in addition to information given by the oldest records, we also have external textual evidence supporting Saqqara as the original provenance of the Brooklyn papyrus.

<h2 style="text-align:center">The Owner, Sobekmose</h2>

The papyrus was made for a man named Sobekmose whose single title is 𓎟𓃀𓏤𓈖𓇋𓏠𓈖 (*nby n ʾImn*)—which means "Goldworker of Amun."[33] Known from a number of New Kingdom sources, the title *nby* ("Goldworker") likely designates a man employed in one of the temple workshops as a jeweler or the like.[34] The addition of the name of a god to the title "Goldworker," here that of the god Amun, is attested in the Eighteenth Dynasty, although it does not appear to have been common.[35] At present, no Sobekmose with this title is known from other Egyptian monuments. The name of his mother, Sa(t)-Montu, is given a number of times along with her title, the ubiquitous "Mistress of the House." No other genealogical information, such as the name or title of his father, is offered.

<h2 style="text-align:center">The Modern History of the Papyrus</h2>

The papyrus was originally acquired in Egypt by Henry Abbott (fig. 28), an English doctor who traveled in Egypt and collected antiquities there during the first half of the nineteenth century.[36] In 1851, Abbott sent his collection to America for public viewing, hoping to earn back some of the money he had spent acquiring it.

Its first presentation was in New York, where the exhibition was received warmly although not with excessive excitement. One enthusiastic reviewer who visited the exhibition on a number of occasions was Walt Whitman, who wrote about Abbott and his "Egyptian museum."[37] Abbott did not reap the income from the exhibition that he had hoped, and in 1854 he decided to leave America with his collection. Against this move, New Yorkers strongly protested and even interceded to prevent the collection from leaving the city or America. With Abbott's death in 1859, a series of negotiations for the sale of the collection began between Abbott's family and the New-York Historical Society. In 1860, the collection was purchased by the Society,[38] where it remained on view from 1861 until 1937. In that year, it was given, along with the Historical Society's other Egyptian holdings, as a long-term loan to the Brooklyn Museum. In 1948, the Brooklyn Museum purchased the collections that comprised the loan.[39]

The *Book of the Dead of the Goldworker of Amun Sobekmose* was one of forty-six papyri in Abbott's collection. When J.J. Clère published his initial study of the Book of the Dead manuscripts in the Brooklyn Museum, in 1968, the papyrus was

Fig. 28 Portrait of Henry Abbott, *c.* **1861**
Dr Abbott is shown here in nineteenth-century Ottoman dress, a practice that was highly fashionable among European travelers in the Near East in the first half of that century.

apparently still unrolled.[40] Its great length led to its being cut first into five large sections, several of which were subsequently subdivided into smaller pieces to accommodate their placement between sheets of glass.

In 2009, the Brooklyn Museum undertook a complete conservation and restoration of the papyrus, to feature it in a new, long-term installation that opened to the public in the spring of 2010. During that period of conservation, the translation in the present volume was first undertaken. Several selections from the translation then in progress were included as wall panels with the installation of the papyrus and can be seen in the gallery today.

Notes

Works cited here in abbreviated form can be found in full in the Reference List.

1 The height of this papyrus fits into the range of the heights of the papyri of the New Kingdom surveyed by Jaroslav Černý in his 1947 lecture published as Černý 1952, and those that Irmtraut Munro surveyed in her study of Eighteenth Dynasty Books of the Dead (Munro 1988).

2 The damaged sheet on which the first group of chapters is written is only slightly narrower than the sheets that follow.

3 The end of the recto of the papyrus shows such treatment.

4 When the terms recto and verso are used to describe the proper front and back sides of a papyrus, respectively, the recto is, generally speaking, the side on which the upper layer of fibers runs horizontally; on the verso, the fibers lie vertically.

5 These terms are invariably used in discussions of the Book of the Dead to designate an individual text that has been presented by a scribe as a discrete textual unit. Over time, many of these individual texts became more or less standardized. Such is not the case, however, with many of the chapters in the *Book of the Dead of the Goldworker of Amun Sobekmose,* probably due to the early date of the papyrus. For example, Chapter 17, an individual and unified text in most papyri of the Eighteenth Dynasty and later, is presented as three different individual and non-contiguous texts in the Brooklyn papyrus; the same feature obtains in the *Book of the Dead of Nebseni* in the British Museum, another papyrus known to come from Saqqara but of a later date, *c.* 1420 BCE.

Several texts in the *Book of the Dead of the Goldworker of Amun Sobekmose* are direct copies of spells from the Coffin Texts; at least one text appears to be an original text not found elsewhere.

6 Now in the British Museum (BM EA 10477). It is approximately sixty-five feet (about twenty meters) long, but inscribed only on the recto. It has 136 individual texts. Nu's title was "Overseer of the Estate of the Treasurer." See Lapp 1997.

7 The exception is the *Book of the Dead of Mesemnetjer* (Louvre E.21324), which dates to the reign of Hatshepsut/Thutmose III. It has forty-three chapters on the recto and twenty-four on the verso; all are written in cursive hieroglyphs except for the final chapter of the verso, Chapter 133. See Munro 1988, pp. 279–80. A few New Kingdom Books of the Dead have a single line of an offering text or simply the name and title(s) of the owner on the verso. See Lucarelli 2010, p. 265.

8 On a number of Books of the Dead of the Eighteenth Dynasty, the offering formula was often written as a single line of text on the verso.

9 The number of lines per column is as follows: Column 1: 21; Column 2: 22; Column 3: 19; Column 4: 21; Column 5: 23; Column 6: 22; Column 7: 22; Column 8: 25; Column 9: 27; Column 10: 26; Column 11: 26; Column 12: 18.

10 John Gee has noted that even a simple distinction between the Coffin Texts and the Book of the Dead is tenuous, especially when looking at early material, such as that from the Seventeenth and early Eighteenth Dynasties. Gee stated that when examining the two, "The picture that emerges is

that this is a single work, whose contents change over time" (Gee 2010, p. 31). But there are certain differences, such as the pronounced interest in the Netherworld, its topography, and its inhabitants found in the Book of the Dead tradition.

11 The phrase is found in the headings for Chapter 64 and Chapter 17$_3$, where it is commonly given as part of the title of these spells. There are several texts that center on "going forth" and "entering," but their focus is restricted to going forth and entering Rosetau or the necropolis.

12 Chapters 68, 92, 72, 71, 65, 8B, 8A, 1, 64B, 2, and 3.

13 The *Book of the Dead of Nebseni* (British Museum BM EA 9900) is the longest Book of the Dead papyrus of the Eighteenth Dynasty, at seventy-seven feet, seven-and-a-half inches (just under twenty-four meters); it has seventy-nine individual chapters, or more if one differentiates those chapters that occur two or even three times in different sections of the papyrus. See Lapp 2004, especially pls 77 and 78 for the vignette of Chapter 136B.

14 See Lapp 2004, pls 79–85.

15 This vignette appears in *Book of the Dead of Nebseni* as well; see Lapp 2004, pls 85, 86.

16 The text of this chapter is composed of various material drawn from the Book of the Dead and the Coffin Text corpora.

17 J.E. 95575 + J.E. 95693, now in the Egyptian Museum, Cairo. Munro has given a date range for that text from the reign of Thutmose III to that of Amunhotep II. Its provenance is Saqqara. Thus, both date and provenance conform generally with those of the Brooklyn papyrus. See Munro 1994, pp. 191–204 and pls. 65–71.

18 See Geisen 2004, pp. 5–10. Our knowledge of the texts on the coffin is based on copies made by the early Egyptian traveler Gardner Wilkinson, whose notes and sketches are now in the Bodleian Library of Oxford University. See Geisen 2004, p. 9 nn. 1–4 and p. 167, n. 1.

19 For example, the *Book of the Dead of Iahmes,* now in the Musée du Louvre, Paris; see Munro 1995, and especially pl. I, for the concurrence of these two forms of writings.

20 The *Book of the Dead of Hatnefer* was written in hieratic. Hatnefer was the mother of Senenmut, an important official in Hatshepsut's court. See Lansing and Hayes 1937, p. 20.

21 Dorman 2014, p. 4.

22 Such as the Book of Caverns, the Book of Gates, and the Amduat papyri.

23 In her survey of New Kingdom Books of the Dead, Munro (1988) documents the sporadic appearance of hieratic signs in cursive hieroglyphic texts. She also lists one Book of the Dead written in hieratic, a text prepared for a daughter of King Ahmose that is currently in the Museo Egizio in Turin, Italy. It is a brief manuscript, containing only five fragmentary spells. To the list of New Kingdom Books of the Dead written in hieratic should be added a Book of the Dead papyrus in the British Museum that was recently unrolled, in 1992. It predates the reign of Thutmose III and is highly fragmentary, but one can identify Chapters 39, 64, 71, 91, and 124. Two other texts in the British Museum belonging to the Eighteenth Dynasty have chapters written in hieratic: the Book of the Dead of a man named Nebimes with Chapters 17/18-22-23-24-25-26-28-27-30A-31, all written in hieratic; and the *Book of the Dead of Khay, the Head Archivist of the Lord of the Two Lands,* written in both cursive hieroglyphs (four chapters) and hieratic (two chapters: Chapters 181-173). Thus, the use of hieratic in early Books of the Dead, although a sporadic phenomenon, is certainly not unknown.

24 The use of hieratic also contributed to the high number of chapters found on this papyrus. Hieratic writing is far more economical than cursive hieroglyphs in terms of the space required, especially when the writing is small and the lines are spaced closely together, as is the case in the Brooklyn papyrus.

25 Note, for example, the extensive use of rubrics in Chapter 17.

26 The *Book of the Dead of Nebseni* shows the writing of this chapter with the writing of the phrase "to be recited" in red at the top of each column. See Lapp 2004, pl. 78.

27 The sequence runs Chapters **23**-**24**-**25**-**26**-**28**-**27**-**43**-**30A**-**31**-**33**-**34**-**35**-**74**-**45**-**93**-*91*-*41*-*61*-*42*-*14*. (The numbers of the recto texts are given here in **bold**, and those of the verso texts in *italics*.)

28 The test gave a range of dates and a probability factor for each date: a probability of 95.4 percent for the range 1620–1430 BCE; and a probability of 50.4 percent for the range 1540–1450 BCE.

29 1479–1458 BCE is the time span of the joint reign; Thutmose III continued to rule until 1425 BCE.

30 Compare the statements in Munro 2010, pp. 55–57.

31 Accession records of the Egyptian collection in the Brooklyn Museum.

32 The *Book of the Dead of Nebseni,* also dating to the Eighteenth Dynasty, is later than the Brooklyn text by, perhaps, three generations or more. A comparison of the vignettes and the cursive hieroglyphic writing in both papyri makes a difference in date for these papyri amply clear. See Lapp 2004.

33 The basic title *nby* ("goldworker") is known as early as the Twelfth Dynasty, in the reign of Sesostris I, and is apparently a Memphite title; for *nby,* see Wb. II 241, 1–7.7; Gourlay 1979, pp. 88–89, 91; Simpson 1979, p. 50; Gaballa 1977, p. 126; de Meulenaere 1977, p. 246. Vercoutter 1959, pp. 120–53, studied titles connected with gold production in regions of southern Egypt and Nubia. For the title *nby,* he suggested a derivation from the verb ⳻ *nbi* ("to melt"), which is written with ⳻, the hieroglyphic sign for gold, as early as the Middle Kingdom. That verb came to mean "to gild" or "to fashion," among other things. Thus, Vercoutter suggested a translation "goldworker," a neutral rendering that covers a range of tasks from processing ore and gold dust to gilding to jewelry making.

34 The title *ḥm.w-nby* (the translation of which would be something like "craftsman-goldworker") is known from demotic texts connected with the temple of Isis at Philae; the title is also attested in Coptic. At least one demotic text connected with the "craftsmen-goldworkers" of Philae indicates that the primary task of such artisans was the transformation of gold

powder or gold from rough ingots into a variety of objects. Another possibility is that Sobekmose was connected with work in the gold mines either in Nubia, the eastern desert, or the Sinai, though such an idea seems far less likely.

35 The statue of a "Goldworker of Amun," a man named Samut, dating to the late Eighteenth Dynasty, is in the Ägyptisches Museum, Berlin. A statue in the Louvre of a similarly named man, also dating to the late Eighteenth Dynasty, bears the title "Goldworker of Min." A related title—although perhaps only generally so—is the title *wᶜb nby.w* ("wab-priest of the goldworkers"), which, as Vercoutter 1959, pp. 120–53, suggested, referred to goldworkers attached to the permanent staff of a temple.

36 Some of the information recorded here is drawn from Raver 1997, pp. 39–45.

37 Walt Whitman, "One of the Lessons Bordering Broadway: The Egyptian Museum," *Life Illustrated,* December 8, 1855.

38 Raver 1997, p. 40, estimated that Abbott spent about one hundred thousand dollars on just six hundred of the objects that he collected, a figure that seems excessively high. In 1849, Samuel Birch, head of the department of antiquities in the British Museum, asked Gardner Wilkinson to examine Abbott's collection for possible purchase. Wilkinson relayed Abbott's offer to the museum to sell the collection for ten thousand pounds on a number of different occasions but the museum rejected the offer. Henry Salt's collection of 1,083 objects though fewer in number than Abbott's was of similarly fine quality. In 1835, that collection sold for £7,168 18s 6d, a figure that seems quite in line with the offer that Abbott allegedly made to Wilkinson. See Thompson 1992, p. 201.

39 The objects acquired by the Brooklyn Museum from the sale numbered well over two thousand, of which number Abbott's share was the greatest. The total number of objects attributed to his collection that are now in Brooklyn is close to sixteen hundred.

40 Clère 1967–68, pp. 88–93.

Translation
of the Recto Texts

Note to the Reader

Short interpretive texts, printed in italics, precede each chapter or sequence of chapters, providing an ongoing explanatory commentary. Those comments marked by the heading CONNECTING THREADS show how a given chapter relates to those that precede and follow it.

The numbering of the chapters in the *Book of the Dead of the Goldworker of Amun Sobekmose* may seem to be out of sequence. This is because the standard, accepted numbering of Book of the Dead chapters, established in the nineteenth century, was based on examples from a much later period in Egyptian history than the Brooklyn papyrus, and with a different sequence of chapters. In this publication, the chapters are printed in the precise order in which they appear in the Brooklyn papyrus, though to make them easier to identify within the Book of the Dead corpus, each carries the later, standard number. Sequences of chapters are shown with hyphens between the individual chapter numbers.

As a convenience to the reader, the translation of each chapter has been divided into paragraphs when appropriate to help elucidate the structure of each text.

General explanatory notes about the translation appear at the foot of the page. Technical notes on alternate readings, transliterations, comparisons with other ancient texts, bibliographical citations, and the like appear as endnotes, following the translation as a whole, and are keyed to each chapter.

The following typographical conventions are used within the translation:

- **Ellipsis points within square brackets [...]** indicate a gap or irrecoverable loss of text in the papyrus.
- **[Words in square brackets]** are restorations of lost text.
- **(Words in parentheses)** are editorial additions intended to give the English translation greater fluency or clearer meaning.
- **Words in red** designate text originally written in red ink in the papyrus.
- **WORDS IN SMALL CAPITAL LETTERS** indicate original chapter headings or titles.
- **Words in this typeface** (*rȝ n tm ... mdw ḥr*) are transliterations, or phonetic renderings, of Egyptian words.

Technical terms are generally defined at first use. For ease of reference, they also appear in the Glossary, which in addition includes divine symbols, divine epithets, place names, and the names of gods.

CHAPTER 105

In this chapter, Sobekmose assures his ka *that he is free of any guilt from moral wrong-doing and promises that he will successfully pass the test of judgment that he is soon to undergo (see Chapter 125, below). As the double of the deceased, the* ka *would be aware of any transgressions committed on earth and thus may be inclined to dissociate itself from the deceased. The claim that his* ka *is now divine and due the prerogatives of a god is a further assertion of innocence. The offerings referred to in the complete version of the chapter (which is only partially preserved here) draw attention to the need for continued provisioning in the afterlife. The text is also a declaration that the deceased, together with his* ka*, will be integrated into the social order of the afterlife. The amulet of Re that is mentioned alludes to personal protection and may also serve as a symbol of the blessed dead, among whom the deceased now claims membership. Note that this spell occurs again among the texts on the verso.*

Chapter 105 (Cols 1–4)

[...] [in]cense (so that) I may purify you with them[1] (and that) [I may purify] your fluids.[2] This evil utterance which I have said (and) this evil wrong which I have done will [not] be put on me,[3] because this papyrus amulet that belongs at the throat of Re and that is given to those in the horizon belongs to me. (If) they flourish, my *ka* flourishes; likewise, the provisions for my *ka* are like (their) provisions. (O) balance-scale, may truth be joyful [at] his nose[4] on this day. (O) my *ka,* you shall not let (my) head (or) shoulder be taken away from me. To me belongs an eye that sees and a *ba* that hears. To me belongs a bull of the animals for slaughter. Are there no invocation offerings from me for those in charge?

---

1 I.e., the natron (salt) and incense mentioned in the lost part of the text, where the beginning of the papyrus is damaged.
2 Bodily fluids, human and divine, were believed to have procreative and protective powers, an idea commonly found in magical, medical, and creation texts.
3 Acknowledgment of wrongdoing but denial of guilt.
4 Objects like lotus blossoms and *ankh*-signs seen at the nose of the deceased in Egyptian reliefs were believed to offer the "breath of life," an allusion to the ability to live on after death. The phrase "truth ... at the nose" used here seems rather to mean something like "be high up" or "directly" in the presence of the god.

Chapters 47-103-104

In the next three texts, the deceased furthers his contention that he is now a member of the retinue of the gods. He asserts his right to sit among the gods and even orders them into his following. His claim to power is based on his rightful inheritance of these gods from his father, their creator. The insistence on certain rights and powers proceeds logically from the first chapter. The word "entourage" introduces the theme of "journeying" that is further developed by the verb "passed by" at the end of the sequence.

Connecting Threads: *The coherence of the three chapters as a group is achieved through the references to "seat" and "throne" found at the beginning and to "sitting" at the end; these references may form a link with the preceding chapter, whose final word has the determinative of a seated deity.*

Chapter 47 (Cols 4–5)

NOT TAKING THE SEAT (AND) THRONE OF A MAN FROM HIM. To be recited by the Goldworker of Amun Sobekmose, justified.[5] He says:

My seat, my throne, come to me. I am your lord. Gods, come into my entourage. I am the son of your lord. You belong to me. It is my father who made you.

Chapter 103 (Cols 5–6)

BEING IN THE ENTOURAGE OF HATHOR. [To be recited] by the Goldworker of Amun Sobekmose, justified. He says:

I am a nobleman who is pure, an *ias*-priest.[6] (O) Ihy, Ihy,[7] I shall be in the entourage of Hathor.[8]

Chapter 104 (Cols 6–8)

SITTING AMONG THE GREAT GODS. To be recited by the Goldworker of Amun-Re Sobekmose, justified. He says:

I have sat among the great gods. I have passed by the house of the evening boat, the cicada bringing me.[9]

---

5 The term "justified" following the name of Sobekmose is an epithet indicating that he has successfully passed judgment after death. See Chapter 125 below.
6 Priests of Hathor with shaved heads who are often depicted as beggars.

7 The son of Hathor and her chief sistrum-player.
8 I.e., for the sake of your mother.
9 "bringing me" in the sense of acting as a guide for me.

CHAPTER 76

The title of this chapter indicates that its theme is transformation. The text, however, simply develops the theme of movement introduced in the preceding sequence. Here, that idea is expanded through allusions to passing by the house of the king and to the pathway on which the deceased wishes to travel.

CONNECTING THREADS: *The phrase "house of the king" and the word "cicada" serve to link this chapter to the sequence that precedes it.*

Chapter 76 (Cols 8–9)

MAKING THE FORMS WHICH (HE) DESIRES. [To be recited] by the Goldworker of Amun-Re Sobekmose, justified. He says:

I pass by the house of the king. It is the cicada who brings me. O (you) who fly to heaven, who illuminates the son of the White Crown and who guards the White Crown. [I] shall be with you, joining the Great God. Make a path for me (so that) I may pass on it.

Chapter 10

The placement of Chapter 10 immediately after Chapter 76 serves to continue the theme of movement but also introduces the theme of the use of force. The deceased asserts that he has not only the power of movement but the efficacious magic to force his way into whatever realms of the cosmos he chooses. In addition, he has regained the ability to eat, through which he can now maintain his strength. The reference to eating and defecation also develops the theme of the restoration of earthly powers to the deceased.

Chapter 10 (Cols 9–12)

ALLOWING the Goldworker of Amun Sobekmose, justified, TO GO FORTH AGAINST [HIS] ENEMIES.

I have hacked up the sky. I have opened the horizon. I have traveled through the earth (to) its edges. I have put the *akhs* (and) the great ones in an uproar because I am one who is equipped with his millions, namely with my magic. I eat with my mouth. I defecate with my anus because I am, indeed, a god, lord of the Duat.[10] I was given these things fixed that make the Goldworker of Amun Sobekmose, justified, prosper.

---

10 The term Duat is one of the Egyptian names for the Netherworld.

Chapter 22

This text is another declaration of power, here that of the ability to speak with the mouth that the deceased has given (back) to himself. Beginning with an allusion to rebirth, the chapter moves on to stress, once again, the deceased's capacity for movement. It also implies that he is now impervious to the dangers of any locality he wishes or needs to enter. Thus, the fire of the Island of Flame offers no threat or menace for him.

Connecting Threads: The reoccurrence of the word "mouth" here as the organ of speech serves as a link to the preceding chapter in which the deceased stated, "I eat with my mouth."

Chapter 22 (Cols 12–14)

GIVING THE MOUTH OF A MAN TO HIM IN THE NECROPOLIS. To be recited by the Goldworker of Amun Sobekmose, justified, born of the Mistress of the House Sa(t)-Montu, justified. He says:

I have arisen from my egg which is in the lands of the secrets. I give my mouth to myself (so that) I may speak with it in the presence of the gods of the Duat. My hand shall not be turned away from the council of the great god Osiris, Lord of Rosetau, this one who is at the top of the dais. I have come (so that) I may do what my heart desires in the Island of Fire, extinguishing the fire which comes forth.

CHAPTERS 86-87-88

These three short chapters continue the theme of transformation, here into animal forms: the swallow, the snake, and the crocodile. The three texts taken together depict a landscape that includes the sky, earth, and water, offering a comprehensive picture of the created cosmos and stating that the deceased has access to whatever places he wishes. His power to change form ensures his unhindered access. The snake and crocodile, in contrast to the swallow, are more commonly encountered as negative cosmic forces associated with the initial stage of creation from chaos. Transformations into non-human forms such as these are central to entering and surviving in the Netherworld.
CONNECTING THREADS: *The references to fire at the end of the preceding chapter and again in the first chapter of this sequence form the link that connects these two groups of chapters.*

Chapter 86 (Cols 14–16)
MAKING THE FORMS OF A SWALLOW. To be recited by the Goldworker of Amun Sobekmose, justified. He says:

I am a swallow, I am a swallow. I am that scorpion, the daughter of Re.[11] How sweet are your odors, the flame that comes forth from the horizon.

Chapter 87 (Cols 16–17)
MAKING THE FORMS OF A SNAKE. To be recited by the Goldworker of Amun Sobekmose, justified. He says:

I am a snake [whose] years are long, who sleeps (and) is born every day. I am a snake who is at the limits of the earth. I sleep. I am born. I am sound every day.

Chapter 88 (Cols 17–19)
MAKING THE FORMS OF A CROCODILE. To be recited by the Goldworker of Amun Sobekmose, justified. He says:

I am in truth the one in the middle of his waters. I am the crocodile who seizes. I am one who takes by robbing. I am the great fish, the great one in Kem-wer.[12] I am the lord of prostration in Letopolis.

---

11 *ḥdd*, the name of a scorpion goddess.
12 A site in Lower Egypt called the "Bitter Lakes."

Chapters 56-5

This pair of chapters is linked through their references to Hermopolis (ancient Wenu), a locality that had especially strong associations with the god Thoth. Though he is not mentioned directly in either of these chapters, Thoth does appear in the text that follows. Again, the power that the deceased lays claim to is both violent and aggressive in nature, as is the reference to his gluttony. The title of Chapter 5 focuses on the threat of being forced to work, a probable allusion to being impressed into work gangs. Impressment was a common practice in Egypt during the time of the Inundation, when the government turned to the masses as a source of labor, since agricultural work was naturally interrupted during the seasonal flood. The Egyptians believed that such unpleasant tasks or responsibilities possibly awaited them in the Netherworld as well.

Chapter 56 (Cols 19–21)

BREATHING AIR ON EARTH. To be recited by the Goldworker of Amun Sobekmose, justified. He says:

O Atum, give the sweet breath which is in your nostril. I am the one who occupies this great seat which is in the middle of Wenu.[13] I have guarded this great egg of the Honker. (If) it is strong, vice versa.[14] (If) I live, it lives. (If) I breathe air, it breathes air.

Chapter 5 (Cols 21–23)

NOT MAKING WORK IN THE NECROPOLIS. To be recited by the Goldworker of Amun Sobekmose, justified. He says:

I am the glutton of the Inert One. I have come forth from Wenu. I am in truth a *ba*. I live on the entrails of the baboon.[15]

13 Wenu is Hermopolis, in Lower Egypt.
14 I.e., "I am strong."

15 Possibly a claim to magical power in the Netherworld.

CHAPTER 96/97

This composite chapter continues the theme of transformation introduced earlier; here the deceased continues his claims to have access to the gods and the power to appease them. The theme of rejuvenation runs through the text as well, as the numerous references to the solar cycle and the Inundation make clear. Although Thoth is mentioned in the heading of the chapter, there is no direct mention of him in the chapter proper; there may be, however, an allusion to him in the phrase "I am the one who is an interpreter of speech," as Thoth was the creator of language in a number of creation texts.
CONNECTING THREADS: *The name Thoth offers a link to the preceding group through the place name Wenu (Hermopolis), where Thoth was the primary deity.*

Chapter 96/97 (Cols 23–30)

EXISTING AT THE SIDE OF **THOTH.** MAKING A MAN BECOME AN *AKH* IN THE NECROPOLIS. To be recited by the Goldworker of Amun Sobekmose, justified. He says:

I give Maat to Re. I have appeased Seth with the spit of the god Aker,[16] bloody ones from the spine of Geb.[17] To be recited. (O) Night-Boat! (O) scepter of Anubis! These four *akhs* who are in the entourage of the lord of offerings are pleased with me. The field is mine by their commands. I am the father of the Inundation[18] who dispels thirst. I am the one who guards the two pools. See me, you elder and great gods, foremost of the *bas* of Heliopolis. I am high above you. I am the effective one among you. See me, cleansing myself for this very great *ba* (of mine). I cannot give myself to this opposition that comes forth from your mouths. It is gone. It will not turn back against me. I am purified in the pool (used) for appeasing judgment. I put on the fillet in Behbeit[19] under the sycamore of the two goddesses of the sky (and) the earth. In truth, *moringa*-oil[20] is pleasing to me. I am vindicated against all of my former enemies.

Draw near, (you) ones who petition Maat through me. I am the one who is ruler, the one who is truly precise, the one who is in the land. I speak of him. I am the one who is an interpreter of speech, the powerful one of the sole lord, Aten, the great one who lives (on) truth that is with him. I will not cause injury to myself thereby, while the day is uncovered in extreme splendor.

---

16 Divine personification of the earth.
17 A divinized name of the earth.
18 A reference to the annual flooding of the Nile.

19 A locale in the Delta in Lower Egypt.
20 This oil was made from pressing the seeds of *Moringa oleifera*, a deciduous tree that grows in tropical and semi-tropical regions. Commonly found in Egyptian tombs, the oil was believed to reverse aging. It continues to be used today as a remedy for dry and wrinkled skin and as a food supplement.

Chapters 117-118

These two chapters were treated as a unit by the scribe who created the papyrus, as Chapter 118 was not given its customary separate heading. Osiris is mentioned in his guise of lord of the realm of the dead, and the Osirian associations are further developed by the mention of Rosetau, a somewhat mysterious and secret place connected with the embalming of Osiris. The theme of movement and "journeying" also continues, as the deceased now has access to Rosetau and the right to walk upon its paths, further developing the motif of transfiguration to the state of an akh.

Connecting Threads: *The theme of transfiguration to an* akh *was first introduced in the preceding Chapter 96/97.*

Chapter 117 (Cols 30–33)

Taking the path in Rosetau.[21] To be recited by the Goldworker of Amun Sobekmose, justified. He says:

The upper path (is) in Rosetau. I am one whom the Great One clothes, who goes forth [with] the *werret*-crown. I have come. I have established offerings in Abydos. I open the paths in Rosetau, (so that) I may ease the suffering of Osiris. I am the one who created the water, [one to whom] his boat is assigned in the valley. Great One, Osiris, Bull of the West—this path of mine, make it (so).

Chapter 118 (Cols 33–34)

I am one who is born in Rosetau. The transfiguration to an *akh* was given to me by the lord of the dignitaries[22] of Pe, namely the purification of Osiris, who receives old age in Rosetau [as] the guide of Osiris. I am one whom they guide [to] the mound of Osiris.

---

21 Originally the name of the necropolis precincts of Giza and Saqqara, it was adopted as a name for the Netherworld or an area thereof, especially in its connections with the embalming of Osiris.

22 I.e., the "mummified ones."

CHAPTER 17₁

This section of Chapter 17 offers the first description of the negative forces that inhabit the Netherworld, all potential threats to the deceased. Apart from Seth, the other beings enumerated here pose threats only to those dead who are impure and who will not pass or have not passed judgment; the slaughtering-places, traps, and kettles mentioned are the instruments of their destruction. Note that the claim of the deceased that he is impervious to the attempted machinations against him is grounded in the statements that he is "one who is pure" and that he is "in the middle of Mesqet." The latter allusion indicates that he is one of the "Imperishable Stars" (i.e., one who has already attained a state of permanence after death).

Chapter 17₁ (Cols 34–42)

O lord of terror, one who is over the Two Lands,[23] lord of red-blood whose slaughtering blocks flourish, to whom the Double Crown and joy were given, to whom was assigned rule among the gods in the presence of the Lord of All, effective *ba* within Herakleopolis, to whom strength was given against sinners, to whom eternity leads. Rescue me from this god who seizes *bas*, who licks up corruption, who lives on what is rotting, the one who belongs to the darkness, whom those in weariness fear. As for this god who seizes souls, who licks up corruption, he is Seth.

O you, Khepri, who is in the middle of his sacred boat, primeval one whose body is eternity, rescue me from these ones to whom examinations belong,[24] to whom the Lord of All has given the magical powers, who stand guard [against] the rebels, who cause slaughter within the slaughtering-place, from whose guard there is no going forth. Their knives shall not enter into me. I shall not come into their slaughtering-places. I shall not descend into their kettles. I shall not sit within their fish-traps. There shall be done to me nothing by these abominations of the gods, because I am one who is pure, who is in the middle of Mesqet,[25] to whom the evening meal is given, namely faience from Tjennet.[26]

---

23 The term Two Lands refers to Upper and Lower Egypt, i.e., Egypt in its entirety.
24 I.e., those who interrogate the deceased at judgment; compare the forty-two judges of Chapter 125.
25 Mesqet is an uncertain area of the night sky originally thought to correspond to the Milky Way; it is the region of the east through which the celestial bodies pass in their risings. It is also one of the areas of the heavens that the deceased is said to travel through.
26 Wordplay on the Egyptian for "faience" (*tjehenet*) and the sanctuary called Tenenet located in Memphis, written *Tjennet*. A gloss on this section of the text that is found in other Books of the Dead of the Eighteenth Dynasty states that the faience referred to here is the "Eye of Horus."

CHAPTER 20-13

Chapter 20 focuses on the vindication of the deceased, namely being found innocent of any of the charges that his enemies may lay against him. (As will be seen in Chapter 125 below, passing judgment in the Netherworld involved a complex declaration of truth on the part of the deceased through which he absolves himself of all wrongdoing.) Because this vindication takes place in a number of councils of the gods, throughout Egypt, where Thoth had vindicated Osiris, this declaration serves as a statement of universal innocence. The councils enumerated here all center on cult places associated with the burial of Osiris, locales where individual parts or relics of the dismembered Osiris were believed to have been interred. This chapter forms a continuation of the Osirian theme presented in the preceding pair of chapters. The focal point of the ensuing Chapter 13 is freedom of movement, in particular the ability to enter and leave the "beautiful West," i.e., the necropolis or Netherworld. The verb "to enter" found here was often used to designate initiation into a religious cult, to denote the privilege of being a member of a sacred circle, or to refer to the right to enter areas of an Egyptian temple that were not accessible to most people, not even to all priests.

CONNECTING THREADS: *The first spell of this sequence is a protection text, just like the preceding Chapter 17. The god to whom the deceased makes his appeal is Thoth. The focus of the deceased in Chapter 13 on the adoration of Osiris links it to the chapters that precede and follow.*

Chapter 20 (Cols 42–51)

O Thoth, who vindicated Osiris against his enemies. Snare [the enemies] of the Osiris, the Goldworker of Amun Sobekmose,[27] justified, in the presence of the council of every god (and) every goddess:[28] in the presence of the great council that is in Heliopolis (on) that night of fighting—that means—of overthrowing the rebels; in the presence of the council that is in Djedet (on) that night of standing up the two *djed*-pillars;[29] in the presence of the council that is in Letopolis (on) that night of the evening offering in Letopolis; in the presence of the council that is in Pe and Dep (on) that night of confirming the inheritance of Horus, namely the property of his father Osiris; in the presence of the council that is in Seshty[30] (on) that night (when) Isis made mourning behind her brother Osiris; in

27 In funerary texts, the deceased is often directly associated with Osiris, essentially becoming "an Osiris" or even "the Osiris."
28 Here begins a list of the councils of the gods and goddesses.

29 Wordplay on a place name in Heliopolis and the *djed*-pillars associated with the spine of Osiris.
30 Seshty is located near Heliopolis in Lower Egypt.

the presence of the council that is in Abydos (on) that night of the Haker-festival, of counting the dead (and) of enumerating the *akhs* (on) the paths of the dead, (on) that night of taking count of the ones who have nothing; in the presence of the council that is in the "great hacking up of the earth"; the one that is in Naref;[31] in the presence of the council that is in Rosetau (on) that night of vindicating Horus against his enemies.

Horus is justified, his heart joyful. The two sanctuaries are appeased because of it. Osiris, his heart (is) joyful.

(O) Thoth, vindicate the Osiris, the Goldworker of Amun Sobekmose, against his enemies in the presence of the council of [every] god (and) every goddess; in the presence of this council of Osiris behind the shrine.

Chapter 13 (Cols 51–52)

To me belongs mankind, giv[en] [wholly to me. I have entered as a falcon; I have gone forth]. Morning star, make a path for me (so that) I may enter in peace into the beautiful West. I belong to the pool of Horus. Act for me so that I may enter (and) I may adore Osiris, Lord of Life.

---

31 The name of the necropolis of Abusir al-Malaq, located on the west bank of the Nile near the entrance to the Faiyum.

CHAPTER 17₂

In this section of Chapter 17, the connections with Osiris are further developed, not only through the assertion by Sobekmose that he is Osiris but through associations as well with Isis and Nephthys, who are the sisters and mourners of Osiris and play a role in his revivification. The deceased also claims that a variety of beings, both human and divine, perform various services for him because his status is equal to that of the gods.

Chapter 17₂ (Cols 52–57)

ANOTHER SPELL. (O) white-mouthed (and) flat-headed one, fall back, because of [my] strength. I act as a guard—do not guard me. I am Osiris. I have flown up. I have alighted, my hair in the middle of my heart as my topknot. I was conceived by Isis, I was begotten by Nephthys. They[32] drive off the ones who interfere with me. My exaltation (and) my awe are at the limits of the elders of the gods. The patricians and the common people encircle me, throwing open the ways for me (and) driving away evils. The gray-haired ones uncover their arms for me. The [odors] which offerings create are provided for me. I cause offerings to be made for Kheraha which is in very great fear of me. I give greetings to the gods. I am Wadjet, mistress of those who are in Anu.[33]

---

32 I.e., Isis and Nephthys.
33 The name of the 8th *nome* (or district) of Lower Egypt.

Chapters 44-50

The formal element that joins these chapters is their "negative" heading: "Spell for not...." In Chapter 44, the deceased claims association with the sun-god Re, a god who routinely overcomes the challenges he faces each night and is able to rise each morning as a result. Associating with Re is a way of ensuring that one "will not die again," a phrase pointing to the cyclical nature of the dangers that the deceased faces in the Netherworld. To overcome them once is not to overcome them permanently. The deceased also claims that certain parts of his anatomy are intact, an allusion to the fact that his body has not suffered the disintegration associated with the death and dismemberment of Osiris by his brother Seth. This physical intactness alludes to his ability to continue to move about and to function normally as he did on earth. In Chapter 50, the deceased explains that his ability to avoid the "place of execution of the god" derives from the power of amuletic knots that various gods have tied around him, possibly a reference to the bands of linen used in mummification. The purpose they serve is to create barriers to any hostile beings or activities.

Connecting Threads: *References to anatomical intactness and to the theme of journeying found here connect this sequence to much of what precedes it.*

Chapter 44 (Cols 57–61)

Spell for not dying again. To be recited by the Goldworker of Amun Sobekmose, justified. He says:

The cavern and the two peep-holes are opened for me (and) sunlight falls within the darkness. I sanctify the Eye of Horus. Wepwawet has nursed me. Conceal me among you, (o) Imperishable Stars.[34] Its neck is (that of) Re. My face is open.[35] My heart is in its place. My utterance (by which) I am known belongs to me. I am Re who himself protects himself by himself. I am ignorant that I have been robbed.[36] I live for you, my father, son of Isis. I am the one who is your son, your eldest who sees your secrets. I appear in glory as king of the gods. I will not die again.

---

34 The Imperishable Stars are the circumpolar stars, those that appear to circle the North Star overhead and never disappear below the horizon.

35 I.e., "I can see properly."

36 I.e., "I know that I have not been robbed."

Chapter 50 (Cols 61–66)

SPELL FOR NOT ENTERING THE SLAUGHTERING-PLACE OF THE GOD. To be recited by the Goldworker of Amun, Sobekmose. He says:

A knot is tied around me in the sky where it connects to earth by Re every day. He has fastened the knot for the Inert One supported upon his thighs (on) that day of cutting off the lock of hair. A knot is tied around me by Seth, (when) the Ennead (was) in his power before discord arose.[37] May you protect me from the ones who slew my father. I am the one who has seized the Two Lands. A knot is tied around me by Nut. I saw her first activity. I saw Maat when there was not yet a birth of the gods (or their) images. I am Penty. I am the sacrilege of the great gods.

37 An allusion to the killing of Osiris
and the subsequent contending
for rightful power by Horus and Seth.

Chapter 38A

Sobekmose now claims that he is Atum, a primeval deity associated with creation. Solar references continue throughout, as does the theme of being in the company of specific divinities.

Connecting Threads: *The claim at the end of the text of "living truly after my death like Re every day" clearly forms a link between this chapter and the two immediately preceding.*

Chapter 38A (Cols 66–73)

SPELL FOR LIVING ON AIR IN THE NECROPOLIS. To be recited by the Goldworker of Amun Sobekmose, justified. He says:

I am Atum. I have gone forth from the Nun to the watery region of the sky. I have taken my seat of the West. I issue commands to the *akhs* whose seats are concealed [from] Ruty. I have made the circuits, rejoicing in the sacred boat of Khepri. I eat there. I have power there. I live on air there. I guide the sacred boat of Re. He opens the mouth of the earth for me. He opens the gates of Geb for me. I have seized those who are in the snare of the Great One. Those who are in their shrines guide me. I pay respects to the Two Lords, Horus and Seth. I lead the children who are above me. I enter. I go forth. My throat is not constricted. I descend into the sacred boat, truth at my side. Those who are in the day-boat (are) at the side of Re when he rises from his horizon. I live after my death like Re every day. I am as powerful as Ruty, living truly after my death like Re every day, the Goldworker of Amun Sobekmose, justified. The land is filled with the lotus anew to appease the Two Lands.

CHAPTER 153

This chapter focuses on the fishers and fowlers found in the Netherworld who try to trap the dead in their nets. The deceased is able to avoid them and their snares through the specialized knowledge that he has: he knows their names and thereby demonstrates the power that he has over them. The theme of netting and trapping may also be an extension of an idea introduced earlier in which the deceased claims to be able to assume a variety of animal forms, some of which are birds and the others aquatic beings. In this we may see the irony that arises from the fact that certain claims to power by the deceased often bring with them a new set of dangers.

CONNECTING THREADS: *This chapter continues the idea of threats by hostile forces that the deceased faces in the Netherworld, one first introduced in Chapter 44.*

Chapter 153 (Cols 73–98)

SPELL FOR GOING FORTH FROM THE NET. To be recited by the Goldworker of Amun Sobekmose, justified, saying:

O one who sees behind him, who has power as fisher (and) fowler, who causes the earth to open. O these fishers, children of their fathers, fishers who go around in the canals of waters. You shall not catch me in these nets of yours in which you catch the Weary Ones, these enclosures of yours in which you enclose the earth wanderers, its floats toward the sky, its weights toward the earth. I have gone forth from the bag of its net. I have appeared as the fish-catcher. Then, I have gone forth from its hands. I have appeared as Sobek. I have made offerings against you, fisher (and) fowler whose fingers are hidden.

I know my spool that is in it. It is the big finger of Sokar. My net-peg which is in it: it is the shinbone of Shesmu.[38] My wooden plug which is in it: it is the hand of Isis. My knife: it is this cutter of Isis with which the navel-cord of Horus was cut. Its floats and its weights: it is the knee and this hock of Ruty. The cords of its fish-catcher: it is the sinew of Atum. The fishermen, (namely) its fishers: they are this earth-god who preceded the Akhby-gods.[39] The arms of its washings: these two arms of the great god, the lord who holds hearings in Heliopolis (on) this night of the half-moon festival in the Mansion of the Moon.

I know the brander(?) of the district ascending over it: it is the district of the firmament upon which the gods stand. This one who receives fish: he is the branding-knife with the tail who belongs to the gods. The path on which he places it: this table of Horus, whom every god placates (and) behind whom every

---

38 Shesmu is a god associated with the wine and oil press.
39 Lit., "the Swallowers"(?).

god sits. He who places it for him: he is this Horus who sits alone in darkness, who is not seen, the one whom those fear who have not praised him. I have come. I appear in glory as the great god. I guide the land through myself in the two great sacred boats. It is the Great One whom I have placed in the middle of the temple of the Great One. I have come before you, fisher, my cleat in my hand, my knife in [my] hand. I go forth (and) I go about. I catch fowl with my net. The cleat that completes the mouth of the wound: this large finger of Osiris. The two fingers that grasp it: it is these two fingers on the hand of Re (and) the fingernails upon the hand of Hathor. The ropes which are upon this cleat: the sinews of the lord of the patricians. The net-peg: it is the shin of Shesmu. Its wooden plug: it is the hand of Osiris. Its cords: the cords of the oldest god. Its nets: it is the time of day.

I know the names of the fishers who fish. They are the earth-gods who are in the presence of Re, the ones who have ceased who are in the presence of Geb. O you who bring what you have eaten, I bring what I have eaten. You have swallowed (and) I have swallowed what Geb (and) Osiris have swallowed. O one whose face is behind him, violent one, fisher (and) fowler, fish-netter of the opening of the earth. O fishers who fish, children of their fathers, hunters (and) trappers within this pillar city of hers. You shall not catch me (like a fish) in your net, not trapping me. You shall not catch me (like a fish) in your net in which you catch the Weary Ones and in which you trap the earth wanderers, because I know it,[40] its floats above, its weights below. Look at me, yes, me. I am come. I shall live, its weights.

Look at me, yes, me, my net-peg is in my hand, my wooden plug in my hand, my slicing-knife in my hand. I have come (so that) I may enter, (and) I may strike, (and) I may fish (with my net). I have come (so that) I may net him (and) I may put him, I may put him in (his) place. I break, stamp flat, strike him (and) I put him in his place. As for this net-peg of mine which is in [my] hand: it is the shin of Shesmu. As for this spool which is in my hand: it is the two fingers of Sokar. As for this wooden plug which is in my hand: it is the fingernail of Hathor. As for this knife which is in my hand: it is the sharp knife[41] of Shesmu.

Look at me, I am come, I am come. I sit in the sacred boat of Re, crossing the Lake of the Two Knives to the northern sky. I hear the words of the gods. I act. I act for them who praise my *ka* thereby.[42] I live on what they live on. The Goldworker of Amun Sobekmose, justified, goes forth upon the ladder which his father Re made for him. Horus (and) Seth hold (him) by his hand.

---

40 I.e., the net.
41 I.e., a razor of sorts.

42 I.e., the gods praise
the *ka* of the deceased.

CHAPTER 124

This is the first of a number of chapters that introduce the theme of descent or entry into various locales in the Netherworld. Throughout the text, Sobekmose emphasizes the orderliness of his existence: he continues to live according to the principles of Maat, just as he did on earth. The references to abominations and the statements about the nature of the food that the deceased eats center on themes of ritual purity and his right to enter any place where ritual purity is a requirement for entrance. At the end of the chapter, the deceased forcefully asserts his rightful presence among the divinities of the Netherworld.

CONNECTING THREADS: *The theme of access to the presence of individual gods continues, as do references to the ability to move about freely without hindrance.*

Chapter 124 (Cols 98–110)

SPELL FOR DESCENDING TO THE DIVINE COUNCIL OF Osiris. To be recited by the Goldworker of Amun Sobekmose, justified, born of the mistress of the house Sat-Montu, justified. He says:

My *ba* has built my fortress in Busiris. I have plowed my field(s) (as) they are (normally) done. My plants are in Pe. (My) *dom*-palm is (that which) Min is upon. The abominations of the Goldworker of Amun Sobekmose, justified—he does not eat his abomination. Feces is an abomination. He will not eat it. Excrement—I will not be harmed by it, (by) not reaching out to it with my two hands. I will not tread (upon it) with the soles of my feet because my bread is white *emmer*-wheat, my beer red barley. It is the night-boat (and) the day-boat that bring them to me. I eat by my pool (and) under (its) branches. I recognize those who bring good (things). Then transformation spells of the White Crown shall be made for me (and) [I] shall be raised up by cobras.

O doorkeeper of the one who appeases the Two Lands, bring to me those who make offerings. May you cause that the ground be raised up for me, that the sun's radiance open (his) arms to me. May the Ennead be silent (and) the sun-people speak with the Goldworker of Amun Sobekmose, justified. The one who guides the hearts of the gods, he protects me. I am powerful in the sky, guarding against that which is evil to me. Any god, any goddess who opposes me is assigned to the ancestors of the light, while the sun's radiance clothes the sky among the Elders. My portion is there with the loaves (for) our mouths. I have entered the sun-disk. I have come forth because of Ihy. He speaks to me. The followers of the gods speak to me. The sun-disk speaks [to me]. His sun-people speak to me. Fear of me (is) in the twilight within Mehet-weret[43] at the side of his forehead.

---

43 Personification of the Inundation.

Truly I am there with Osiris. My mat will be his mat among the Elders. I speak the words of men to him. I repeat the words of the gods to him. Come, my equipped *akh*. You make Maat rise up to the one whom she loves. I am an equipped *akh*, one more equipped than all of the *akhs*.

Chapters 119-102-7

Chapter 119 begins as a resurrection text but shifts its attention to Osiris's joining the entourage of Re in his solar travels. Chapter 102 seems an almost direct continuation. The mention of the solar boat at the beginning and the references to the rejuvenation at the end make this chapter a bridge from Chapter 119 to Chapter 7, the text concluding the sequence. The reference in Chapter 7 to passing by the vertebrae of Apophis continues the theme of the solar journey. Through his claim to an association with Atum and through the references to his secret name, Sobekmose alludes to his presence at the initial acts of creation, thus emphasizing his eternal nature.

Connecting Threads: *The focus on the solar travels of Re echoes the theme of journeying introduced earlier; references to "abominations" are also found in the preceding and succeeding chapters.*

Chapter 119 (Cols 110–114)

Spell for knowing the name of Osiris (and) entering (and) going forth from Rosetau. To be recited by the Goldworker of Amun Sobekmose, justified. He says:

I am the Great One who makes his (own) light. I have come before you, Osiris, (so that) I may worship you, (so that) I may be purified [by] the effluxes that pour from you, making the name of Rosetau the moment it descends into it. Greetings, Osiris, in your power, in your might. You are powerful in Rosetau. Raise yourself up, Osiris, through your power, through your might. Raise yourself up, Osiris, through this power of yours in Rosetau, through this might of yours in Abydos (so that) you may circle heaven (and) you may be rowed in front of Re (and) you may see the common people. Sole one, Re indeed circles with you. Now, look at me. I say to you, Osiris: To me belongs the dignity of a god. I say what comes to pass. I will not be turned away from you.

Chapter 102 (Cols 114–120)

Spell for descending to the sacred boat of Re. To be recited by the Goldworker of Amun Sobekmose, justified.

O Great One who is in his sacred boat, bring me to your sacred boat (so that) [I] may draw near your staircase, (so that) I may govern for you your sailing voyages in these duties of yours allotted to the Unwearying Stars. My abominations: I will not eat my abomination. Feces is an abomination. I will not eat it. Excrement—I will not be harmed by it. I will not reach out to it with my two hands. [I] will not tread (upon it) with the soles of my feet because my bread is white *emmer*-wheat, my beer red barley. It is the night-boat (and) the day-boat that are brought to me. The wealth of the villages is upon the altar of the souls of Heliopolis. Greetings to you, Great One who makes the ferryings of the *shen*-cakes of Tjeni (which) these dogs[44] partake of. I am not languishing. I have come myself (so that) I may rescue this god from those who would make him suffer from these sicknesses (in) the thigh, the arm, and his legs. I have come (so that) I may spit on the thigh, rejoin his arm, lift up the leg. "Descend (and) sail," Re commands.

Chapter 7 (Cols 120–123)

Spell for passing by the vertebrae of Apophis. To be recited by the Goldworker of Amun Sobekmose, justified. He says:

O sole one (made of) wax[45] who plunders (and) seizes by robbing, who lives on the Weary Ones. I shall not be weary for you. I shall not languish for you. Your poison shall not enter my limbs. My limbs are the limbs of Atum. As for not being weak, I am not weak for you. Your weakness shall not enter these limbs of mine. I am the one who is foremost of the Nun. My protection is that of the gods, lords of eternity. My protection is that of the gods, lords of eternity. I am one who is among them. I have gone forth together with Atum. I am one who is not examined. I am in a state of great well-being.

44 Thought to be an allusion to Seth and his accomplices.

45 An allusion to the wax image of an enemy that will be burned in an apotropaic ritual.

CHAPTERS 136A-136B
(SEE FIG. 29 FOR VIGNETTE)

These chapters are solar texts through which the deceased attains two goals. In Chapter 136A, he ascends with the sun-god Re in his solar boat of the daytime and reaches the upper sky, where the planets are located. In Chapter 136B, the deceased identifies himself directly with Re. By doing so, he is able to pass by the Ring of Fire, one of the dangers encountered in the journey through the Netherworld.
CONNECTING THREADS: *The continued focus on the solar journey of Re.*

Chapter 136A (Cols 124–126)
SPELL FOR SAILING IN THE GREAT SACRED BOAT OF RE by the Goldworker of Amun Sobekmose, justified. He says:

Behold, all the stars that arise in Kheraha. The god is born, the one who puts on his fillet, who grasps this steering oar of his. Assign me (to) the shipyard of the gods (so that) I may take the sacred boat from there, flowers at its head.[46] I will go forth to the sky; I will sail in it to Nut. I will sail together with Re. I will sail in it with the ape. I will turn away the waves of Nut to the stairway of Sebeg.

Chapter 136B (Cols 127–142)
SPELL FOR SAILING IN THE GREAT SACRED BOAT OF RE TO PASS BY THE RING OF FIRE. To be recited:

This fire is bright behind Re, bound together—to be recited—behind him. The storm fears the sacred boat, bright (and)—to be recited—sacred. I have come today with Seku-her[47] from the middle of his sacred pool—to be recited—I have seen the ones who have attained truth as well as the Double Lions who belong there—to be recited—being the ones who are in coffins, more numerous than (those in) the Field of Reeds (whom) I have seen there.

To be recited—we are rejoicing, and their greater gods are in joy—to be recited—their smaller ones in good fortune. Make a path for me in the front of the sacred boat.—to be recited—I am raised up in his sun-disk. I am white with the radiance of—to be recited—cobras. He is provided with his requirements, sheltered as this lord of truth. Who—to be recited—is the underling? says the Ennead.

To be recited—The kite of Osiris. Behold, his father bears witness for him, lord of—to be recited—those within. I have removed wrongdoing from him. Replacement [I] have brought—to be recited—Tefnut to him (so that) he may live.

46 I.e., at its bow and stern.
47 The name of a divinity.

48 The reference to jaws and backbone here are to the body parts of the wounded or dismembered god mentioned in this text and in Chapter 102, which forms part of this sequence; in all likelihood, this god is Osiris.

To be recited: Come and go, come and go, he shall say (and) truth shall bear witness to the lord of greatness. Go, call out in the evening at his hours, look at me, I am come. I have brought to him the jaws of Rosetau—to be recited: I have brought to him the backbone[48] that was in Heliopolis. I have unified what was many. I have turned away Apophis.

To be recited—I have spit on (his) wounds for him. Make paths for me (so that) I may pass among you. I am the eldest one of those who are with the gods.

To be recited—Come, pass by for the Lord of Perception. You are the heir of the eldest. To be recited—Dampen the fire. Extinguish—to be recited—the fire. Make a path for me, fathers (and) their offspring (so that) I may enter into the horizon (and) pass by the side of the elders. I bear witness for the one who is in his sacred boat. I have passed by the Ring of Fire behind the lord of braided hair. Recorded in writing by the herald.

To be recited—On your faces, (you) *hefau*-snakes. The *fentu*-snakes grant it to me that I may pass by. I am the mighty one, the lord of the mighty ones. I am the noble one, the lord of truth whom Wadjet engendered. The protections of Re [are my protections]. Look at [me], namely the one who encircles the Field of Offerings. I am Re, a god [greater] than you, who reckons his Ennead among those who give offerings.

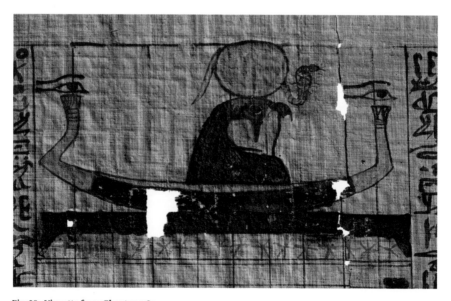

Fig. 29 Vignette from Chapter 136B
The purpose of this chapter is to help the deceased pass by a dangerous location called the Ring of Fire by traveling in the solar boat of Re. The god Re is shown in a solar boat as a falcon head with a sun-disk equipped with a *uraeus*. The boat rests on a sky-sign surmounting a field of stars. These details suggest that the journey on which the deceased will embark takes place in the celestial realms.

Fig. 30 Detail of vignette from Chapter 149: Mound Six
The vignette of Chapter 149 consists of individual depictions
of each of fourteen mounds that the deceased encounters
and must pass by. In his addresses, the deceased outlines
the knowledge he possesses about the nature of the mounds
and the potentially dangerous divinities that inhabit them.
Such knowledge enables him to pass safely through or by each
one. Mound Six, called Imhet, or "Cavern," is designated
as "secluded, hidden," and "dangerous" for the gods and
the *akhs* in the accompanying text. Its resident divinity,
shown as a fish-like snake or perhaps a centipede, is named
the One Who Makes the *Buri*-Fish Fall.

Fig. 31 Detail of vignette from Chapter 149: Mound Nine
Mound Nine, called Iksy, is curiously depicted as a jar with
a crocodile nuzzling its opening. The accompanying text,
saying of the jar that "there is no coming forth (for) the ones
who enter it," helps explain the meaning of the vignette.
In some contemporaneous papyri, the crocodile is named
He Who Is Watching What He Will Seize, making it amply
clear why "there is no coming forth."

Fig. 32 Detail of vignette from Chapter 149: Mound Ten
Mound Ten, in other texts called "That Which Is at the Entrance
of the District," is shown as a rectangle with diagonals. Beside it
stands a human-headed deity holding two knives, above whose
head appears a cobra. The accompanying text calls it the "city
of Qahu," whose inhabitants seize *akhs* and have power over the
shades (of the deceased).

Fig. 33 Detail of vignette from Chapter 149: Mound Eleven
Mound Eleven, called "Idu-town," is shown as a rectangular
area with steps on the right side that lead, ostensibly, to the sky.
Its deity is depicted as a falcon-headed divinity holding
a knife. One can still see the figural outline in red that the
scribe was intended to follow carefully, but apparently did not.

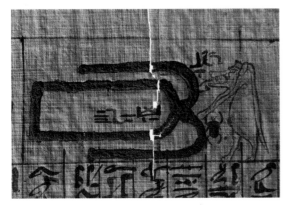

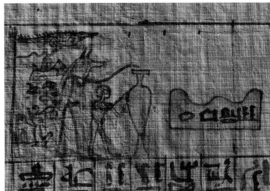

Fig. 34 Detail of vignette from Chapter 149: Mound Thirteen
Mound Thirteen, shown as a composite, with the shape
of Mound Three within that of Mound Six, is named the "Mound
of the District of Water" or perhaps the "Mound of the Water-
District." The accompanying text calls it simply "mound of water"
but describes the water as made up of waves of flame that
cannot extinguish thirst. The focus of the text on water and
the references to the god Hapi, the divine embodiment of
the annual Inundation and the Nile itself, may help to explain the
two figures shown on the vignette. The standing hippopotamus
with crocodile tail is named He Who Opens His Mouth,
a possible allusion to Hapi, who floods the land by doing so.
The scarab in front of him is not only an image associated with
the manifestation of the sun at dawn called Khepri but is also
a writing of the Egyptian verb whose meaning is "come into
being." Thus, these two images may also allude to the beginning
of the Inundation, a symbol of rebirth and regeneration.

Fig. 35 Detail of vignette from Chapter 149: Mound Fourteen
The depiction of Mound Fourteen, "Mound of Kheraha," is
the most complex of this group of vignettes. The central focus of
the accompanying text is once again the god Hapi, personification
of the Inundation. Hapi does not appear in the vignette but
instead a jackal-headed god with an outstretched arm holds that
position. This gesture, however, points to an Egyptian verb that
means "summon," and some contemporaneous texts actually
show the writing of that verb next to this figure. The composition
then makes a clear allusion to the summoning of the annual flood,
symbol of rebirth and regeneration, as the jar likely alludes to
the Inundation as well. Thus, the fourteen detailed sections of the
vignette of Chapter 149 indicate that not only has the deceased
successfully made his way past these mounds but that he is once
again connected with the life-giving rise of the Nile.

CHAPTERS 149-150
(SEE FIGS 30–39 FOR THE VIGNETTES TO THESE CHAPTERS)

This pair of chapters often follows Chapter 136A-B, as it does here, and in many Books of the Dead of this period it forms the conclusion of the papyrus. Chapter 149 is a list of a series of mounds that the deceased must pass by. Each mound has its own name, designating it as a separate entity; all belong to the house of Osiris and are located in the Field of Reeds. By offering the deceased the information needed to identify and to utter the name of the mound, the text gives the deceased the power to safely enter into or pass by it. Chapter 150 is essentially a set of vignettes that serve as the illustrations for Chapter 149.

CONNECTING THREADS: *The link between this pair and the preceding two is that both present an obstacle consisting of a dangerous locale the deceased must pass by. In the first pair, he does so through his identification with the god Re. In the present pair, he is able to pass by through the specialized, secret knowledge in his possession.*

Chapter 149 (Cols 143–215)

(First Mound) To be recited by the Goldworker of Amun Sobekmose, justified. He says:

O you mound of the West. One lives in it on *shenes*-cake (and) flowers. Take off your head-cloths when I approach, like (you would) indeed for the great one who is among you. May he unite my bones. May he make my limbs fast. Bring Ihy to me, the lord of hearts, (so that) he may (re)build my bones, (so that) he may make fast the *werret*-crown of Atum. Set my head in place for me, Nehebkau. Fill and make the balance-beam firm (so that) you may rule with the gods, (o) Min the builder.

(Second Mound) To be recited by the Goldworker of Amun Sobekmose, justified. He says:

I am one great of possessions in the Field of Reeds. O you Field of Reeds, its walls are of metal, the height of its barley is seven cubits, its ears (of corn) are two cubits, its stalk is five cubits. It is *akhs*, nine cubits tall thereof, who cut it down at the side of Re-Horakhty. I know the gate in the middle of the Field of Reeds from which Re goes forth in the east of the sky. Its south is by the pool of the *kheru*-geese; its north is at the water of the *ra*-geese, the place Re sails from (by) wind (and) by rowing. I am the one in charge of the tackle in the boat of the god. I am a rower who does not grow weary in the sacred boat of Re. I know these twin sycamores of turquoise from which Re goes forth, going through the two props of Shu at the eastern gate from which [he][49] comes forth. I know this

---

49 I.e., Re.

Field of Reeds of Re, the height of its barley is four cubits, its *emmer* seven cubits. It is *akhs* of nine cubits who cut it down at the side of the *bas* of the east.

(Third Mound) To be recited by the Goldworker of Amun Sobekmose justified. He says:

O you mound of the *akhs* upon which there is no sailing, it[50] holds (up) the *akhs*, while her flame is a flame of fire. O you mound of the *akhs*, you whose faces are downward, you whose ways are sacred, purify your mounds. That means: it is an order (given) by Osiris (Lord) of Eternity that you will do for me. I am the red flame that is on the forehead of sunlight, that causes the Two Lands (and) everyone to live by the heat of its mouth, and that saves Re from Apophis.

(Fourth Mound) To be recited by the Goldworker of Amun Sobekmose, justified. He says:

O one in charge of the secret mound, o you high mountain that is in the necropolis, above which the lower heaven hovers, three hundred cubits in its length, ten cubits in its breadth, there is a snake on it—Thrower of the Two Knives is his name—who is seventy cubits when he moves quickly.[51] He lives by beheading the *akhs* (and) the dead in the necropolis. I stand against you[52] (so that) the sailing courses may be true (since) I have seen the path toward you. I am one who has been reassembled. I am the one who is the male. Cover your head. [I am] healthy. I am one great of magic. Your eyes are given to me (so that) I have the power of an *akh*. Who is that, the one who goes upon his belly, you whose strength is your twin mountains? Look at me, I am gone forth for sure, your strength with me. I am the one who displays strength. I have come (so that) I may look after the earth-gods for Re. He has been appeased for me in the evening. I circle this sky while you are in your fetters, that which was ordered for you from before.

(Fifth Mound) To be recited by the Goldworker of Amun Sobekmose, justified. He says:

O you mound of the *akhs*, upon which one cannot pass; the *akhs* who are in it, six cubits from their buttocks, they live on the shadows of the Weary Ones. O you mound of the *akhs*, open your paths (so that) I may pass to the beautiful West. That means: it is ordered by Osiris, the *akh* (who is) lord of the *akhs*, who lives through my power. I am one [who partakes in] the new-moon festival, (who is) witness to the full-moon festival. The Eye of Horus which is in my possession

---

50 I.e., the mound.
51 Possibly an allusion to the goddess Meretseger, who was the personification of the tall peak that rose above the Theban necropolis; she was often portrayed in the form of a cobra.
52 I.e., the snake.

serves me in the entourage of Thoth. As for any of the gods (or) any dead man who licks his mouth in my presence on this day, [he] shall fall to the deep.

(Sixth Mound) To be recited by the Goldworker of Amun Sobekmose, justified. He says:

O you cavern, secluded from the gods, hidden from the *akhs*, dangerous for the gods. The god who is in it—the One Who Makes the *Buri*-Fish Fall is his name. Hail to you, you cavern. I have come to see the gods who are in [it]. Open your faces.[53] Take off your head-cloths at my approaches. I have come to make your *pat*-cakes.[54] The One Who Makes the *Buri*-Fish Fall does not have power over me. The *kharu*-demon[55] shall not come after me. The male adversary[56] shall not come after me. I live on the offerings that are within you.

(Seventh Mound) To be recited by the Goldworker of Amun Sobekmose, justified. He says:

O you, Ises,[57] too far to be seen, whose hot breath is fire in whom there is a snake—Rerek is its name—who is six cubits in length in his backbone [who lives on] the *akhs* (and) is equipped with their power. Back, you, Rerek who is in Ises, whose mouth bites, who blinds with his eye. You are broken. Your poison is weak in me. Fall (and) lie down, your fevers in the ground, your lips in a hole. His *ka* falls because of a *sedeh*-snake and vice versa. I am protected. You are beheaded by Mafdet.[58]

(Eighth Mound) To be recited by the Goldworker of Amun Sobekmose, justified. He says:

O you who descend calmly, very great one, this one whose waters within no one can have control over because of fear of it and because of the height of its roaring—the Exalted God is his name. It is he who guards it so that it cannot be approached. I am that *nur*-bird that is above heaven without boundary. I bring the things of the earth to Atum at the time of enriching crews. I have put my terror in the ones overseeing the sanctuaries. I have put my awe in the possessors of offerings. I shall not be seized for the slaughtering-block of the god for the destruction which they desire for me. I am the one who guides the northern horizon.

(Ninth Mound) To be recited by the Goldworker of Amun Sobekmose, justified. He says:

---

53 I.e., clear your vision.
54 Cakes given as part of funerary offerings.
55 A malevolent being routinely encountered in books of protection.
56 Another such being.

57 Name of the mound.
58 A god who appears in lynx or ichneumon form as the enemy of dangerous snakes associated with the Netherworld.

O Iksy,[59] hidden [from] the gods, whose name the *akhs* are afraid to know, there is no coming forth (for) the ones who enter it except this august god who places his fear in the gods, his terror in the *akhs*. Its opening is fire, its breath is destructive to nostrils. He has done this for those who are in his following, so that they do not breathe the air except this august god who is in his egg. He has done this for those who exist in it so that there was no approaching it except on the day of the great doings. Hail to you, august god who is in his egg. I have come before you (so that) I may be in your entourage. Let me come forth (and) let me enter Iksy. Let it be opened (so that) I may breathe the air which is in it (and so that) I may have power over its offerings.

(Tenth Mound) To be recited by the Goldworker of Amun Sobekmose, justified. He says:

O you city of Qahu who seize the *akhs*, who have power over the shadows, who eat what is fresh (and) gulp down what is corruption because of what their eyes see, whose guarding the land does not exist, who are in their mound. Place yourselves upon your bellies. [No one shall seize] my *akh* (or) have power over my shade. I am a divine falcon. Let myrrh be brought to me. Let incense be burned for me. Let offerings be presented to me,[60] Isis (at) my head (and) Nephthys behind me.[61] Let the path of this *nau*-snake[62] be cleared for me, (and that of) the bull of Nut, Nehebkau.[63] I have come before you, you gods. May your *akhs* save me. [Give] to me the power of an *akh* for eternity.

(Eleventh Mound) To be recited by the Goldworker of Amun Sobekmose, justified. He says:

O you city of Igeret whose body is concealed that has power over the *akhs*. There is no entering into it because of the fear of revealing what is in it. The gods with him see [it] as his marvel; the dead with him see it as his awe, except the gods who exist in him as his secrets about the *akhs*. O you Idu-town that is in the necropolis, let me pass by. I am Great of Magic, with the knife that came forth from Seth. My feet belong to me forever. I am present in glory (and) I am mighty through this Eye[64] that raised up my heart after weariness. One transfigured in heaven, mighty on earth, I have flown as a falcon. I have honked as a *semen*-goose. Alighting upon this district of the pool is granted to me. I have stood upon it. I have sat upon it. I have appeared as a god. I have eaten from the sustenance

---

59 Name of the Ninth Mound.
60 Myrrh, incense, and offerings all associate their recipient with the divine.
61 An allusion to Osiris as well as to a coffin, as images of these goddesses were often represented on the head and foot, respectively.

62 Lit., "the slippery one," a path-blocking snake found in that capacity as early as the Pyramid Texts.
63 Deity associated with the *kas* of various gods, Atum in particular.
64 I.e., the Eye of Horus.

of the Field of Offerings. I have descended to the shore (where) the stars perish. I have opened the doors of truth. I have passed the waters of heaven. I have raised up a ladder to heaven among the gods. I am one who is with you. I have spoken as a *semen*-goose, (and) the gods hear my voice. I speak to Soped.

(Twelfth Mound) To be recited by the Goldworker of Amun Sobekmose, justified. He says:

O you mound of Wenet which is in front of Rosetau, whose hot breath is fire. The gods cannot ascend to it. The *akhs* [do not] unite with it. The cobras upon it—destroyers are their names. O you mound of Wenet, I am the Great One among the *akhs* who are in you. I am among the Imperishable Stars that are in you. I will not perish. My name will not perish. The odor comes, so they say. (O) gods who are in the mound of Wenet, I am together with you. I live together with you. (O) gods who are in the mound of Wenet, may you love me more than the gods, (and) I will be together with you for eternity.

(Thirteenth Mound) To be recited by the Goldworker of Amun Sobekmose, justified. He says:

O you mound of water over whom the *akhs* do not have power. Its water is fire, its waves are flame, its hot breath is a flame of fire, so that there is no drinking (from) its water to allow thirst to be extinguished by that which is in it, on account of the greatness of their fear, (and) the greatness of its awe. The gods see (and) the *akhs* see her water from far off, (but) there is no extinguishing of their thirst. There is no appeasing their hearts so that there is no approaching by them. The river is filled (with) plants, like the flood from the effluxes that come forth from Osiris. Let me have power over the waters. Let me have an abundance of waters like this god who is in the mound of water. It is he who guards it because of fear that the gods will drink her waters while it is keeping (them) far [from the *akhs*.] Hail to you, you god who is in the mound of waters. I have come before you (so that) I may have power over her water (and) drink from her water like you did for this great god for whom Hapi came, for whom vegetation came into being, for whom plants grew strong (when) the like was given to the gods at his coming. May you be gracious (and) may Hapi come for me (so that) I may have power over plants. I am this one of your body forever.

(Fourteenth Mound) To be recited by the Goldworker of Amun Sobekmose, justified. He says:

O you mound of Kheraha that diverts Hapi to Busiris, (and) that causes Hapi to come measured by the *heqat*-measure.[65] He is led to the mouth of the eater, who gives divine offerings to the gods, invocation offerings to the *akhs*.

---

65 An allusion to a good Inundation.

This snake that belongs to it is from the two caverns of Elephantine, the mouth of Rosetau.[66] Hapi, he comes with water (and) he stops at this district of Kheraha at the council upon the waters (so that) he is seen at the hour of the silencing of the night. (O) gods who are in the waters of Kheraha, council that is upon the waters, open your canals for me, open your swamps for me (so that) I may have power over the water, (so that) I may be appeased by the water, (so that) I may eat grain, (so that) I may be satisfied with your sustenance. Let me be raised up. Let my heart be great. (O) images that are in Kheraha. Let your offerings be made, (and) let me be provisioned from the effluxes that come forth from Osiris without me being parted from him.

Chapter 150: Large Vignette (see figs 36–39)
Captions (reading vertically from left to right):
The Field of Reeds
The Horns of Fire. The god who is in it is Lifter of Braziers
The Great High Mountain
The Mound of *Akhs*
The Cavern. The god who is in it is He Who Makes the *Buri*-Fish Fall
Iseset
Hasret. The god who is in it is Raiser of the Sky
Iksy. The god who is in it is He Who Sees What He Would Seize
The Horns of Qahu
Idu. The god who is in it—Soped
The Mound of Wenet. The god who is in it is Destroyer of *Bas*
The Horns of Water. The god who is in it is Great One of the Powerful Ones
The Mound of Kheraha. The god who is in it is Hapi.
The Pool whose River Burns with Fire.
The Beautiful West. The gods live in it on *shenes*-cakes (and) wine jars.

66 I.e., the entrance to Rosetau.

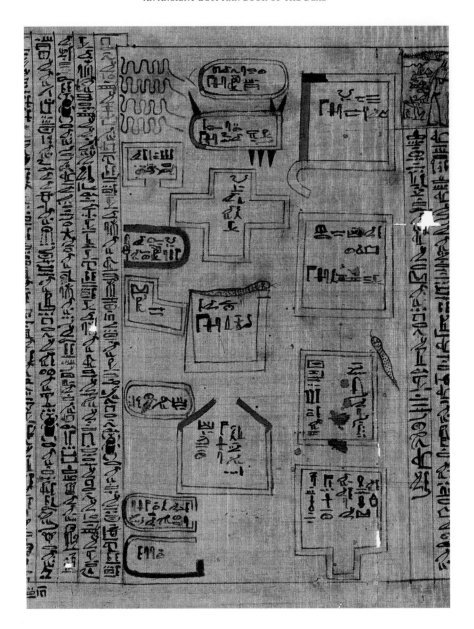

Fig. 36 Vignette from Chapter 150
This vignette essentially reiterates the vignettes that accompany the preceding Chapter 149, but here the mounds number fifteen instead of fourteen. They are also depicted differently than they are in Chapter 149. No extended texts accompany the vignette of these mounds; rather they are described simply by short phrases that give their names.

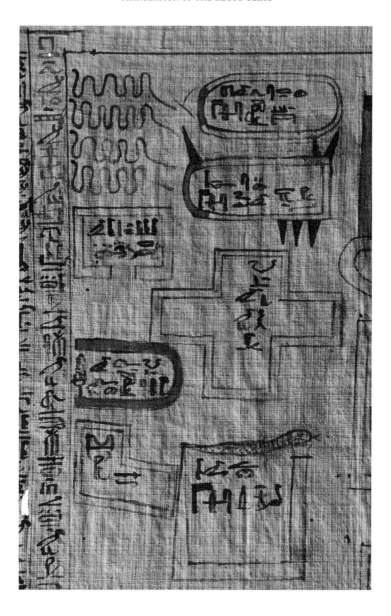

Fig. 37 Detail of vignette from Chapter 150
The rectilinear mound surmounted by a snake in the bottom center of the photograph appears
to connect it with Mound Eleven of Chapter 149, as its name Idu-town suggests. The short text
states: "The god within it—Soped." Soped is associated with the constellation Orion as well
as the star Sirius. The hieroglyph ⌂ used in the writing of the god's name can be seen mirrored
in the shape of the left-hand side of the mound.

 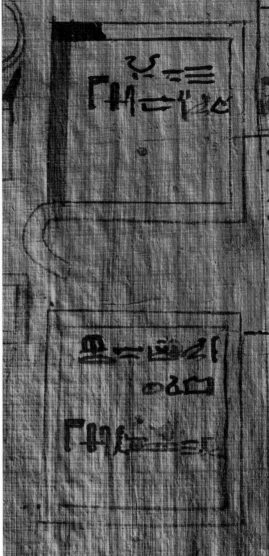

Fig. 38   Detail of vignette from Chapter 150
The rectangle with the snake in its upper-right corner is named The Pool Whose River Burns with Fire, suggesting at least some connection with Mound Thirteen of Chapter 149, which was described as having waves made of flame. The mention of a pool and river also alludes to the Inundation, a term regularly encountered in the text that accompanies Mound Thirteen as well.

Fig. 39   Detail of vignette from Chapter 150
The name of the rectangular field visible in the bottom of the photograph is Mound of Kheraha, recalling the name of Mound Fourteen in Chapter 149. The god who is in it is named Hapi as well, the personification of the Inundation.

CHAPTER 64

This is another solar text. Once again, the deceased claims identification with Re and, thus, is able to "go forth by day" and cross the earth just as the sun-god crosses the sky by day. The deceased declares that he possesses secret knowledge.

CONNECTING THREADS: *The theme of the solar journey resonates with that found in the paired Chapter 136A-B. There are also several references to judgment, the major focus of the next chapter, Chapter 125. The phrase "not dying again" hints at a successful passing of judgment.*

Chapter 64 (Cols 214–235)

COMING FORTH BY DAY (AND) NOT PREVENTING THE *BA* of the Goldworker of Amun Sobekmose, justified, born of the mistress of the house Sat-Montu, justified, (FROM) ENTERING, COMING FORTH, MAKING FORMS AS ANYTHING THAT IS THE WISH of the Goldworker of Amun Sobekmose, justified, (and) not dying again. The record that Thoth made for the Osiris the Goldworker of Amun Sobekmose, justified, namely the specification (in) writing for that, namely what came forth from the mouth of Atum to create other forms for him. He says:

To me belongs yesterday which is pregnant with tomorrow. Its births will rise on another occasion of his. (I am) the one whose *ba* is secret, who made the gods, who gives offerings to the protector of the west (side) of the sky, the steering rudder of the east, lord of two faces whose rays are seen, lord of the elevations who goes forth at twilight, manifestations [...]

O (you) [two] falcons of his who are in charge of their council, who hear (what) the tongue (says), who guide those who die to the things that are secret, who drag Re, who follow from the seat of the shrine that is above [the sky], [lord] of the shrine that stands in the enclosure wall of the earth. I am he (and) vice versa. Faience is molded (and) Hapi is in charge of his metals. Re, cry out, let your heart be pleased by your beautiful truth of this day. Enter from the under-sky, go forth from the East, (you) whom the elders and the ancestors worship. Make your paths pleasant for me, broaden your roads for me (so that) I may cross the earth in the manner of (crossing) the sky, your sunlight upon me.

(O) *ba* of three,[67] I am approaching the god who speaks in the ears in the Duat. There are no sins of my mother against me.[68] May you save me, may you protect me from the one who makes his eyes blind at night, who makes everything

---

67 I.e., Khepri, Re, and Atum.
68 I.e., my heart will not bear witness against me.

unrecognizable in the darkness. I am the abundant flood. Kem-wer is my name. The back which conceals its inside is filled.

O you, great one whose island does not exist, summon those who are in their sedge plants [at] the hour of supporting the god.[69] Speak, please, to the one who is in charge of his flood: "Behold, the foreleg is joined to the neck, the buttocks are on the head." Give to me what is the two great birds. Do not cause me to weep at what I have seen. Let me sail from the dam in Abydos. (O) door-bolts, move the gates quickly, your faces downcast. Your arm is your tent, your face is the hound [that sniffs at the shrine.] I [move] my feet [quickly] as Anubis has arrived at (the place called) No Limit. [...] I know the depths more than my name. The needs of the *akhs* are taken care of, that is four million, six hundred thousand, with one thousand two hundred offerings on top of their things, (their) water holes more than the hours of the day. The day of examining what pertains to the shoulders of Orion, one-twelfth from that which passes united by giving one from them.[70] It is one-sixth then thereof, the foremost hour of the day of making the rebel fall, (and) I come (back) from there in triumph. It is these who are at the opening of the Duat. It is these who provided for Shu. I have arisen as lord of life because of my good truths of this day: blood that is cool, wounds that are fresh, interment. I have separated the two horns from joining the crocodile against me.

(O you) whose nature is secret, do not turn me back, (you) ones upon their bellies. I have come with a message of the lords to greet Osiris. Do not let the eye swallow its tears. I am the distraught one of the house of the one who is in his chapel. I have come from Letopolis to Heliopolis to make the phoenix[71] know the affairs of the Duat.

O Igeret[72] which is secret, which is with its double, that creates my forms like Khepri, let me go forth with the sun-disk and the sunshine (which) I make linger in the west of the sky.

69 This sentence seems to allude to the creator-god at the moment of creation, when he was in search of a place to stand (i.e., the island mentioned here) and needed something to support him.

70 Reference to the twelve hours of the day or night.

71 In Egyptian creation myths, the phoenix, or *benu*-bird, was the *ba* of Re, the god who created himself.

72 A name of the realm of the dead, known first in the New Kingdom.

CHAPTER 125

The deceased has successfully navigated two major obstacles: the Ring of Fire and the Mounds of the Field of Reeds. He has also declared that he has the ability to go forth by day, just as the sun-god does daily. The deceased now arrives at the Hall of the Two Truths, where he will undergo judgment. His judgment consists of proving that he was a functioning and properly integrated member of society when alive. He appears before a tribunal of forty-two judges, a number equal to that of the Egyptian nomes, territorial divisions that collectively made up the country. Thus, he is making his declaration of innocence before the whole of Egypt. The deceased begins his defense with a series of statements, in each of which he declares what he has not done. He reinforces his claims by restating them a second time but in somewhat different language. He presents each statement to one of forty-two judges, addressing him by name. Each name is preceded by the vocative marker "O" written in red ink. By naming each one, he demonstrates once again his possession of specialized and secret knowledge through which he emphasizes his power over each and every judge. He then asks for protection, acknowledging that he is pure of mouth and body. He demonstrates as well that he is able to answer a series of questions put to him, again because he possesses the requisite knowledge. He is then told he may enter, but only after he correctly names the parts of the entranceway, which he does successfully. He is then allowed to enter because he has now been identified as Osiris. The text ends with a detailed description of how the deceased should dress and instructions about how this chapter should be written. By following those instructions, he guarantees his entry into the Hall of the Two Truths.

Chapter 125 (Cols 236–314)

WHAT IS SAID AT THE ARRIVAL AT THE BROAD HALL OF THE TWO TRUTHS. To be recited by the Goldworker of Amun Sobekmose, justified.

Hail to you great god, lord of the Two Truths. I have arrived before you, my lord. One brings me to you so that I may see your beauty. I know you. I know your name. I know the names of the forty-two gods who exist with you, in this broad Hall of the Two Truths, who live on the protectors of evil, (and) who swallow their blood (on) this day of reckoning (their) characters in the presence of Wennefer. Behold, the two daughters whom his two eyes love—lord of truth is your name. Behold me, I am come.

I have brought truths to you. I have dispelled wrongdoing for you. I have not done wrong against anyone. I have not impoverished (my) associates. I have not done what is wrong in place of what is right. I have not known that which is not (to be known). I have not done anything evil. I have not made at the beginning of each day work in addition to what I had (already) made.[73] My name has not reached the sacred boat of the controller. I have not [spoken ill of] the god. I have not deprived the orphan. I have not done the abominations of the gods. I have not slandered a servant to his superior. I have not caused pain. I have not caused grief. I have not killed. I have not ordered killing. I have (not) directed suffering upon anyone. I have not deducted food offerings from the temples. I have not destroyed the offerings of the gods. I have not seized the food offerings of the *akhs*. I have not committed rape. I have not acted lasciviously. I have not added to (and) I have not decreased a requisition. I have not decreased [an *aroura*][74] nor encroached upon the fields. I have not increased the balancing of the balance-scale. I have not frustrated the movement of the plummet of the balance-scale. I have not taken milk from the mouth(s) of children. I have not deprived small cattle of their herbage. I have not trapped birds belonging to the harpoons of the gods. I have not caught fish in their[75] marsh waters. I have not diverted water in its season. I have not dammed up a dam against water that moves quickly.[76] I have not extinguished a fire in its time. I have not disobeyed the days for choice cuts of meat.[77] I have not turned back cattle from the god's property. I have not prevented the god in his goings forth.

I am pure. I am pure. I am pure. I am pure. My purity is the purity of this great phoenix that is in Herakleopolis because I am this nose of the lord of breaths who makes all people live on this day of filling the Sound Eye in Heliopolis in this second month of Peret, last day, in the presence of the lord of this land. I am one who sees the filling of the Sound Eye in Heliopolis. There is no evil that can happen to me [in this land, in this Hall of] Two Truths because I am one who knows the names of these gods who exist in it.[78]

O one broad of strides who came forth from Heliopolis, I have not engaged in wrongdoing.

O one who embraces the flame, who came forth from Kheraha, I have [not] robbed.

O Beaky who came forth from Hermopolis, I have not been covetous.

O one who swallows shadows who came forth from the cavern, I have not seized.

O fierce of face who came forth from Rosetau, I have not killed people.

---

73 The meaning is the deceased never increased the workload of those employed by him beyond what was agreed upon.
74 An *aroura* was a unit of area used to measure fields; equivalent to about two-thirds of an acre.

75 I.e., the marsh water belonging to the gods, or possibly the sacred lakes belonging to temples.
76 The reference is to the time of the Inundation.
77 The reference here seems to be to an act of religious obligation.

78 Beginning here is a section of text known as the Negative Confession or Declaration of Innocence. It consists of a series of statements, each beginning with the name of one of the forty-two divine judges followed by a denial of specific wrongdoing.

O Ruty who came forth from the sky, [I] have not damaged what was required.[79]

O one whose eyes are flint who came forth from Letopolis, I have not done crookedness.

O flame that came forth as one going backward, I have not seized the property of the god.

O bone-breaker who came forth from Herakleopolis, I have not spoken falsehoods.

O one whose flame is sturdy, who came forth from Memphis, I have not carried off food.

O inhabitant of the twin caverns who came forth from the West, I have not been sullen.

O white tooth who came forth from the Faiyum, I have not transgressed.

O blood-eater who came forth from the slaughtering block, I have not slaughtered the cattle of the god.

O entrail-eater who came forth from the Tribunal of Thirty, I have not made obstruction.

O lord of truth who came forth from the Two Truths, I have not stolen offering portions.

O traveler who came forth from Bubastis, I have not eavesdropped.

O pale one who came forth from Heliopolis, I have not run at the mouth.

O double evil who came forth from Anedjty, I have not engaged in disputes except over my property.

O *wammty*-snake[80] who came forth from the place of execution, I have not committed adultery.

O one who sees what he is brought, who came forth from the house of Min, I have not acted lasciviously.

O one who is in charge of the Elder who came forth from Imu,[81] I have not created terror.

O destroyer who came forth from Guey,[82] I have not transgressed.

O reciter of words who came forth from Weryt, I have not been hot-tempered.

O child who came forth from Heqa-Andju,[83] I have not been deaf to words of truth.

O prophesier who came forth from Wensy,[84] I have not made a disturbance.

O Bubastite who came forth from Shetyt,[85] I have not acted shamefully.

79 I.e., reduced the amounts or measurements of what was required for any kind of transaction.
80 Snake associated with Apophis and fire in a number of texts.
81 Kom el-Hisn, a town on the western edge of the Delta.
82 Possibly Xoïs, a town in the Delta.
83 Capital of the Heliopolitan *nome*.
84 Place name in the 19th *nome*, or district, of Upper Egypt.
85 Name of the sanctuary of Sokar in Memphis.

O one whose face is backward who came forth from his hole of eternity, I have not had sexual relations, I have not committed rape, I have not copulated.

O hot-foot who came forth from twilight, I have not been regretful.

O darkness that came forth from Kenmet,[86] I have not quarreled.

O one who brings his offering who came forth from Sais,[87] I have not been active.[88]

O lord of faces who came forth from Nedjfeti,[89] I have not been impatient.

O slanderer who came forth from Wetenet,[90] I have not falsified my character. I have not been vindictive (against) the god.

O lord of two horns who came forth from Asiut, I have not been vulgar in (my) talk.[91]

O Nefertem who came forth from Memphis, I have been free of wrongdoing. I have not done evil.

O Tem-sep who came forth from Busiris, I have not quarreled against the king.

O one who acts as he wishes who came forth from Tjebet,[92] I have not waded in the water.

O Ihy [who came forth from] the Nun, I have not been loud of voice.

O one who makes the common people flourish, I have not reviled the god.

O one who provides what is good, I have not done sinful actions.

O Nehebkau, I have not made distinctions for myself.

O one whose head is raised, my requirements have not been large except my property.

O one who brings his portion, I have not weakened my town god.

Hail to you, you gods. I know you, I know (your) names. I shall not fall to your knives. You will not present my evil to this god whose following you are in. No fault of mine shall come before you. You will tell the truth about me in the presence of the register of the Lord of All because I have done what is right in Egypt. No case of mine came before the king who was in his day.

Hail to you who are in the broad Hall of the Two Truths, (you) with no falsehoods in their bellies, who live on truth in Heliopolis, who swallow from their excesses in the presence of Horus who is in his sun-disk. May you save me from Baba[93] who lives on the entrails of the Elders on this day of the great reckoning. Behold me, I am come before you. No sin of mine exists. No displeasure of mine exists. No evil of mine exists. No witnesses (against) me exist. There is

---

86 Unknown toponym that forms a play on the Egyptian word *kenmet* ("darkness") here.
87 Ancient and well-known religious center in the Delta; Neith was its principal deity.

88 I.e., in some negative way.
89 One of two similarly named places in Upper Egypt.
90 Name of a site in Punt or Nubia.
91 Probably a reference to gossip or the like.

92 Antaeopolis (lit., "Sandal-Town"), in the 13th Upper Egypt *nome,* or district.
93 A divinity who is associated with or seems to personify lack of virility and vital strength; associated with the theme of "weariness."

no one against whom I have done things. I live on truth. I swallow down truth. I have done those things which men say, those things with which the gods are pleased. I have appeased the gods with what they love, providing bread to the hungry, water to the thirsty man, clothing to the naked man, a ferry to the one who is boat-less. I have made divine offerings to the gods, invocation offerings to the *akhs*. Save me, then; protect me, then. You will not report against me in the presence of [the great god]. I am one pure of mouth, pure of hands to whom "Welcome! Welcome!" is said by those who see him, as I heard this word that the ass spoke with the cat in the house of the one whose mouth is opened. I bear witness before him. He gives forth [cries]. I have seen the splitting of the Ished-tree within Rosetau. I am the *semwy*-priest of the gods, namely one who knows the matters of their bellies. I have come here to bear witness to the truth, to bring the balance to its proper position within the silent places.

O one high upon his standard, lord of the *atef*-crown, who makes his name as lord of the winds, may you rescue me from your emissaries, who send forth injury, who bring punishment to pass without compassion on their faces. I have done the truth for the lord of truth. I am pure, my heart pure from abomination, my buttocks clean, my middle in a pool of truth, my limbs not lacking truth. I am purified in the southern pool. I rest in the northern town, in the field of locusts in which the crew of Re is purified in this fourth hour of the night, the fifth hour of the day, calming the hearts of the gods after they pass through it by night [or by day].

They speak to me. Who are you?, they say to me. What is your name?, they say to me. I am the spike of the underside of the papyrus clump. The one who is in the *moringa*-tree (is) my name. You passed through what?, they say to me. I passed through a town north of the *moringa*-tree. What did you see there? It was a leg bone and a thigh. What did you say to them? I have seen rejoicing in the lands of the Fenkhu-people. What did they give [to] you? It was a torch of fire and a green stone of faience. What did you do with them? I buried them on the shore of Maak as an evening meal. What did you find there on the shore of Maak? It was a scepter of flint, Giver of Breath is its name. What did you do with the torch of fire and the green stone of faience after you buried them? I lamented over them. I took them. I extinguished the flame. I broke the green stone, throwing (them) into a pool. Come, then, enter through this door of this broad Hall of the Two Truths, since you know us.

I will not let you enter through me, said the doorpost of this gate, unless you say my name. Plumb Line of Truth is your name. I will not let you enter through me, said the right door-leaf of this gate, unless you say my name. Scale Pan for Weighing the Truth is your name. I will not let you enter through me, said the left door-leaf of this gate, unless you say my name. Scale Pan Weighing Wine is your name. I will not let you pass by me, said the floor of this gate, unless you say my name. Ox of Geb is your name. I will not open to you, said the bolt of this gate, unless you say my name. Toe of Iunmutef is your name. I will not open to you, said the threshold of this gate, unless you say my name. Living [Eye] of Sobek, lord of Bekhu[94] is your name. I will not open to you, you will not enter through me, says the doorkeeper of this gate, unless you say my name. Breast of Shu which he gave as a shadow (to) Osiris is your name. We shall not let you pass through us, say the cross-timbers of this gate, unless you say our names. Children of Renennutet are your names. You know us. You may then pass through us.

I will not let you tread upon me said the floor of the broad Hall of the Two Truths. But why? I am surely one who is pure. Because we do not know the feet with which you tread upon us. I (must) know the names of the feet with which you tread upon us. You shall say them to me. Swellings of Min is the name of my right foot. Wenpet of Nephthys is the name of my left foot. Then, you may tread upon us as you know us.

I will not announce you, says the doorkeeper of the broad hall, unless you say my name. Perceiver of Hearts, Prober of Bellies is your name. To what god who is in his hour shall I announce you? You shall say it to the interpreter of the Two Lands. Who is the interpreter of the Two Lands? He is Thoth. Behold, says Thoth, what have you come for? I have come here to make an announcement. What is your condition? I am pure from baseness. I am excluded from quarrels of their days. I shall not associate with them. To whom shall I announce you? You shall announce [me] to this one whose forecourt is of fire, its walls of living cobras, the floor of his house is water. Proceed. Who? He is Osiris.

Proceed, then. Behold, you are announced. Your bread is the Sound Eye. Your beer is the Sound Eye. Your going forth at the voice is the Sound Eye. How good it is for a man who acts as one should (in) the broad Hall of the Two Truths, namely the words which a man says who is pure (and) clothing given to him, shod with white sandals, anointed with the finest oil of myrrh, and he presents a young bull, fowl, incense, bread, beer, vegetables. Now make for yourself this guide in writing on clean ground adorned with soil upon which a lion has not trod. As for the one on behalf of whom this book roll was made, he shall be vigorous (and) the children of his children without hunger. He shall be an intimate of the king, together with his courtiers. One shall give to him a *shen*-cake, a *des*-jar, a *pesen*-loaf, a great portion of meat upon the altar of the great god. He shall not be restrained from any doorway of the west. He shall be towed[95] together with the kings of Upper Egypt (and) Lower Egypt. He shall be in the entourage of Osiris. Truly effective millions of times.

94 A mythical location.

95 I.e., through the Netherworld in a divine boat.

Chapter 126: Large Vignette

(SEE FIGS 40, 41)

This large vignette of baboons seated around a pool of fire with no accompanying text was one of the options available to the illustrator of Books of the Dead of the Eighteenth Dynasty. Another option includes the vignette accompanied by text. This vignette was chosen in place of the judgment scene often found accompanying Chapter 125.

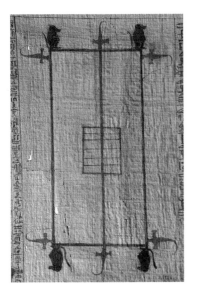 

Fig. 40 Vignette from Chapter 126
This vignette is sometimes accompanied by its own separate text, known as Chapter 126, while in other papyri it serves as one of the illustrations for Chapter 125. The six fire signs (𓊮) that surround the rectangular field help demarcate it as a lake or pool of fire that the deceased must pass to gain entrance to the Netherworld. In the text that sometimes accompanies the vignette, the four baboons are described as divine guardians found in the prow of the solar boat of Re. It is to them that the deceased makes his appeal to be allowed entrance and access to the Netherworld.

Fig. 41 Detail of vignette from Chapter 126
Here we see one of the four baboon guardians flanked by two of the fire signs that designate the pool in the center of the vignette as composed of fire.

TEXT X – COFFIN TEXT 901 – TEXT Y – CHAPTER 119

The following four texts draw largely from material found in the Coffin Texts, supplemented by material not known from elsewhere. Only the fourth, Chapter 119, belongs to the Book of the Dead corpus. Following Chapters 125-126 (a chapter pairing that deals with judgment), the present group locates the deceased squarely in the Netherworld. In the first two texts, the deceased declares that he has the specialized knowledge that allows him to cross the Field of Reeds and to navigate his way through a series of chambers. Once again, his ability to articulate the names of the obstacles that he encounters allows him to pass through or by them. In the third text, apparently one not known to either the Coffin Text or Book of the Dead traditions, the deceased lists the powers that he has, thereby declaring that he is divine. The text also stresses the power that comes through knowledge. In Chapter 119, the deceased claims that he has come before Osiris in Rosetau, a hidden region in the Netherworld whose secrecy is due to its connections with the embalming of Osiris. As in the other chapters of this sequence, the deceased emphasizes his divinity and his ability to fend for himself.

Text X (Cols 315–322)

BEGINNING OF THE GATES OF THE FIELD OF REEDS OF THE HOUSE OF OSIRIS. To be recited by the Goldworker of Amun Sobekmose, justified.

I am this sole *ba* (on) the day of the centipede, whose pupils are open, whose ears are open. I have rescued the effluxes of my father. I have come to this land. I am transformed to an *akh* by my magic. I am not without knowledge of the sky. I am not without knowledge of the water. I am not without knowledge of the gates. I am not without knowledge, I am not without knowledge.

(O) Thoth, I know the Two Combatants of the *akh* who falls in the doorway of the slaughterer. The doorkeeper of Shu is his name. He exists [...] whose name is foremost of the valley which he is in; the name of the two who sit (and are) found at the entrance of the Duat. They make their forms as the neighbors of the two lions. Then a man shall say: Do not descend upon me, (o) Two Combatants. I have come, a possessor of *akhs*. My magic is known just as my protections perform it before Osiris according to the wish of Tekem.

The name of the scribe (?) is He Who Drives Backwards. The name of the ferryman is The One Who Finds Faces, Who Uplifts Faces. The name of the ferry (is) The One Who Finds Faces, Who Uplifts Faces. The name of the steering oar is Precision (and) Accuracy. The name of the prow rope is Stinker (is) its name. The name of its mast is Pool of Wounds. The name of the bailer (is) Report That Its Excellence Has Spread. The name of the river is (He) Who Sees *snš*. The name of the west is Beautiful.

I sail across the Field of Reeds.

Coffin Text 901 (Cols 323–329)

First gate. Chamber of secrets, mistress of holiness before the gods.

Second gate. Chamber of Sebtef, mistress of the revered ones.

Third gate. Chamber of the great one, mistress of the shrine before Re in his sacred boat.

Fourth gate. Chamber of the holy one, mistress who forbids, guardian who gives bread to those upon their bellies.[96]

Fifth gate. Chamber of the one who seals everything, the offerings which the gods consume.

Sixth gate. Chamber of the district, mistress of the horizon, who knows Re in his name.

Seventh gate. Chamber of the concealed one, mistress of the paths, who guides Horus (and) Seth when she passes by.

Text Y (Cols 330–334)

I have brought to pass what has come to pass (and) what will come to pass (and) vice versa. I am the one who comes forth from the egg which the Nun created, whose flood waters raise you up as one who is made divine. I am the one whose faces are numerous, whose name is not known. Save him from everything done to him, an *akh* whose magic is great, a *ba* within his shrine, lord of fear, whose great awe exists every day. I am one who enters counted, who comes forth numbered. I am not at the slaughtering-block of the gods (and) Asha-khet.[97] I am one against whom you do not seal your doors.

To be recited: If a man knows these things upon the earth, he shall exist in the beautiful West after he goes to rest with his *ka*, then not dying again in the necropolis. He shall exist as an *akh-iqer* among the *akhs* for eternity, an offering loaf in his mouth therein like he existed on earth while doing all that he did there, like he existed while living.

Chapter 119 (Cols 334–338)

SPELL FOR KNOWING THE NAMES OF OSIRIS by the Goldworker of Amun Sobekmose, justified, entering (and) going forth from Rosetau.

I am the Great One who makes his own light. I have come before you, Osiris [to] adore you. I am purified [by] the effluxes pouring from you, making its name at Rosetau the moment it descends there. Hail to you, Osiris. Your power, your might (are) in Rosetau. Raise yourself up, Osiris, through your power, through your might. Raise yourself up, Osiris, through this power of yours in Rosetau,

---

96 I.e., snakes.

97 A deity whose name means the One Whose Possessions Are Numerous.

through this might of yours in Abydos. You circle the sky; you are rowed in front of Re (so that) you see the common people. Sole one, circle about (as) Re (does). Look at me now, I have spoken to you, Osiris. To me belongs the dignity of a god.[98] I say what comes to pass for me. I will not be turned away from you.

---

98 I.e., the state of being mummified.

Chapters 18-17₃

In many Book of the Dead manuscripts, Chapters 18-17 were treated as a unit. Even though Chapter 17 has been divided into three separate sections in the Brooklyn Book of the Dead, the third of those sections follows Chapter 18 in the papyrus. Chapter 18 is essentially a litany to Thoth, the god responsible for ensuring that Osiris was vindicated before his enemies in the tribunals after his death. The chapter of this text has two objectives: to list the tribunals of Egypt before which Osiris appeared, and to appeal to those tribunals to vindicate Sobekmose just as they had vindicated Osiris. The section of Chapter 17 that follows is a transfiguration text, one in which the deceased asserts that he has become an akh. The text of the chapter consists of a series of questions and answers presented to elucidate the true identity of a number of divine beings. The variant texts that are added in places have been interpreted in a number of ways. One thought is that they represent attempts on the part of Egyptian scribes or priests to make sense of textual allusions that they no longer understood. Another explanation is that the variant answers were added when the writer had a particular interest in emphasizing solar or creation mythology. A third is that they represent diverse local traditions that were compiled when the precursor text of Chapter 17, Coffin Text 335, was originally created. The reader will see that the content of many of the variants has to do with Re, the sun-god, or Atum, one of the manifestations of the creator-god.

Connecting Threads: *The focus on Osiris continues from the preceding group of chapters. The content of Chapter 17 further develops the theme of power that comes from the possession of secret and specialized knowledge.*

Chapter 18 (Cols 338–369)

O (you) who vindicated Osiris against his enemies. Vindicate the Goldworker of Amun Sobekmose, justified, against his enemies in the great council which was in Heliopolis (on) this night of the evening meal, (on) this night of fighting (and) guarding against the rebels, this day on which the enemies of the Lord of All were annihilated. As for the great council which is in Heliopolis: it means Atum, it means Shu, (and) it means Tefnut. As for guarding against the rebels: it means the confederates of Seth were annihilated again for his crime.

O Thoth (who) vindicated Osiris against his enemies, vindicate the Goldworker of Amun Sobekmose, justified, against his enemies in the great council that is in Busiris (on) this night of erecting the two *djed*-pillars in Busiris. As for the great council that is in Busiris: it means Osiris, it means Isis, it means Nephthys, (and) it means Horus, avenger of his father. As for making the two *djed*-pillars stand: it means the two shoulders of Horus Khenty-irty. They were behind Osiris with a binding of cloth.[99]

O Thoth (who) vindicated Osiris against his enemies, vindicate the Goldworker of Amun Sobekmose, justified, against his enemies in the great council that is in Letopolis (on) the night of the evening meal in Letopolis. As for the great council which is in Letopolis: it means Horus Mekhenty-irty, (and) it means Thoth who is in the council of Naref. As for this night of the evening meal: it means the dawn of the burial of Osiris.

O Thoth, (who) vindicated Osiris against his enemies, vindicate the Goldworker of Amun Sobekmose, justified, against his enemies in the great council that is in Pe (on) this night of erecting the snake shrine of Horus, namely that the inheritance of the possessions of his father Osiris be established for him. As for the great council which is in Pe (and) Dep: it means Horus, Isis, Imsety, (and) Hapi. As for erecting the snake shrine of Horus: it means Seth said to those in his following: Erect a Snake Shrine (is) its name.

O Thoth, (who) vindicated Osiris against his enemies, vindicate the Goldworker of Amun Sobekmose, justified, against his enemies in the council that is in the banks of Seshty[100] (on) this night (when) Isis passed the night watching over (and) mourning for her brother Osiris. As for the council that is in the banks of Seshty: it means Isis, Horus, (and) Imsety.

O Thoth, (who) vindicated Osiris against his enemies, vindicate the Goldworker of Amun Sobekmose, justified, against his enemies in the great council that is in Abydos (on) this night of the Haker-festival with the numbering of the dead, with the counting of the *akhs* when jubilation singing happens in Tjeni. As for the great council which is in Abydos: it means Osiris, Isis, and Wepwawet.

O Thoth, (who) vindicated Osiris against his enemies, vindicate the Goldworker of Amun Sobekmose, justified, against his enemies in the great council that is in the roads of the dead (on) this night of making a counting of the have-nots. As for the great council that is in the roads of the dead: it means Thoth, Osiris, Anubis, (and) Isdes. As for making a counting on the roads of the dead: [it means] offerings were kept back from the *bas* of the children of the Weary Ones.

O Thoth, (who) vindicated Osiris against his enemies, vindicate the Goldworker of Amun Sobekmose, justified, against his enemies in the council that is in the hacking up the earth in Busiris (on) this night of hacking up the earth (and) blood for the vindication of Osiris against his enemies. As for the great council that is in the hacking up the earth in Busiris: it means (when) the confederates of Seth came (and) they made their forms as goats (and) slaughter arose in the presence of these gods until blood descended from them. Then it was given by [...] to those in Busiris.

---

99 A reference to mummification.

100 Seshty is located near Heliopolis in Lower Egypt.

O Thoth, (who) vindicated Osiris against his enemies, vindicate the Goldworker of Amun Sobekmose, justified, against his enemies in the great council that is in Naref (on) this night of making secret the one whose forms are great. As for the great council that is in Naref: it means Horus, Baba, Re, (and) Osiris. As for this night of making secret the one whose forms are great: it means one was burying the forearm, the head, the flank, and the thigh of Wennefer.

O Thoth, (who) vindicated Osiris against his enemies, vindicate the Goldworker of Amun Sobekmose, justified, against his enemies in the great council that is in Rosetau (on) this night (when) Anubis spent the night, his hands upon his head behind Osiris for the vindication of Horus against his enemies. As for the great council that is in Rosetau: it means Osiris, Horus (and) Isis. Horus, his heart was pleased. Osiris, his heart was joyful. The two sanctuaries were contented on account of it.

(O) Thoth, (who) vindicated Osiris against his enemies, vindicate the Goldworker of Amun Sobekmose, justified, against his enemies in the council that is with Re, that is with Osiris, in the council of all the gods (and) goddesses, in the presence of the Lord of All (when) he dispels all of the male enemies, all of the female enemies of the Goldworker of Amun Sobekmose, justified, (and) he dispels every evil pertaining to him.

A man should say this spell being pure. It means going forth by day after his death, (as) an *akh* in the beautiful West (and) making his form from all forms which he desires, coming into being in it, being in the following of this great god, appeased by the food offerings of Wennefer. As for one reciting all of it for himself (while) pure: it means prospering upon the earth. He comes forth from every fire. No evil shall encircle him. Truly effective millions of times. I have seen it happen often.

Chapter 17₃ (Cols 370–478)

THE BEGINNING OF THOSE THINGS WHICH UPLIFT, THOSE THINGS WHICH TRANSFIGURE (FOR) GOING FORTH AND DESCENDING FROM THE NECROPOLIS (FOR) BEING AN *AKH* IN THE BEAUTIFUL WEST. SPELL FOR GOING FORTH BY DAY, MAKING HIS FORMS FROM THE FORMS WHICH HE DESIRES, PLAYING SENET (WHILE) SITTING IN THE BOOTH, GOING FORTH AS A LIVING *BA* by the Goldworker of Amun Sobekmose, justified, AFTER HE DIES. (It is) effective for the one who does it upon the earth. The words of the lord of mankind come to pass, namely: I was alone in the Nun (as) Re in his appearances in glory when he began to rule what he had made.

Who is he? It means Re when he began to rule what he had made; it means when Re began to appear as king, when the props of Shu[101] had not (yet) come into existence. He saw the slope that was in Heliopolis.[102] Then the children of the Weary Ones were given to him by the gods who are in Hermopolis.

I am the great god who created himself.

Who is he, the great god who created himself? It means water; it means the Nun, the father of the gods. Variant: It means Re (when) he created his names, the lord of the Ennead.

Who is he? It means Re (when) he created the name of his limbs; it means (when) these gods who are in his following came into existence (and) he was not turned away by the gods.

Who is he? It means: Atum who is in his solar-disk. Variant: Re in his risings in the eastern horizon of the sky.

To me belongs yesterday. I know [tomorrow].

Who is he? As for yesterday, it is Osiris. As for tomorrow, it is Re. It is the day (when) the enemies of the Lord of All were annihilated and his son Horus was made to rule. Variant: It is the day (of) We Endure;[103] it means (when) the burial of Osiris was ordered by his father Re (and) the battlefield of the gods was made according to my order.

What is it? It is the West (and) it was made for the *bas* of the gods according to the order of Osiris, lord of the necropolis of the West. Variant: It is the West. It is that to which Re made every god descend. Then he fought him on account of it.[104]

I know this great god who is in it.

Who is he? He is Osiris. Variant: He who acclaims Re is his name. He is the *ba* of Re who copulates with it himself.

I am this phoenix that is in Heliopolis, the examiner of that which exists.

Who is he? He is Osiris. As for that which exists, it means his injuries. Variant: It is eternity together with forever. As for eternity, it means the day. As for forever, it means the night.

I am Iahesy[105] in his goings forth. I have placed the two feathers on my head.

Who is he? Iahesy means Horus, the avenger of his father. As for his goings forth, it means his birth. As for his two feathers on his head, it means that Isis and Nephthys set out (and) they placed themselves upon his head when they were two kites when he indeed was ill (in) his head. Variant: It is two very large cobras who are on the brow of my father Atum. Variant: The two feathers on his head (are) his two eyes.

I existed in my land (and) I came into my city.

What is it? It means the horizon of my father Atum.

---

101 The four supports that separate the sky from the earth, one at each of the cardinal points.

102 The primal mound on which the creator-god established himself at the moment of creation.
103 The name of a festival day.

104 This sentence refers to a cosmic battle between the solar deity and his enemy.
105 A divine name.

My injustices have been driven away. My evils have been cleared away.

What is it? The navel-cord of the Goldworker of Amun Sobekmose, justified, has been cut.

My evil which pertained to me has been removed.

What is it? I am purified (on) the day I am born. I am cleansed in the two very great swamp waters which are in Herakleopolis (on) the day of the food offerings of the common people (for) this great god who is in it.

What is it? Millions is the name of one. Great-green is the name of the other. It means a pool of natron and the pool of Maet.[106] Variant: Guide of millions is the name of one. Great-green is the name of the other. Variant: Begetter of millions is the name of one. Great-green is the name of the other. Now as for this great god who is in it: Re himself.

I set out upon [a road I know] by the island of the just.

What is it? It means Rosetau. The south gate is [in] Naref. The north gate is in the Mound of Osiris.[107] Now as for the island of the just, it is Abydos. Variant: It means the road on which my father Atum set out when he proceeded to the Field of Reeds.

I arrive at the island of the just. I go forth at the sacred gate.

What is it? It is the Field of Reeds which produces food offerings for the gods behind the shrine. Now as for this sacred gate: this gate of the props of Shu. Variant: It means the gate of the Duat. Variant: It means the door-leaves through which Atum departs when he proceeds to the eastern horizon of the sky.

(O you) who were before (me), give me your hands. I am the one who came into being from you.

What is it? This blood which descended from the phallus of Re on his ways (when) he made his cuttings himself. Then (they) came into being as the gods who are in the presence of Re. It means Shu and Sia.[108] I exist in the following of my father Atum daily.

I filled my eye after its damage.

It means the day of the Two Comrades fighting.

What is it? It means the day on which Horus fought with Seth (when) he made wounds on the face of Horus, when Horus seized the testicles of Seth. It was Thoth who did these things with his fingers.

I raised up the hair from the Sound Eye in its time of raging.

106 Unknown word, but possibly referring to a locale near Giza.
107 The two gates seem to refer to terminal points on the road.

108 The god who is the personification of "Perception."

What is it? This Right Eye of Re when it raged against him after he sent it forth. It was Thoth who raised up the hair from it when he brought it alive, prospering, (and) in health without any of its weakness. Variant: It means the Eye was sick when it was weeping for its double. Then Thoth spat upon it.

I saw this Re who was born on yesterday from the rump of Mehet-weret. (If) I am sound, he is sound. (If) he is sound, I am sound.

What is it? It means these waters of the sky. Variant: It means the image of the Eye of Re at his births every day. Now as for Mehet-weret, it is the Sound Eye of Re.

I am one from those who are in the following of Horus. I say that which his lord loves.

What is it? Imsety, Hapi, Duamutef, Qebusenef.[109]

Hail to you, gods, lords of truth, the council behind Osiris, who put terror in the sinners who are in the following of Hetepes-khues.[110] See, I am come before you (so that) you may drive out all the evil which pertains to me like those things that you did [for] these seven *akhs* who are in the entourage of the lord of the primeval ones whose seats Anubis made (on) that day of Come, then, from there.

What is it? As for the council behind Osiris, it means Imsety, Hapi, Duamutef, Qebusenef who are behind the Great Bear in the northern sky. As for those who put terror in the sinners who are in the following of Hetepes-khues, it means Sobek (and) those who are in the water. As for Hetepes-khues, it means the Eye of Re. Variant: It means Nesret[111] who is in the following of Osiris, burning up the *bas* of his enemies. Now as for the evil which pertains to me: that which the Goldworker of Amun Sobekmose, justified, has been doing since he descended from the womb. As for these seven *akhs* Imsety, Hapi, Duamutef, Qebusenef, Then I Saw My Father, The One Under His Moringa Tree, (and) Horus Mekhenty-irty. It means the ones Anubis placed as protections (of) the burial of Osiris. Variant: As for these seven *akhs*, Nedhedhu, Qedqed, the Bull to Whom the Flame from His Heat was Given, the One Who Enters with the One Who Is in his Hour. As for these lords of truth, it means Seth together with Isdes, lord of the red West who is in his house of bright red linen, Flame of Face who came forth going backwards, he who sees in the night what he will bring forth (in) the day. As for the chief of this council of Naref: Horus. Now as for that day of Come then to me, Osiris said to Re: Come then from there (so that I) may see you. So he said (in) the West.

I am his two *bas* who are in the midst of his two fledglings.

---

109 Traditionally, the four sons of Horus.

110 Lit., "she is content when she protects." The gloss a few lines later explains who this goddess is.

111 Lit., "the Flame."

What is it? It means Osiris when he entered Busiris. He found the *ba* of Re (and) one embraced the other. Then (they) became the two *bas*. Now as for the two fledglings, it means Horus avenger of his father together with Horus Khenty-irty. Variant: As for his twin *bas* in the midst of the two fledglings, it means the *ba* of Re (and) it means the *ba* of Osiris, the *ba* who is in Shu (and) the *ba* who is in Tefnut. It means the *ba* of Mendes.

I am this cat at whose side the Ished-tree in Heliopolis was split on the night of the fighting and making guard (against) the rebels on that day of annihilating the enemies of the Lord of All.

Who is he? Now as for this great cat it means Re himself. He was called cat when Sia[109] said He is similar in these things which (he) has done and this his name of cat came into being.[112] Variant: It means Atum was making a will for Geb (and) for Osiris. Now as for the one for whom the Ished-tree was split in Heliopolis, it means the children of the Weary Ones were given over to justice for what they had done. Now as for that night of fighting, it means they entered into the east of the sky.[113] Then there arose war in the sky (and) on all the earth.

O Re who is in his egg, who shines from his disk, who rises from his horizon, who swims upon his copper (sky), whose equal among the gods does not exist, who sails over the props of Shu, who produces a breeze with the burning heat of his mouth, who illuminates the Two Lands with his sunlight: may you save the Goldworker of Amun Sobekmose, justified, from this god whose forms are secret, whose eyebrows are the arms of the balance-scale (on) that night of reckoning with the "robber."

Who is he? He is the one who removes his portion. As for that night of reckoning with the robber, this night of Nesret (and) blood sacrifices, who causes the lassoing of sinners for his slaughtering-block for *bas*.

Who is he? It means Shesmu; it means the mutilator of Osiris. Variant: It means Apophis; he exists with one head in possession of truth. Variant: It means Horus; he exists with [two] heads. The one is in possession of truths, the other in possession of falsehoods. He gives falsehood to the one who does (false-hood), truth to the one who comes in possession of it.[114] Variant: It means Horus the great one, who is foremost in Letopolis. Variant: It means Thoth. Variant: It means Nefertem, son of Bastet. (O) council that keeps away the enemies of the Lord of All.

---

112 The meaning of this passage turns on the wordplay between *miu* ("cat") and *miuty* ("similar").

113 Allusion to the battle between the sun-god and his enemies just before dawn.

114 I.e., one who comes in a state of truth or in possession of truth.

Save the Goldworker of Amun Sobekmose, justified, from those keepers of aggression, the slaughterers, the ones whose fingers are sharp, who cause pains, the beheaders who are in the following of Osiris. They will not have power over me. I will not descend into their cauldrons.

Who is he? It means Anubis; it means Horus Mekhenty-irty. Variant: The council that keeps away the enemies of the Lord of All. Variant: It means the chief of the physicians of the court. Their knives will not be in me. I shall not descend into their cauldrons because I know them. I know the names that belong to (them). I have known this enforcer among them who belongs to the house of Osiris, who shoots with his eye while he is not seen, who encircles the sky with his flame, who announces Hapi, while he is (yet) not seen.[115] I am one who was prosperous on earth with Re, who died along with Osiris. Your offerings shall not come to pass from me for the ones in charge of their altars because I am in the entourage of the Lord of All according to the writings of Khepri. I fly as a falcon; I honk as a *semen*-goose. I pass eternity like Nehebkau.

What is it? Those who are in charge of their altars: it means an image of the Eye of Re together with an image of the Eye of Horus.

O Re-Atum, lord of the [great]-house, sovereign of all the gods. May you save the Goldworker of Amun Sobekmose, justified, from this god whose face is that of a hound, whose eyebrows are those of a man. Variant: His skin is that of a man. He lives on blood sacrifices. It means the one who belongs to this winding of the lake of fire, who swallows corpses, who snatches hearts, who inflicts injuries while he is not seen.

Who is he? He who swallows millions, he exists in the pool of Wenet. As for this lake of fire, it means that which is in between Naref and the court. As for anyone treading upon it, let him beware lest he fall to the massacres. Variant: By the knife man. It means the doorkeeper of the West. Variant: The One in Charge of His Affairs is his name.

O lord of terror, chief of the Two Lands, lord of blood, whose slaughtering-blocks prosper, who lives on entrails.

What is it? It means the heart of Osiris. It is he who eats all this slaughtering. To him was given the *werret*-crown (and) the joy before Herakleopolis.

What is it? As for the *werret*-crown given to him (and) the joy before Herakleopolis, it means Osiris. To him was assigned rule among the gods (on) that day of uniting the land in the presence of the Lord of All.

---

115 An allusion to the beginning of the Inundation.

Who is he? As for the one to whom rule among the gods was assigned, (it is) Horus, son of Isis, made to rule in place of his father Osiris. As for that day of uniting the land, (it means) the Two Lands joined to bury Osiris, the efficacious *ba* who is in Herakleopolis, who gives life force (and) drives away sinners, who guides the way to the paths of eternity.

Who is he? It means Re himself.

May you save the Goldworker of Amun Sobekmose, justified, from this god who takes away *bas*, who licks up corruption, who lives on what rots, who guards the darkness, who is in darkness, whom the Weary Ones fear.

Who is he? It means Seth. Variant: It means the great wild bull; it means the *ba* of Geb.

O Khepri, who is in the middle of his sacred boat, primeval one whose body is eternity, may you save the Goldworker of Amun Sobekmose, justified, from these ones to whom belong examinations, to whom the Lord of All has given *akh*-powers to guard (against) his enemies, who cause slaughter within the place of punishment, from whose guarding there is no going forth. Their knives shall not be sent into me. I shall not enter into their places of punishment. I shall not descend into the interior of their slaughtering-blocks. I shall not sit within their fish-traps. Nothing shall be done to me through these abominations of the gods, because I am one who passed by pure, who is in the middle of the eastern region, to whom supper was brought, namely faience which is from Tjennet.

Who is he? As for Khepri who is in the middle of his sacred boat, it means Re himself. As for those to whom examinations belong, it means the two baboons. It means Isis; it means Nephthys. As for those abominations of the gods, it means excrement; it means falsehood. As for one who passed by pure in the middle of the eastern region, it means Anubis. He is behind the chest which contains the entrails of Osiris. As for him (to whom) there were given suppers, namely faience which is from Tjennet, it means Osiris. Variant: As for suppers, namely faience which is from Tjennet, it means the sky; it means the earth. Variant: It means Shu flattened the lands in Herakleopolis. As for faience, it means the Eye of Horus. As for Tjennet, it means the house of Osiris.[116]

How (well)-built is your house, Atum. Your house is (well)-founded, Ruty. Run, run to this. (If) Horus is divine, Seth is divine. Vice versa. I have come into this land. I have moved with my feet. I am Atum. I am in my town. Back, lion, whose mouth is white, whose head is stamped flat. Turn back because of my might. Variant: Turn back, (you) who attack me. (O you) who make guard while he is unseen guarding. I am Isis. You found me, the hair on my face disheveled, the

116 I.e., his tomb.

hair on my brow disordered. I conceive as Isis. I beget as Nephthys. Isis restrains those who guard me (and) Nephthys drives off those who interfere with me. Terror (of me) is behind me; awe of me is in front of me. Millions bend their shoulders to me. The common people surround me. The people trap my enemies for me. The greybeards bare their arms to me. Food is permanently provided for me which those in Kheraha create for me, as well as those who are in Heliopolis. Every god is greatly afraid because I take counsel with the one who vilifies. I scatter amulets (so that) I may live according to my desire. I am Wadjet, mistress of those who are in the flame. They ascend to me (but) few among them.

What is it? Secret of Forms, the Arms of Hemen is the name of the trap. The One Who Sees What He Takes Away Immediately is the name of the storm cloud. Variant: The name of the slaughtering-block. As for the lion whose mouth is white, whose head is stamped flat, it means the phallus of Osiris. Variant: It means the phallus of Re. As for the hair on my face disheveled, the hair on my brow disordered, Isis is at Shetyt. Then she rubbed her hair. As for Wadjet, mistress of those who are in the flame, it means the Eye of Re. As for they rise up to me (but) few among them, it means the confederates of Seth were drawing near her, since what draws near her is fire.

CHAPTERS 23-24-25-26-28-27-43-30A-31-33-34-35-74-45-93-91-41-61-42-14-68-69-70-92-63A-105-95-72

These chapters form a long sequence that begins near the end of the recto and runs into Column 5 of the verso. There are logical subdivisions within that sequence, and the texts that follow, both here and in the translation of the verso, are grouped according to these shorter sequences.

CHAPTERS 23-24-25-26-28-27

This group of texts is one of the oldest and best-attested sequences from the earliest appearance of the Book of the Dead. The overall focus of these texts is the restoration and protection of the physical properties of the deceased, the mouth and heart in particular, two organs whose functions distinguish humans from animals. The mouth is needed for gaining sustenance and for the recitation of protection texts like these very ones. The heart is closely related, being the organ of thought and the seat of the conscience. Thus, it was believed that the heart could "speak against" the deceased, that is, bear witness against him at judgment. Chapter 23 focuses on the restoration of the power of speech after death so that the deceased is able to both speak his magic and speak against the magic of others who intend to threaten him. Chapter 24 develops the theme of magic, stating that the deceased is in full possession of all the magic available to him. In Chapter 25, the theme of remembering one's name appears to be something of a shift but actually serves to shed light on the relationship that exists between the mouth and the heart. The heart was considered part of an individual's persona and the seat of true memory, while the mouth is capable of speaking both truth and falsehood. Chapter 26 develops the theme of physical regeneration. Once the deceased has his heart (and mouth), he has the power to declare that he is not dead, that he is not physically disintegrated, but is rather a unified whole, an individual who has regained all powers of speech, thought, mobility, sight, and physical strength. Note that these claims are, in essence, a denial of the effects of death as well as a denial of the effects of aging. Chapter 28 and Chapter 27 close this sequence, both introduced by the formula: "Spell for not (having something happen)...." The allusions in Chapter 28 are quite cryptic and elusive, but the focus of the chapter seems to be on the ability of the deceased to keep his heart through the use of specialized knowledge. Chapter 27 is an appeal to beings who have the power to take the heart away, asking that they not do so. There is also an appeal by the deceased not to allow his heart to make reproaches or accusations against him.

CONNECTING THREADS: *The theme of not allowing the heart to speak against one will be developed in Chapter 30A, a text that follows in the next sequence.*

Chapter 23 (Cols 478–483)

SPELL FOR OPENING THE MOUTH of the Goldworker of Amun Sobekmose, justified, FOR HIS MAGIC.

My mouth is opened by Ptah. What was on my mouth was loosened for me by my city god. Thoth comes then, full (and) equipped with magic, and he loosened the things belonging to Seth that were on my mouth. The hands of Atum warded (them) off and cast away what was on my mouth. My mouth is opened. My mouth is split open by Ptah with the metal harpoon [of his] with which he opened the mouth of the gods. I am Sakhmet, Great of Magic. I sit at the western side in the sky. I am Orion in the midst of the *bas* of Heliopolis. All the magic, all the words said against me, may the gods stand against [them], the Ennead all together, these gods of theirs all together.

Chapter 24 (Cols 483–489)

SPELL FOR BRINGING MAGIC to the Goldworker of Amun Sobekmose, justified.

I am Khepri who fashions himself on the lap of his mother, who gave jackals to those who are in the Nun, hounds to those who are in the council. This magic of mine was assembled for me from every place it was in, every man it was with, running faster than a hound, swifter than a shadow.

O (you) who brings the ferryboat of Re, may your rope be strong when your ferryboat swims[117] to the Island of Twin Flames in the necropolis. Now, assemble for yourself this magic of mine from every place it was in, (from) every man it was with, faster than a hound, swifter than a shadow. Variant: swifter than Shu. The *nur*-bird was created, the gods were held silent; the *nur*-bird was made to cry out, submission to the gods. Now, this magic of mine is given to you from every place it was in, every man it was with, faster than a hound, swifter than a shadow. Variant: swifter than sunlight.

Chapter 25 (Cols 489–491)

SPELL FOR CAUSING the Goldworker of Amun Sobekmose, justified, TO REMEMBER HIS NAME IN THE NECROPOLIS.

My name is given to me in the shrine of Upper Egypt. I remember my name in the shrine of Lower Egypt (on) this night of counting the years (and) numbering the months. I am one who is within the primeval one. I sit on the eastern side of the sky. Every god who does not come following me, I shall say his name afterward.[118]

---

117 I.e., "travels by water."

118 I.e., "to those who come afterward," the people yet to be born.

Chapter 26 (Cols 492–497)

SPELL FOR GIVING THE HEART OF the Goldworker of Amun Sobekmose, justified, TO HIM IN THE NECROPOLIS.

(O) heart which is in the house of hearts, (o) heart which is in the house of hearts, I have my heart (and) it is pleased. I will not eat the cakes given (to) Osiris on that eastern side of the narrows, (in) the boat when you sail downstream or (you) sail upstream (or) descending (to) the boat which you are in.

I have my mouth to speak, my legs to proceed, my arms to make my enemies fall. The two entrances in the earth are opened for me.[119] Geb, the prince of the gods, has opened his jaws for me (and) my eyes which were blocked; he stretches out my legs which were crooked; Anubis strengthens my thighs. I am raised up indeed (and) Sakhmet the goddess who exists in the sky stretches me out. Orders shall be made in Memphis.

I am [not] ignorant in my heart. I have power over my heart. I have power over my arms. I have power over my legs.

Chapter 28 (Cols 497–504)

SPELL FOR NOT LETTING THE HEART OF the Goldworker of Amun Sobekmose, justified, BE TAKEN AWAY FROM HIM IN THE NECROPOLIS.

O lion. I am Re. Your temple is an abomination. This heart of mine shall not be taken away from me by the fighters in Heliopolis.

(O you) (bone) breakers of Osiris when he saw Seth. O turn back after the one who struck him. He has caused my destruction. This heart of mine sits, (and) it itself bewails itself in the presence of Osiris, his staff in his hand. He has asked from me, (and) I have given to him. I have assigned to him the ones whose heart(s) are secret in the house of the broad-faced one. I have conveyed sand to him at the entrance of Hermopolis. This heart of mine shall not be abandoned [by] me. You have not advanced his seat, binding hearts to him in the field of fresh offerings.

(O) one powerful against his abominations, lord of power because your striking power is safe in your grasp (and) because of your strength. This heart of mine shall be placed in the annals of Atum. He guides the way (to) the caverns of Seth. Has he not given it to me, my heart that his heart made in the council that is in the necropolis? A wrapped leg (is what) they found and they buried.

---

119 A reference to the East and the West;
thus, the deceased can enter and go forth.

Chapter 27 (Cols 504–508)

SPELL FOR NOT LETTING THE HEART OF the Goldworker of Amun Sobekmose, justified, BE TAKEN AWAY FROM HIM IN THE NECROPOLIS.

O (you) who seize hearts, who rip out hearts, who (re)create the heart of a man into that which acts against him. Now, it has forgotten him because of you. Hail to you, lords of forever, who establish eternity. Do not take this heart of mine away from me. Do not reproach this heart of mine. Do not let the heart fashion this reproach of evil against me, because this heart of mine is the heart of the One Great of Names. The great god speaks through his limbs. Do not reproach this heart of mine. It shall not say what I have done. I am the one who has power over his limbs himself. Obey me, my heart. I am your lord. I shall not be defied. I am the one who commands that you obey him in the necropolis.

Chapters 43-30A

In early New Kingdom Books of the Dead, Chapters 43-30A close the sequence that has just preceded. Chapter 43 focuses on corporeal integration, a theme begun in the preceding texts, Chapters 28-27. It is also an Osirian text, through which the deceased assimilates himself to the dying and then rejuvenated god. Just as the head and heart of a man are not to be taken from him, so the heart that remains in him is not to cause mischief or problems for him either. The idea of judgment continues, as does the theme of not dying a second death.

Connecting Threads: *Chapter 43 forms a link with a number of the short texts preceding it that focused on avoiding corporeal dissolution. It also forms a link with the following Chapter 30A, a heart-text that resonates with many of the chapters of the preceding sequence as well.*

Chapter 43 (Cols 509–511)

Spell for not letting the head of the Goldworker of Amun Sobekmose, justified, be cut off from him in the necropolis.

I am an Elder (god), son of an Elder (god), a Flame (god), son of a Flame (god). His head shall be given to him after it is cut off from him. The head of Osiris shall not be taken away from him. My head shall not be taken from me. You shall raise me up. You shall make me new. You shall rejuvenate me. I am Osiris.

Chapter 30A (Cols 511–515)

Spell for not (letting) the heart of the Goldworker of Amun Sobekmose, justified, contend against him in the necropolis.

My heart of my mother, my heart of my mother, my heart from when I was upon the earth. Do not stand against me as my witness at the side of the lord of offerings. Do not say against me: he has done it in truth (about) what I have done. Do not fashion things against me at the side of the great god, lord of the West.

Hail to you, my heart. Hail to you, my heart. Hail to you, my entrails. Hail to you, you gods who are foremost of the ones with braided hair (and with) these hands upon their scepters. Speak my good (deeds) to Re. Make me flourish for Nehebkau. Now, he is interred within those who are great, who endure (upon) the earth, who do not die (in) the West, (as) an *akh* in it.

Chapters 31-33

Chapter 31 focuses on warding off the threats of the crocodile, an aquatic being associated with the margins of the created universe. A manifestation of the god Seth, the crocodile was also to be feared since it was a symbol of the forces dedicated to the destruction of the body. Chapter 33 pairs nicely with Chapter 31 as it focuses on warding off the threats of the snake, a terrestrial being also associated with pre-creation and the chaos at the edge of the civilized world. The reference to Geb and Shu "standing against" the snake is an allusion to creation, as each of these gods is the manifestation of a differentiated state of the cosmos as it came into being: Geb is the earth (dry land) and Shu is the sky (dry atmosphere). Snakes that naturally feed on mice are understood here as being unaware of the proper workings of the newly created cosmos: since they eat what the gods abominate, there is no chance for their ultimate survival in the ordered realm of creation.

Connecting Threads: *The theme of threats to corporeal unity continues, running through virtually all of the chapters of the section following Chapter 125.*

Chapter 31 (Cols 515–520)

Spell for driving back a crocodile that comes to seize the magic of the Goldworker of Amun Sobekmose, justified.

Back you! Retreat! Back you, crocodile. Do not come against me. I live on my magic. Let me not say this name of yours to any great god who allows you to come. Messenger is the name of one. Badty is the name of the other. Your face belongs to truth.

The sky has encircled its hours, and my magic has encircled its settlements. My mouth has encircled the magic that is in it. My teeth are flint. My tusks are from the Viper Mountain.

O spiny one, you who act against this magic of mine. You shall not seize it, (o you) crocodile who lives on magic.

Chapter 33 (Cols 520–521)

Spell for driving back any snakes by this Goldworker of Amun Sobekmose justified.

O Rerek-snake, behold, Geb (and) Shu stand against you. You have eaten a mouse, the abomination of Re. You have chewed on the bones of a cat that is rotting.

Chapters 34-35

These two short texts are anti-snake spells that use the formula: "Spell for not (having something happen)," thus continuing a theme begun with Chapter 28. The focus here is specifically on not letting the body of the deceased be defiled in any way, ensuring his continued existence in the tomb and the Netherworld.

Connecting Threads: *The concern with continued existence will also be addressed in the three texts that follow, especially in Chapters 45-93. It also connects with the preceding Chapter 33.*

Chapter 34 (Cols 521–523)

Spell for this Goldworker of Amun Sobekmose, justified, not being eaten by that which is in the funerary chapel.

O cobra, I am the flame that shines (upon) the brow of millions, the standard of the divine years. Variant: the standard of fresh plants[120] upon it. Be far from me. I am Mafdet.

Chapter 35 (Cols 523–526)

Spell for this Goldworker of Amun Sobekmose, justified, not being eaten by snakes in the necropolis.

O Shu, says Busiris (and) vice versa. The one(s) who wear the head-cloth of Hathor, they make Osiris happy. Is there one who will eat me? O one who alights, care for me. Pass me by, (o) *zekzek*-snake. It is the *sema*-plant that guards this Osiris. These[121] he shall ask (for) when he is buried. The eyes of the Elder have fallen—cleared—on you. Truth apportions (when) assessing what has accumulated.

---

120 Wordplay on the Egyptian for "years" and "plants."

121 I.e., the *sema*-plant.

CHAPTER 74

At first glance, Chapter 74 seems to be a departure from the themes of the chapters immediately surrounding it, all of which are texts whose heading is: "Spell for not...." However, the word senek *("darkness"), if that is the correct reading here, certainly has negative or "reversed" associations. Note, also, that the text focuses on the struggle between two opposing forces, namely the inertness associated with death and the power of the sun to rise and shine forth, after overcoming the forces of chaos and darkness overnight.*

Chapter 74 (Cols 526–528)

SPELL FOR MAKING THE FEET HURRY AND FOR GOING FORTH FROM THE EARTH by the Goldworker of Amun Sobekmose, justified.

You shall do that which you do,[122] Senek, Senek, with what is in his funerary chapel (and) what is in the stairway in the necropolis. I am the one who shines, the one who is above the district of the sky. I go forth to the sky. I climb upon the sun's rays. O, I am weary, I am weary, (yet) I proceed—(though) I am weary, I am weary—upon the banks of those who assemble in the necropolis.

---

122 I.e., do what you are supposed to do.

CHAPTERS 45-93

These two chapters invoke the theme of avoiding a second death in the necropolis. Chapter 45 addresses the question of putrefaction and the disintegration of the body. Avoidance of such is achieved through the deceased's identification with Osiris. Chapter 93 continues this theme, focusing on the fear of being carried off to the East. This motif is a slightly complex one, as being carried to the East alludes to the idea of "the reversed order of being." The East in funerary literature was not only the location of the sun rising at dawn but also the place of the execution of the enemies of the sun-god, an idea likely originating in the association between the blood of battle and the red color of dawn each morning. The East is thus envisioned as a place where the solar deity triumphs over Apophis right before sunrise (though in certain Egyptian funerary texts, the defeat and triumph over Apophis happen during one of the middle hours of the night). Chapter 93 ends with a threat formula that states what will happen to the gods Khepri and Re, both manifestations of the sun-god, if the deceased is carried off to the East. The reversion that he suffers will, in turn, be inflicted on the cosmos, with a specific disruption of the solar cycle.

Chapter 45 (Cols 528–530)
SPELL FOR NOT HAVING the Goldworker of Amun Sobekmose, justified, ROT.

Weariness, weariness is in Osiris. Weary is the limb of Osiris. It will not be weary. It will not rot. It will not come loose. It will not go away. May you do likewise (for me). I am Osiris.

Chapter 93 (Cols 530–535)
SPELL FOR NOT CROSSING the Goldworker of Amun Sobekmose, justified, TO THE EAST FROM THE NECROPOLIS.

O you phallus of Re, made soft indeed by the uproar. The weariness of Baba has come to pass. He is stronger through me [than] the strong ones. If I am crossed over to the East, (my) horns bound[123]—Variant: If anything bad (or) evil is done at the feast of the rebels against me by the binding of horns,—then, indeed, the phallus of Re will swallow the head of Osiris.

Now, I am led to the fields of the one whom the gods have beheaded where they give answer. Then, indeed, the horns of Khepri shall be bound. Then ulcerations[124] shall exist in the Eye of Atum, the annihilator, because I am seized, because I am carried off to the East, because a rebel-feast is made from me, because a slaughtering was evilly done to me.

---

123 I.e., "against my will." The text of this phrase continues after the "Variant."   124 I.e., "swellings."

Translation
of the Verso Texts

Chapter 91

The chapters of the verso begin with a text that emphasizes the mobility of the ba *of the deceased and its innate power. The text also lays claim to the right of the* ba, akh, *and shadow of the deceased to receive provisions in the next world. Thus, two central concerns of the deceased—mobility and food provisions—are realized through the power of this chapter.*

Connecting Threads: *The early texts of the verso emphasize the divinity of the deceased by locating him in the company of a number of different deities, with whom he will claim to have physical connections. Thus, Chapter 91 continues the themes—provisioning, self-willed mobility, and an unchallenged presence in the divine world—that we saw in the texts at the end of the recto. Chapter 91 also has the heading "Spell for not (having something happen...)," continuing the pattern we saw in Chapters 45-93, the final two texts of the recto.*

Chapter 91 (Col. 1; ll. 1–3)

SPELL FOR THE *BA* of this Goldworker of Amun Sobekmose, justified, NOT BEING CONFINED.

O lofty one who is adored, great of power, *ba* whose awe is great, who puts his fear in the gods, who appears in glory upon his great thrones. Give thought so that my *ba*, my *akh*, my shadow are provided for. I am a provisioned *akh*. Make a path for me to the place where Re (and) Hathor are.

CHAPTERS 41-61-42-14

These chapters continue and develop the theme of "Going forth by day" with their focus on mobility, access to requisites, and the ability to overcome any attempts to impede the deceased's movement.

Chapter 41 (Col. 1; ll. 3–10)
Chapter 41 is somewhat rare and is found in New Kingdom Books of the Dead only in the Eighteenth Dynasty. The crucial word in the text is šꜥd ("slaughtering"), an apparent reference to the negative activity of hostile beings in the Netherworld, against whom the deceased must be armed. The deceased claims divinity and outlines his various powers—the ability to eat, to enter, to leave, and to speak at will. At the end of the text, he declares that he is Osiris. Thus, his power and divine nature combine to ensure his immunity to danger.
CONNECTING THREADS: *In this chapter, as in the preceding one, the deceased explicitly claims to be in the company of the gods; the references to eating and living on air continue the theme of being provisioned with the requisites of continued life that was central to the preceding chapter.*

SPELL FOR WARDING OFF SLAUGHTER by the Goldworker of Amun Sobekmose, justified, IN THE NECROPOLIS.

I am Atum. I am more *akh*-like than Ruty. He has opened the gate of Geb (so that) I may kiss the god who is hidden. O you gatekeeper of the City of the Bee which is in the West—I eat, I live on air. I lead Imyadjwer [to] the sacred boat of Khepri. I speak to the crew which is in the evening. I enter, I go forth (so that) I see the one whom I shall raise up (and so that) I may speak to him the words of the one whose throat is constricted. I live indeed after death.

O one who brings offerings, who opens his mouth, who brings forward the writings, who gives offerings, who establishes what is right, who brings forward injury, who establishes the goddess. I am Osiris who counts his seasons, who hears these (things), who raises the right arm (when) he judges the Elders whom he sends into the council.

Chapter 61 (Col. 1; ll. 10–11)
This short chapter continues the claims of the deceased found in the previous chapter. Here, his connection with the annual flood ensures for him the ubiquitous presence of water, another essential in the Netherworld. The heading given in the Brooklyn papyrus for this chapter is, properly speaking, that of Chapter 62.

SPELL FOR DRINKING WATER by this Goldworker of Amun Sobekmose, justified.

I am the one who goes forth from the flood (and) to whom the Inundation has been given (so that) he may have power over [it] as Hapi (does).

Chapter 42 (Col. 1; l. 11–Col. 3; l. 4)

This long text returns to the theme of avoiding slaughter in the Netherworld introduced in Chapter 41. Here the deceased declares that each part of his body, through connection with a specific divinity, is divine and therefore impervious to danger. He then identifies himself directly with a number of different gods known from the Osirian myth cycle, like Horus and Wennefer. He also claims to exist within the Sound Eye, a reference to the undamaged Eye of Re or Horus, well known in Egyptian thought as a symbol of powerful protection.

CONNECTING THREADS: *The theme of being in the company of the gods largely ties this chapter to the one that precedes it and the group that follows; these early texts of the verso lay heavy emphasis on the claims of the deceased to be associated with specific divinities.*

SPELL FOR WARDING OFF SLAUGHTER IN HERAKLEOPOLIS by this Goldworker of Amun Sobekmose, justified.

The land belongs to the staff. The White Crown belongs to the images of the standards of Min. I am the child. Four times.[125] O Ibu-weret,[126] you have said today: the place of execution is equipped with what you know. You have come to it, viscera of the Eldest. I am one whose praise is established. I am the divine vertebra that lives within the tamarisk-tree. How (much) more beautiful today is than yesterday. Four times. I am one whose praise is established. I am the vertebra within the tamarisk.

How (much) more beautiful today is than yesterday. Four times. (If) I prosper, one prospers, this day prospers.

My hair is the Nun.[127] My face is Re. My eyes are Hathor. My ears are Wepwawet. My nose is Khenty-khas.[128] [My] lips are Anubis. My teeth are Khepri. My neck is Isis the divine one. My arms are Khnum, lord of Busiris. My chest is Neith, mistress of Sais. My back is Seth. My phallus is Osiris. My flesh is the lords of Kheraha. My breast is Aa-shefshefet.[129] My belly (and) my backbone are Sakhmet.

---

125 Instructions for how many times to repeat this section of the text. The recitation of a passage four times is commonly encountered in magical texts as an instruction to recite the passage to the four cardinal geographic points in order to maximize its effectiveness.

126 The name of a deity who plays the role of protector in a number of different contexts.

127 Beginning here is a list of statements in which the deceased claims direct connection between the parts of his body and specific deities.

128 Lit., Foremost One of Xoïs.

129 Lit., He Whose Awe Is Great.

My buttocks are the Eye of Horus. My thighs (and) my calves are Nut. My feet are Ptah. My fingers (and) my toes are living cobras. There is no limb of mine devoid of a god. Thoth is the protections of my entire flesh.

I am Re every day. I shall not be grasped by my arms. My hands shall not be seized. No men, gods, *ahks*, dead people, patricians, any of the common people, (nor) any of the sun-people shall rob anything from me.[130]

I am one who goes forth prospering, whose name is not known. I am yesterday. The one who sees millions of years is my name. Go, go upon the path of the Chief Examiner.

I am the lord of eternity. May I be counted like Khepri. I am the lord of the *werret*-crown.

I am the one within the Sound Eye. (O) egg, egg. I have allowed them to live. I am the one within the Sound Eye, (even if) closed, I am in its protections. I have gone forth, I have risen, I have entered (and) I live. I am the one within the Sound Eye. My seat is my throne. I sit in my structure before it.

I am Horus who treads on millions. My throne has been assigned to me (so that) I may rule from it with a mouth that speaks (and) is silent. I am precise. Look, my form is upside down.

I am Wen[nefer]. Season by season, his requisites are with him, one by one, (as) he makes his circuit. I am the one within the Sound Eye. No evil condition of mine exists. Strife, it does not exist against me.

[I am one who] opens a gate in the sky. I rule (from my) throne, judging those born on this day. There is no child who treads upon the road of yesterday. This day belongs to me, man as man.

I am your protector for millions (of years). Do you exist, you of the sky, of the Two Lands, of the South, of the North, of the West, of the East? (Is) your fear of me in your bellies? I am the one who fashions with his Eye. I do not die again. My striking power [is] in your bellies. My forms are within me. I am one who cannot be known. The red ones, their faces (are) against me.

I am one who is joyful. No season is found when it[131] (can) act against me. Where is the sky? Where is the earth? Children of misfortune are united. My name passes by it, namely, everything evil. With words I speak [to] you.

I am the one who rises, shining down on wall by wall, one by one. No day is free of its responsibilities. Pass by! Pass by! Pass by! Pass by! See, I have spoken.

---

130 The reference is to losing any of the parts of his reintegrated physical being.
131 I.e., "season."

I am the blossom that came forth from the Nun—that means my mother. O one who created me, I am one who does not tread,[132] the great commander within yesterday. My condition of commander is within my hand.[133] The one who knows me is not known. The one who should grasp me does not grasp me.

(O) Egg! Egg! (O) Egg! Egg! I am Horus who is foremost over men, (my) scorching heat against your faces whose hearts would be sick against me. I have ruled (from) my throne. I pass this time [upon] paths that I have opened. I am released from all evil.

I am the baboon of gold of three palms (and) two fingers, who has no legs, who has no arms, the foremost one of Memphis. (If) I am sound, the baboon of gold, of three palms (and) two fingers, the foremost one of Memphis, is sound.

Say this word: May you illuminate the one you are driving away.

Chapter 14 (Col. 3; ll. 4–6)

The Coffin Text on which Chapter 14 was modeled makes it clear that mobility and the power to cross the sky are dependent on the ability of the deceased to appease the anger of the gods and to enlist their help by claiming to be free of wrongdoing.
CONNECTING THREADS: *The assertion of the deceased that he has power over the individual members of his body strongly links this group with the immediately preceding text Chapter 42. The theme of divine association continues to be stressed as well.*

DRIVING AWAY ANGER FROM THE HEART OF A GOD for this Goldworker of Amun Sobekmose, justified.

Ah to you whose striking power descends, foremost one of all secrets. See, my words are spoken. So says the god. Wrongdoing floods, and it falls to the responsibility of the lord of truth. May you drive off the harm which is in me, which is evil. The god unites with Truth. May this god be kind to me. Drive away my harm to another.

O lord of offerings, great powerful one, see, I bring to you a propitiation offering (so that) you may live on it (and that) I may live on it. Be kind to me. Drive away all the anger which is in your heart against [me].

---

132 Possibly a metaphor for "who does not offend."

133 Possibly a reference to a scepter or some symbol of power.

CHAPTERS 68-69-70-92

Chapters 68-69-70-92 are all spells for "Going forth by day." Note that in Chapter 68, the deceased claims to have power over the individual members of his physical body, further developing the theme of Chapter 42, in which the deceased claimed that his body parts were actually individual gods. In Chapter 69, he once again claims direct association with a number of divinities. In Chapter 70, he states that he has power over the winds, in Egyptian thought an allusion to the ability to breathe. A number of references to resurrection occur as well. Chapter 92 is another text for "Going forth by day." It brings together the ba, akh, *and shadow once again, this time insisting that they shall not be restrained in any way from movement. The deceased associates himself with Horus, the son of Osiris. Therefore, the normal modes of restraint exercised by the "keepers of the limbs of Osiris" do not apply to him. He and his otherworldly manifestations are free to move about at will.*

CONNECTING THREADS: *The theme of "Going forth by day" links these chapters, presenting them as another unit within the thematic context of the chapters that precede and follow.*

Chapter 68 (Col. 3; ll. 6–15)

SPELL FOR GOING FORTH BY DAY by the Goldworker of Amun Sobekmose, justified.

The doors of heaven are opened for me. The doors of earth are opened for me. The door-bolts of Geb are opened for me. The house top (and) peep-hole are revealed for me. It is the one who guards me who releases me. It is the one who binds his arm on me who thrusts his arm from me to the ground. The mouth of the pelican is opened for me. The mouth of the pelican is revealed to me. The mouth of the pelican grants to me that I go forth by day to any place my heart desires.

I have power over my heart. I have power over my heart. I have power over my mouth. I have power over my legs. I have power over my arms. I have power over all of my limbs. I again have power over my invocation offerings. I have power over air. I have power over water. I have power over the flood. I have power over the river. I have power over the riverbanks. I have power over males who act against me. I have power over females who act against me in the necropolis. I have power over those ordered to act [against me] on earth.

What you have said about me is a lie: "he lives on the bread of Geb." It is my abomination. I have not eaten it. I live on the red *emmer*-bread of Hapi in the pure place. I swallow red-wheat beer of Hapi in the pure place. I sit under the branches of the *ima*-tree[134] in the vicinity of Hathor, foremost one of the broad

134 Tree sacred to Hathor.

solar-disk, while she departs for Heliopolis in possession of the writings of the god's words,[135] the book of Thoth.

I have power over my heart. I have power over my heart. I have power over my feet. I have power over my arms. I have power over invocation offerings. I have power over water. I have power over air. I have power. I have power over the flood. I have power over the river. I have power over the riverbanks. I have power over males who act against me, over females who act against me in the necropolis. I have power over those ordered to act against me.

Raise me from my left side to my right side. Raise me from my right side; place me (so that) I am seated, (so that) I stand up (so that) I shake off my dust. My tongue (is) connected to me as a skilled guide.

Chapter 69 (Col. 3; l. 15–Col. 4; l. 4)

Variant: I am the burning one, brother of the burning one, Osiris brother of Isis. My son and his mother Isis have saved me from my male enemies (and) my female enemies who would do everything evil (against me). Their bonds were placed on their arms, on their hands, (and) their feet because they did their evil against me.

I am Osiris, eldest of (my) generation, eldest of the gods, heir of my father, Geb. I am Osiris, lord of people, whose foreside lives, whose backside is strong, whose phallus is hard, who is within the boundaries of the common people.

I am Orion who reaches his land, sailing in front of the stars of the sky (on) the belly of (his) mother Nut. She conceived me in accordance with her desire. She gave birth to me in accordance with her wish.

I am Anubis (on) the day of the centipede, the bull, the one who is foremost of the field.

It is I who am Osiris, for whom his father and his mother sealed this day when the great slaughter was done. Geb is (my) father; Nut is my mother.

I am the Elder (on) the day of ascending (the throne).

I am Anubis, the centipede.

It is I who am the Lord of All. I am Osiris. (O) eldest who has entered, [say] to the collector of writings (to) the doorkeeper of Osiris that I am come. I am an *akh*. I am counted.[136] I am powerful. I am divine. I have come, (and) I have protected my body myself. I sit on the birth-brick of Osiris (so that) I may drive away his painful suffering. I am a powerful one; I am a divinity who is upon on the birth-brick of Osiris. I was born together with him, the extremely youthful one. I wrap these knees of mine (and) the lower part of Osiris. I open the mouth of the gods

135 I.e., "hieroglyphs."

136 Denotes recognition among the blessed dead.

because of it. I sit at his side as Thoth goes forth gladdened: one thousand loaves of bread and beer upon the offering table of my father Osiris with my spotted cattle, with my long-horned cattle, with my red cattle, with my bulls, with my *ra*-geese, with my *hetep*-geese. I make an offering to Horus. I make a presentation to Thoth, a slaughtering for the one who is chief of Teryt.

Chapter 70 (Col. 4; ll. 4–7)

Variant: I moor for the one who is chief of refusal, the scribe of the one whose heart is sound. I satisfy (myself) at the offering tables of my father Osiris. I rule Busiris. I wander over its two banks. I breathe in the east wind by its tresses. I grasp the north wind by its braids. I grasp (and) I seize the west wind by its curls. I circle this sky to its four corners. [I grasp] the mouth of the south wind by its plaits. I give my breath to the revered ones among those who eat bread. As for one who knows this bookroll while upon earth, he goes forth by day, (and) he will proceed upon earth among the living. His name cannot perish for eternity.

Chapter 92 (Col. 4; ll. 7–14)

OPENING THE TOMB FOR THE *BA* AND THE SHADOW (TO) GO FORTH BY DAY. SPELL FOR HAVING POWER OVER THE LEGS by this Goldworker of Amun Sobekmose, justified.

What is open is to be open! What is sealed is to be sealed!

(You who) sleep, what is open is to be open for my *ba* which is within it.[137] (O) Eye of Horus, I have been saved (and) my beauty is fastened on the forehead of Re.[138] Far-strider, leg-stretcher, make way for me, great one, (my) flesh is made fast.

I am Horus, avenger of his father. I am the one who brings his father (and) who brings the Great One[139] by his staff. Open the ways for one who has power (over) his feet (so that) he may see the great god within the sacred boat of Re, in which *bas* are counted. My *ba* is therein at the front together with the one who counts the years.

Come, take my *ba* for me, (o) Eye of Re, (so that) he may fasten adornments on the forehead of Re while the twilight is upon your faces, you keepers of the limbs of Osiris. You cannot imprison my *ba*. You cannot restrain the shade of this Goldworker of Amun Sobekmose, justified. Open the ways for my *ba*, for my shade, for the *akh* (so that) he may see the Great God within the shrine (on) the day of counting the *bas* (and so that) he may repeat the words of Osiris.

137 I.e., the tomb.
138 An allusion to the protective *uraeus* on the brow of the sun-god.
139 Name of a goddess, often alluding to the *uraeus*.

(O) ones whose seats are hidden, keepers of the limbs of Osiris, who restrain *bas* (and) *akhs*, who put seals upon the shades of the dead, both male and female, who would do evil against me, (and) those who have done evil against me. Go, go far away because your *ka* is with my *ba*. The *akhs* who are equipped, they will guide (you so that) you may sit before the elders whose seats are foremost. You shall not be imprisoned by the keepers of the limbs of Osiris who restrain (and) put seals upon the shades of the dead, both male and female. Are you held by the sky?

CHAPTER 63A

This chapter has more to do with the ability of the deceased to move than it does with his need to obtain water as the title seems to suggest. Again, the focus seems to be on the deceased's ability to move freely, regardless of the obstacles presented to him, here a dehydrating fire that either threatens him or through which he must move.

CONNECTING THREADS: *Osirian motifs and allusions to going forth in the reference to the solar boat of Re continue themes that have run through many of the preceding chapters.*

Chapter 63A (Col. 4; ll. 14–16)

SPELL FOR DRINKING WATER (AND) NOT BEING DEHYDRATED BY FIRE by this Goldworker of Amun Sobekmose, justified.

O Bull of the West, bring me to you. I am this paddle of Re with which he rows the elders. I am Baba, the first son of Osiris to whom the gods within his Eye of Heliopolis are joined. I am the heir who unwrapped the Elder (god), the Weary One. My name flourishes for me. I have prevented another from living on me.

Chapter 105 ii

This is the second appearance of this chapter in the papyrus, as it is the first extant chapter of the recto as well. Repetition is not an uncommon feature of Books of the Dead, particularly when the second text shows slight alterations or additions, as it does here. The declarations of the deceased that he, as a powerful ba, *brings appeasement offerings to his* ka *serve to link this text with those preceding. The chapter not only helps the deceased unite with his* ka *but continues to emphasize his powers.*

Connecting Threads: *The claims of the deceased that he has power over himself and his environs continue the themes of the previous chapters.*

Chapter 105 ii (Col. 4; ll. 16–20)

Spell for appeasing the *ka* of this Goldworker of Amun Sobekmose, justified.

Hail to you, my *ka*, my lifetime. See, I am come before you. I am risen, I am a *ba*. I am powerful. I am healthy. I bring to you natron (and) incense (so that) I may purify you with them (and so that) I may purify your fluids with them.

This evil utterance which I have said (and) this evil impurity which I have done will not be put on me because this papyrus amulet that belongs at the throat of Re and is given to those who are in the horizon belongs to me. (If) they flourish, my *ka* flourishes like them, the provisions of my *ka* like theirs.

You who balance the scale, truth rises to the nose of Re on that day. (O) my *ka*, do not let my head be taken from me. To me belongs an eye that sees, an ear that hears. To me belongs a bull of the animals for slaughter. Are there no invocation offerings from me for those who are in charge? Variant—those who are in charge of the lower sky.

CHAPTER 95

The epithet "you who balance the scale" in the previous chapter was an allusion to the god Thoth mentioned in this chapter. The deceased's juxtaposition with the god Thoth accords him mighty powers.

CONNECTING THREADS: *The claims of power and divine authority continue.*

Chapter 95 (Col. 4; l. 20–Col. 5; l. 1)

SPELL FOR BEING AT THE SIDE of Thoth by this Goldworker of Amun Sobekmose, justified.

I am the terror in the storm who guards the great one [in] the conflict. Sharp Knife strikes for me. Ash god provides coolness for me. I act on behalf of the great one in the conflict. I give strength to the knife, namely the sharp knife that is in the hand of Thoth in the storm.

Chapter 72

The deceased now states that he has powers that guarantee him access to food and drink in the Netherworld, as well as the right to move about freely. In Chapter 72, the powers he possesses come through the fact that he is already an akh and has possession of magic as well. He instructs the lords of truth to protect him because he knows their names, a knowledge that gives him power over them.

Connecting Threads: *The themes of "Going forth by day" and specialized knowledge continue in this chapter.*

Chapter 72 (Col. 5; ll. 1–8)

Spell for going forth by day (and) opening Imhet[140] by this Goldworker of Amun Sobekmose, justified.

Hail to you, lords of truth, free from wrongdoing, who exist forever and forever. I have reached you (because) I am an *akh* with my forms. I am powerful through my magic. I am organized with my magical spells. Save me from this crocodile of the land of the righteous. My mouth belongs to me (so that) I may speak with it. My gifts are given to me in your presence because I know you (and) I know your names. I know the name of this great god at whose nose you place offerings— Tekem is his name. He penetrates to the eastern horizon of the sky. He alights in the western horizon of the sky. He departs, I depart. I am sound, he is sound.

I shall not be driven away from Mesqet.[141] The rebels shall not have power over me. I shall not be turned back at your gates. You shall not seal your doors against me, because my bread is in Pe (and) my beer is in Dep. The excess of my hands is in the temple. (My) father Atum has given to me (and) he has established for me my house upon the earth, barley and *emmer* in it beyond count. Offerings shall be made for me there by the son of my body. You will give to me an invocation offering (consisting of) incense, oil, every good (and) pure thing that (a god) lives on, (and) existence forever in any form that I want.

I will travel north. I will travel south from the Field of Reeds (and) enter the Two Fields of Hotep because I am Ruty.

As for one who knows this book-roll upon earth or if it is made in writing on his coffin, he goes forth by day in any form (that) he wants and (re)enters to his seat. He cannot be turned back. He is given bread, beer, a great (piece) of meat which is on the offering table of Osiris. He ascends to the Field of Reeds. He is given barley (and) wheat there. He shall exist, flourishing as he exists upon earth. He does whatever he wants like these gods (who are) there. Proven effective millions of times.

---

140 A name of the Netherworld.

141 As noted earlier, Mesqet is an uncertain area of the night sky once thought to correspond to the Milky Way; it is the region of the east through which the celestial bodies pass in their risings.

CHAPTERS 71-106

Chapter 71 (Col. 5; ll. 8–18)

In Chapter 71, the powers of the deceased are said to stem from his identification with certain gods and sacred plants, as well as from his knowledge of the gods and their names. Chapter 106 specifically focuses on the town of Memphis and the god Ptah, its most important deity.

CONNECTING THREADS: *The theme of "Going forth by day," prevalent in the texts of the verso, continues to link each spell with those that precede and follow.*

SPELL FOR GOING FORTH BY DAY by this Goldworker of Amun Sobekmose, justified.

O falcon who rises from the Nun, lord of the great flood. May you make me sound like you make yourself sound.

"Loosen him. Set him free. Place him on the ground. Grant what he wishes." So says the lord, the single-faced one, concerning me.

"I am the falcon within the shrine. I penetrate to the one who makes the fringed garment." So says Horus, son of Isis. (O) Horus son of Isis, may you make me sound like you make yourself sound.

"Loosen him. Set him free. Place him on the ground. Grant what he wishes." So says the lord, the single-faced one, concerning me.

"I am the falcon in the southern sky. I am Thoth in the northern sky who appeases the raging fiery cobra who presents truth to the one whom she loves." So said Thoth. O Thoth, may you make me sound like you make yourself sound.

"Loosen him. Set him free. Place him on the ground. Grant what he wishes." So says the lord, the single-faced one, concerning me.

"I am the blossom of Naref, the *nebheh*-plant of the hidden season." So says Osiris. (O) Osiris, may you make me sound like you make yourself sound.

"Loosen him. Set him free. Place him on the ground. Grant what he wishes." So says the lord, the single-faced one, concerning me.

O you whose feet are bound who is in his moment. Variant: O one whose terror is in his feet who is in his moment, Lord of the Two Fledglings. As the Two Fledglings live, may you make me sound like you make yourself sound.

"Loosen him. Set him free. Place him on the ground. Grant what he wishes." So says the lord, the single-faced one, concerning me.

O [...] who is in his egg, Lord of the Great Flood, may you make me sound like you make yourself sound.

"Loosen him. Set him free. Place him on the ground. Grant what he wishes." So says the lord, the single-faced one, concerning me.

Rise up, Sobek who dwells on his hill. Rise up, Neith who dwells on her riverbanks.

"Loosen him. Set him free. Place him on the ground. Grant what he wishes." So says the lord, the single-faced one, concerning me.

O you seven knots, the arms of the balance on this night of reckoning up the Sound Eye, who cut off heads, who sever necks, who seize hearts, who snatch up hearts, who make a slaughtering in the Island of Fire. I know you, I know your names. May you know me like I know your names. I reach you, you reach me. You live through me, I live through you. You make me flourish by the life that is in your hands, by the scepter that is in your fist. May you assign me to life (on) the first of the years[142] (so that) he may give many years upon years of life, many months upon months of life, many days upon days of life, many nights upon nights of life until I go forth. May I rise to my image, breath at my nose. My eyes, may they have sight among those who are in the horizon (on) this day of reckoning with the robber.[143]

Chapter 106 (Col. 5; ll. 18–20)

The mention of Memphis and Ptah, the god most closely associated with Memphis, in this chapter is particularly apt as Memphis is quite possibly where Sobekmose resided while on earth. Ptah is mentioned in a number of funerary texts in connection with food offerings, as he is in this text.

CONNECTING THREADS: *The deceased asserts the right to be given food offerings worthy of a divinity.*

SPELL FOR GIVING OFFERINGS to this Goldworker of Amun Sobekmose, justified, IN MEMPHIS (AND) IN THE NECROPOLIS.

O you provisions.

O eldest, foremost one of the upper house, you who give bread to Ptah, give bread to me (and) give beer. My breakfast (is) a calf bone[144] together with a *seshret*-cake.

O you ferryman of the Field of Reeds, bring me to this bread of your waters as if to (your) father, the eldest, who has gone in the ship of the god.

---

142 I.e., grant me this request each year on the first day of the year.

143 A reference to judgment after death.
144 Lower part of the leg.

CHAPTER 9

The deceased now directly associates himself with Osiris and Thoth, the gods who played central roles in the original myth of judgment. Here Osiris is said to be the father of the deceased who claims to be Thoth. He also claims to be an akh-iqer, *a particularly efficacious form of an* akh *for whom no obstacles are impassable or impenetrable.*

CONNECTING THREADS: *Just as the deceased has asserted the right to "Go forth by day," a theme common from a number of the preceding texts, here he claims to have the power to (re)enter the Netherworld, where, like the sun-god, he will dispel the darkness and unite with Osiris.*

Chapter 9 (Col. 5; ll. 20–22)

SPELL FOR PENETRATING THE DUAT by this Goldworker of Amun Sobekmose, justified.

(O) ram great of majesty, look at me, I am come (so that) I may see you. I penetrate the Duat (so that) I may see my father Osiris. I remove the darkness. I am his beloved. I have come. I have seen my father Osiris. Open for me all the paths that are in the sky. I am his father's beloved. I have come. I am ennobled. I am an *akh*. I am one who is equipped.

O every god, every *akh*, make a path for me. I am Thoth (when) he ascends.

CHAPTERS 83-84-85-82-77-86-99

Here begins a long sequence of transformation texts in which the deceased takes on the form of a variety of birds and animals and a number of different deities. Embedded in the transformation to bird form is the idea of freedom of movement as well as ascension, a clear solar allusion. The specific mention of birds such as the phoenix and the heron continues the solar theme but also introduces an Osirian one, as these birds are associated with Osiris as well. Thus, the themes of rebirth and renewal lie at the center of this group of texts. In Chapter 99, the final text of the sequence, the deceased, now in the sky, engages in a lengthy dialogue with the celestial ferryman that has the form of an initiation text. The deceased is asked questions about the nature of the various parts of the ferry, all of which he is able to answer. Power over the ferryboat is necessary if he is to use it as a means of going forth. He thus demonstrates, once again, that the specialized knowledge that he possesses gives him access to food provisions and total freedom of movement.

CONNECTING THREADS: *The themes of going forth and of the assertion of power through possession of specialized knowledge link this group of texts to those that precede it. The nautical motifs of Chapter 99, the final chapter of the group, will link the whole to Chapters 38A and 39, the two texts that follow.*

Chapter 83 (Col. 5; l. 23–Col. 6; l. 2)

TAKING ON THE FORM OF A PHOENIX by this Goldworker of Amun Sobekmose, justified.

I have flown as the Primeval One. I have become Khepri. I have grown as shoots (grow). (I) have clothed myself as a turtle. I am the fruit[145] of every god. I am yesterday, this fourth of the cobras that came into being in the West, Horus who illuminates with his body. He is a god against Seth. Thoth was among them in this judgment of the foremost one of Letopolis together with the *bas* of Heliopolis, the flood that was between them. I have come by day. I am one who appears in glory in the footsteps of the gods. I am Khonsu, the rage of the lords.

Chapter 84 (Col. 6; ll. 2–7)

TAKING ON THE FORM OF A HERON by this Goldworker of Amun Sobekmose, justified, the powerful one among the bulls with flint upon their heads, the braids which are on their bald-headed ones, the aged ones, those of the sunshine, whose strike is sharp. The (might) of this Goldworker of Amun Sobekmose, justified, is against the sky, his terror against the earth (and) vice versa.

---

145 The word "fruit" is a metaphor for "essence" or the like.

It is my power that has created victory, making[146] the height of the sky greet me respectfully (and) making the wideness of my strides (stretch) to my city (and) settlements. I proceed as one tousled, as one who is bald. I abandon the gods upon their paths. I seek out the ones who are resting in their shrines. Do I not know the Nun? Do I not know Tatenen? Do I not know the red ones who drag with their horns? Do I not know Heka[147] when I hear his words? I am this Masu[148] found in the writings. Words to be said by the gods while they lament.

Yesterday is beyond us. It has come before me. Dawn comes (but) you are unaware. You are unaware of those who guard you. My fault is in my belly. What Hu says to me is (what) I say. I shall not speak of lies yesterday (and) truth today. Truth runs upon my eyebrows (at) the time of night. The foremost one sails south, standing vigil. Is the aged one who guards her land drunk?

Chapter 85 (Col. 6; ll. 7–16)

TAKING ON THE FORM OF A *BA* (AND) NOT ENTERING THE PLACE OF EXECUTION by this Goldworker of Amun Sobekmose justified. He says:

I am a *ba*. I am Re who goes forth from the Nun. The god who created Hu[149] is my *ba*. Wrongdoing is my abomination. I have not seen it. I think about truth (and) I live on it. I am Hu who does not perish in this name of mine—*ba*. I came into being myself together with the Nun in this name of mine—Khepri. I have come into being as him every day. I am the lord of light. Mooring[150] is my abomination. I shall not enter into the place of execution of the Duat.

I am the one who gives offerings to Osiris, who appeases the hearts of those who follow (him) (and) the underlings. They cause fear of me, (and) they create their awe for those who are in their midst. Lo, I am high upon my standard of the Nun, upon this seat of mine. I am the Nun. The ones who do wrongdoing will not harm me.

I am the eldest of the Primeval One. The gods, the *bas* of eternity, are my *ba*. I am the one who creates darkness, who makes his seat in the region of the sky. My *ba* comes to me here, far from the aged ones (where) I make darkness in the region of the sky. (If) I wish to reach their region, I proceed on my feet. I have control. I cross the firmament which they have made. I remove the darkness (and) the snakes who are hidden. I remove my steps from the lord of the two regions. The *ba* of my body is my *ba*. It is the two cobras. It is the image of eternity, the lord of years. It is the ruler of eternity.

---

146 I.e., "reaching" (?).
147 Personification of magic.
148 Possibly a miswriting of the word *semau* ("wild bull").

149 Personification of divine "uttered authority."
150 Common Egyptian metaphor for dying.

I am the one who is exalted, the lord of Ta-bu.[151] Youth in the cities, young man in my field is my name. My name cannot perish. I am the *ba* that created the Nun, making his seat in the necropolis. My nest has not been seen. My egg has not been broken. I am an exalted lord. I have made a nest in the region of the sky. I descend to the land of Geb. I drive away my evil. I see my father, lord of the evening. This Goldworker of Amun Sobekmose, justified, kisses his body which is in Heliopolis. Commended to me are the [...] upon the western mounds of the ibis.

Chapter 82 (Col. 6; ll. 16–22)

SPELL FOR TAKING ON THE FORM OF Ptah (AND) EATING BREAD, DRINKING, EXCRETING FROM THE BUTTOCKS, (AND) EXISTING ALIVE IN HELIOPOLIS by this Goldworker of Amun Sobekmose, justified.

I have flown (and) I have honked as a *semen*-goose. I have alighted on that side of the mound of the great festival. My abomination, my abomination—I have not eaten my abomination. Excrement is [my] abomination. I have not eaten it. The abomination of my *ka*—it will not enter into my belly.

What then do you live on? they say, the gods (and) the *akhs*. I live (and) I have power through bread. Where then will you eat it? they say, the gods (and) the *akhs*. I have power (and) I eat under the foliage (and) branches of the *ima*-tree of Hathor, my mistress who provides food offerings, who provides bread, who provides beer in Busiris (and) corn in Heliopolis.

I will be clothed with a loincloth from Tayet upon me. I will sit in the place I want to be in. My head is Re joined with Atum. The four suns, the gifts of the land of Re—four times. I have gone forth. My tongue is Ptah. My throat is Hathor. I remember the words of Atum for my father with my mouth (when) he destroyed the servant of the wife of Geb, fire upon him. Fear him (and) do not repeat it. Woes will follow.

(I) have been assigned the inheritance of the lord of the earth, Geb, my protector there. Geb cools me. He gives his crown to me. Those who are in Heliopolis bow their heads before me. I am their lord. I am their bull. I am more powerful than the lord of striking power. I copulate; I have power over millions.

Chapter 77 (Col. 6; l. 22–Col. 7; l. 3)

TAKING ON THE FORM OF A FALCON OF GOLD by this Goldworker of Amun Sobekmose, justified.

I appear in glory as a great falcon who goes forth from his egg. I fly (and) I alight as a falcon whose back is four cubits. My wings are green-stone of Upper Egypt. I have gone forth from the chest [to] the night-boat. My heart is brought to

---

151 An unknown place name.

me from the eastern mountain. I alight in the day-boat. Those who are with their primeval ones come to me (and) are brought to me, as they bend down to one who is arisen (and) reassembled as a falcon of gold atop the *benu*-stone.[152]

Re has entered every day making his judgments. I sit among these gods, the elders of the sky. The Field of Offerings is set aside for me in my presence (so that) I may eat from it; I have the power of an *akh* from it; I have abundance from it to the fulfillment of my heart. The grain goddess gives to me my throat (so that) I may have power [over] my head.

Chapter 86 (Col. 7; ll. 3–9)

TAKING ON THE FORM OF A SWALLOW by the Goldworker of Amun Sobekmose, justified.

I am a swallow, I am a swallow. I am that scorpion the daughter of Re. O gods, how sweet is your odor, the flame in the two horizons.

O you who are in the cities, bring to me the one who guards his coils. Give me your hand, (as) I have spent my time on the Island of Fire. I proceeded on a mission (and) I have come bearing its report. Open for me (and) then I shall say what I have seen.

O Horus, namely the one who governs the sacred boat. The throne of his father is given to him while that Seth, son of Nut, is in bonds because of what he did against him.

I have examined what is in Letopolis. I have bent my arms to Osiris. I proceeded to make an examination (and) I have come to speak. Allow me to pass (so that) I may make a report of my mission. I am one who enters counted, who comes forth reckoned (at) the gate of the Lord of All. (I) have purified myself in this great district. I drive away my evil. I drive off my sins. I have driven to the ground the evil that belonged to my flesh. Gatekeepers, make a path for me. I am your equal. I go forth by day. I proceed on my feet. I proceed in the footsteps of the sunlight. I am one who knows the path of secrets (and) the Gate of the Field of Reeds. I exist therein. See me, I am come. I have overthrown my enemies upon the earth.[153] My corpse, it is buried.

As for one who knows this spell, he enters after he goes forth from the West. As for one who does not know this spell, he cannot enter after he goes forth, not knowing how to go forth by day.

---

152 The triangular-shaped capstone atop a pyramid or obelisk.

153 Refers either to one's earthly enemies or the fact that he has thrown his enemies to the ground.

Chapter 99 (Col. 7; l. 9–Col. 8; l. 7)

SPELL FOR BRINGING THE FERRYBOAT IN THE NECROPOLIS by this Goldworker of Amun Sobekmose, justified.

O you who bring the ferryboat of the Nun over this dangerous sandbank, bring to me the ferryboat, tie the rope for me in peace. Come! Come! Approach me! Approach me! I have come to see my father Osiris. O lord of red linen who has power over joy. O lord of storms, the male who sails. O you who sail over this vertebra[154] of Apophis. O you who fasten heads (and) who make necks firm when wounds come forth. O you in charge of the secret ferryboat, who guard Apophis, bring the ferryboat to me. Tie the rope for me so that I may go forth in it [from] this dangerous land where the stars in it fall [upon] their faces (and) they raise themselves up. (O) Henswa the tongue of Re, Inbedu who guides the Two Lands, Nebgu who is in their mouths, it is the power of Re that opens the disk, whose face is red. Let me be brought. Do not leave me boat-less. This *akh* is coming who crosses to the place which you know.

Tell me my name, says the mooring-post. Lady of the Two Lands in the Shrines is your name. Tell me my name, says the mallet. Leg of Apis is your name. Tell me my name, says the prow-rope. Braid of the Mooring-Post of Anubis in the Work of Embalming is your name. Tell me my name, says the steering-post. Columns of the Path of the Necropolis is your name. Tell me my name, says the mast-step. Aker[155] is your name. Tell me my name, says the mast. He Who Brought the Great One After She Was Far Away is your name. Tell me my name, says the mast-head. Throat of Imsety is your name. Tell me my name, says the sail. Nut is your name. Tell me my name, says the oar-loop. You Were Made from the Hide of the Mnevis-Bull (and) the Tendons of Seth [is your name.] Tell me my name, say the oars. It is Fingers of Horus the Elder. Tell me my name, says the bailer. It is Hand of Isis Bailing Blood from the Eye of Horus. Tell me my name, say the ribs which are in its timbers. Imsety, Hapi, Duamutef, Qebusenef, He Who Plunders, He Who Seizes by Robbery, He Who Sees His Father, He Who Made His Own Name are your names. Tell me my name, says the beam. Foremost One of the Gardens is your name. Tell me my name, says the oar-handle. Meret is your name. Tell me my name, says the steering-oar. Precision is your name. What rises from the water, you whose oar blades are secret. Tell me my name, says the boat. It is the leg of Isis which Re cut with a knife in order to bring blood to the night-boat. Tell me my name, says the master. Rebuffer is your name. Tell me my name, says the breeze, since you are carried by me. North Wind that Comes Forth from Atum to

154 Wordplay on the similarity of the Egyptian words for "sandbank" and "vertebra."   155 The name of the earth-god.

the Nose of Khenty-imentyu is your name. Tell me my name, says the river, since you cross over by me. The One Who Sees Them is your name. Tell me my name, says the riverbank. He Who Destroys the One Who Stretches Out His Arm in the Pure Place is your name. Tell me my name, says the ground. Nose of the Sky Which Comes Forth from the Embalmer Who is in the Field of Reeds Who Goes Out [in] Joy from It [is your name.]

That which is said before them:

Hail to you, whose *kas* are perfect, possessors of offerings, who exist forever (and) forever. This Goldworker of Amun Sobekmose, justified, penetrates [to you] (so that) you may give to me funerary offerings at his side (so that) I may eat from it, the *sheser*-cake that Nephthys baked in the broad hall in the presence of the hands of the Goldworker of Amun Sobekmose, justified.

I know this god to whose nose you give provisions—his name is Tekem. He reveals (himself) in the eastern (part) of the sky. He travels in the west. Tekem. He departs, I depart. He seizes Mesqet.

The rebels do not have power over my flesh. My bread is in Pe; my beer is in Dep. Your offerings of this day are mine—they are offerings of barley (and) *emmer*; they are offerings of myrrh (and) clothing; they are offerings of ox-meat (and) fowl; they are offerings of life, prosperity (and) health; they are my offerings, (I) who come forth by day in any form I want, going out in it in the Field of Reeds.

As for one who knows this spell, he goes forth in the Field of Reeds (and) one will give to him a *sheser*-cake, a *des*-jar, a *pesen*-loaf, fields with barley (and) *emmer* of four cubits by the Followers of Horus who will reap it for him. Then he will chew on this barley (and) *emmer* (and) he will rub his body with them (and) his body will be like these gods. He will go forth from the Field of Reeds in any form in which he wishes to go forth.

Chapter 38A

Chapter 38A is another chapter through which the deceased claims to "live on air," a direct allusion to power over the winds that allows him to guide the solar boat of Re, which proceeds not only through the sky by day but also through the Netherworld at night. Note that this is the second appearance of this chapter in the papyrus, as we saw it earlier on the recto. Such "repeats" are a common feature of longer Books of the Dead of the New Kingdom and Third Intermediate Period.

Connecting Threads: *This chapter, like the preceding Chapter 99, emphasizes the deceased's total freedom of movement. It also continues the nautical theme of the preceding chapter.*

Chapter 38A (Col. 8; ll. 7–12)
Spell for living on air in the necropolis by this Goldworker of Amun Sobekmose justified.

I am Atum. I have come forth from the Nun to sit [in] the portico. I have received my seat of the West. My words are commanded to the *akhs* whose seats are hidden (and) more powerful with [...] than Ruty. I make my circuit in the *henhen*-boat of Khepri. I eat there. I have power there. I live there on air. I guide the sacred boat of Re. He opens the mouth of the earth for me. He has thrown open the gates of Geb for me. I have seized those who are in the nets of the great one. I have guided those who are in their shrines. I associate with Horus (and) Seth. I have sent the Elders on my behalf. I have entered (and) I go forth without my throat being blocked. I ascend to the sacred boat of the lord of truth. I praise those who are in the day-boat at his side, Re who shines in the horizon. I will live after my death like Re every day. I am more powerful than Ruty, giving spoken orders in the evening to the crew of Re (and) orders I have written to these four winds. I am more powerful than Ruty. I live after death like Re every day.

CHAPTER 39

In the preceding chapter, the deceased declared that he had the power to guide the solar boat. The focus of Chapter 39 is on the snake Apophis, the archenemy of the sun-god, who must be turned away or even annihilated in order for the solar boat to proceed and usher in the dawn each day. The Rerek-snake mentioned in the title is known from several chapters from the Coffin Texts as a menace that the deceased must face. In this chapter, the deceased and the sun-god each face their respective threats—both snakes—and succeed, as the final sentence of the chapter makes clear: "Re triumphs over Apophis."

CONNECTING THREADS: *The presence of Apophis in this chapter continues the theme of traveling in the solar boat as he is the archenemy of the sun-god.*

Chapter 39 (Col. 8; ll. 12–23)

SPELL FOR DRIVING AWAY REREK FROM THE NECROPOLIS by this Goldworker of Amun Sobekmose, justified.

Back, you! Glide away! Move away, you great one! Go! Swim to the pool of the Nun [to the place] where your father [ordered] that your slaughter be done. Be far from this birth-brick of Re, in the place where you tremble. I am Re at whom he trembles. Back, rebel, from the knives of his light. Re has made your words fall. Your face is turned over by the gods. Your heart is seized by Mafdet. Your bonds are placed (on you) by Hedjedjet.[156] Your injuries are placed (on you) by Maat. Those who are on the paths have overthrown [you]. Fall! Glide away, Apophis, enemy of Re. O leave the desert margins in the east of the sky at the sound of the roaring storm.

May the gates of the horizon open before Re (when) he comes forth weary with wounds. I do what you desire, I do what you desire, Re. I do what is good, I do what is good. I act by appeasing Re, making a throwing down of your bonds, Re. Apophis falls to your binding. The gods of the South, the North, the West, the East bind their bonds on him. Rekez has made him fall (and) the one who has authority over writing binds him. Re is appeased. Re is appeased. Re proceeds in peace. Apophis is fallen.

O Apophis, enemy of Re, what you have tasted is greater than the taste in the heart of the scorpion. What she has done against you is great. You are sick because of her (and) her needs forever. You have not escaped; you have not fled. (O) Apophis, enemy of Re, turn aside your face, which Re hates, (so that) you see

---

156　A goddess whose form is that of a scorpion.

what is behind you, one whose head is cut off, one who is passed by on the side of the two paths. Your head is cut off (by) the one who is in his earth. Your bones are broken. Your limbs are cut off. He assigns you to Keket.[157]

Apophis, enemy of Re, your crew is powerful, your chosen ones. Hurry, hurry, (so that) you may rest content therein. Your property, bring (it), bring (it) to the house. Bring what you have made to the house. Bring what is good. No evil obstacle has come forth from your mouth against me, namely what you may do against me. I am Seth who raises the tumult of the storm within the horizon of heaven as he is one who licks his heart.

Says Atum: raise up your faces, army of Re. Turn back the Bristler from the council for me. Says Geb: may you establish those who are on their thrones which are in the middle of the sacred boat of Khepri. Take your paths (with) your weapons given to you upon your arms. Says Hathor: take your weapons. Says [Nut]: come, we shall turn back this Bristler (so that) the one who is in his shrine may come (and) he may cross himself in solitude, the Lord of All who is not turned away.

O you gods who are in their primeval places, who encircle the pool of turquoise. Come, let the adoration be great (and) let us rescue the great one [in] his shrine from whom the gods came forth. Let what is beneficial be done for him. Let praises be given to him. Announce him to yourselves and to [me]. So says Nut of that pleasant one. Those who are among the gods say: may he go forth (and) may he find the path. May he make plunder from the gods. May he set in motion the one before Nut (so that) Geb stands up. O Terror, the Ennead is hurrying, the mouth of Hathor is trembling. Re triumphs over Apophis.

157 One of the eight primeval gods, the personification of darkness. Or possibly Keker, the earth god.

Chapter 65

Another spell for "Going forth by day." The associations of the deceased with the sun-god Re who has just triumphed over his archenemy Apophis suggest that he, too, should be allowed to go forth to triumph over his enemies. Any attempts to restrain him will result in cosmic chaos: the god Hapi, the personification of the Nile flood, will rise to the sky and the sun-god Re descend to the waters. Such threats of cosmic reversal are common in Egyptian religious and magical texts.
Connecting Threads: *The solar themes that have predominated in the preceding chapters continue.*

Chapter 65 (Col. 8; l. 23–Col. 9; l. 4)
Spell for going forth by day (and) having power over the enemy by this Goldworker of Amun Sobekmose, justified.

Re sits as the foremost one over his millions. He has united the Ennead, namely those whose faces are secret, who are in the mansion of Khepri, who eat abundance, who drink the gods' drink, who bring the sky to dawn and vice versa. Do not seize me as plunder for Osiris. I was never with the accomplices of Seth.

O one who sits upon his coils before the one whose *ba* is powerful. See, I am sitting upon the seat of Re, taking my body before Geb. I cause Horus to go forth triumphant against Seth. The dreams of Seth belong to the dreams of the crocodile, [those whose faces are] hidden. The foremost one of the mansion of the kings of Lower Egypt, who clothes the gods on the sixth-day feast, he has snared those who are in eternity; he has tied up eternity. I have seen Ibka placed in bonds, lies [placed under] his guard. Ibka is released. Lies are unloosened. Lo, I go forth in the form of a living *ba* whom the common people on earth praise.

O sick one who does this against me, remove yourself from the hand that is the power of Re. You will let me go forth against my enemies (and) triumph over him in the council in the presence of the Great Ennead. If you do not let me go forth triumphant from the council in the presence of the Great Ennead, you will not go forth from the Great Ennead. Then Hapi will go forth to the sky (and) he will live on truth (and) Re will go forth from the waters (and) he will live on fish. But if you allow me to go forth against my enemies (and) I triumph in the council of the great god, Hapi will not go forth to the sky (and) he will not live on truth. Re will not descend from the waters (and) he will not live on fish. Repression will dispel its condition from the land. I have come against that enemy (and) he is given to me, put to an end under my will in the council.

Chapters 8B-8A

This short pair of texts continues the theme of "Going forth by day," adding to it the parallel theme of entering into the West. Complete freedom of movement for the deceased meant not just ascending from the Netherworld at dawn but reentering it at night as well, thus leading to the idea of Re and Osiris as a balanced pair, assimilated into one. Note that in both chapters, the deceased associates himself with a number of deities, all of whom played a major role in the myth cycles that dealt with "judgment by the tribunal."

Connecting Threads: *The theme of "entering and going forth by day" continues.*

Chapter 8B (Col. 9; ll. 4–5)

Spell for penetrating to the West (and) going forth by day by this Goldworker of Amun Sobekmose, justified.

This one who is in the West is this Osiris. Osiris knows [this spell]. He does not exist in it. I do not exist in it. I am Seth who is with the gods. I have not ceased to exist.

Chapter 8A (Col. 9; ll. 5–7)

Another spell for penetrating to the West (and) going forth by day by this Goldworker of Amun Sobekmose, justified.

Hermopolis is open. My head is sealed. (O) Thoth, the Eye of Horus is excellent. The Eye of Horus saves me. The ornaments on the brow of Re, the father of the gods, are magically effective. This one who is in the West is Osiris. Osiris knows the day on which he will not exist, (and) I will not exist on it. I am Seth who is with the gods. I have not perished. Stand up, (so that) Horus may count you among the gods.

Chapters 60-62

This pair of short texts details the deceased's access to the cool waters found in the sky, couched in language alluding to the annual flood of the Nile, a common metaphor for rebirth and renewal.

Connecting Threads: *This pair of texts puts further emphasis on having access to what is necessary for continued existence in the next life.*

Chapter 60 (Col. 9; ll. 7–8)

ANOTHER SPELL FOR DRINKING WATER by this Goldworker of Amun Sobekmose, justified.

Open for me are the double doors of the sky. Undone for me are the double doors of the cool waters of the sky by Hapi, that means the Hapi of the sky at sunrise. May you allow me to have power over the water just as Seth plundered his enemies that day when the Two Lands raged. The Elders have watched over the shoulder that is in the corner (of the sky).

Chapter 62 (Col. 9; ll. 8–9)

ANOTHER SPELL FOR DRINKING WATER by this Goldworker of Amun Sobekmose, justified.

Open is the great flood of cool waters for Osiris. Undone are the cool waters of the sky for Thoth, waters for Hapi, the lord of the horizon in this his name of flattener of the earth.[158]

---

[158] During the Inundation, Egypt appeared like a flat sheet of water covering all of the agricultural land.

CHAPTER 1

Essentially an Osirian text, Chapter 1 lays emphasis on the power of the transfigured deceased. The theme of triumphing over one's enemies is developed largely through addresses that Thoth makes to certain tribunals located at a number of sacred sites throughout Egypt. At the end of the chapter, the deceased, like Osiris, is said to be vindicated. As its title indicates, this chapter belongs to the genre of texts for "Going forth by day."

CONNECTING THREADS: *This chapter continues the theme of triumphing over one's enemies, a theme developed in several chapters encountered earlier; the idea of "entering and going forth" continues as well.*

Chapter 1 (Col. 9; ll. 9–20)

SPELL FOR THE DAY OF BURIAL, **ENTERING AFTER GOING FORTH.** WORDS TO BE RECITED by this Goldworker of Amun Sobekmose, justified.

(O) Bull of the West, says Thoth [to] the king of eternity. I am the god of protection who fought on your behalf. I am one of these gods of the council that vindicated Osiris against his enemies (on) this day of judgment. I belong to your people, Osiris. I am one of these gods, the children of Nut, who slay the enemies of Osiris (and) imprison the rebels for his sake. I belong to your people, Horus. I fought on your behalf. I watched over your name. I am Thoth who vindicated Osiris against his enemies (on) this day of judgment in the mansion of the great elder which is in Heliopolis. I am a Busirite, the son of a Busirite. I was conceived in Busiris (and) born in Busiris. I was with the male mourners of Osiris (and) the female mourners of Osiris on the Shores of the Washerman. Vindicate Osiris against his enemies, as Re said to Thoth. Vindicate Osiris against his enemies, as (he) said, is what I, Thoth, did. I was with Horus the day of clothing the Teshtesh-figure,[159] opening the caverns of the weary-hearted ones, (and) making secret the entrance of the secrets in Rosetau. I was with Horus as protector of this left shoulder of Osiris[160] which is in Letopolis. I went forth (and) I entered into the consuming flame (on) the day of driving out the rebels from Letopolis. I was with Horus (on) the day of celebrating the festivals of Osiris. I made offerings to Re, the sixth- (and) seventh-day festivals in Heliopolis. I am a *wab*-priest in Heliopolis, an exalted one in the high place. I was a *hem-netjer* priest in Abydos (on) the day of the uplifting of the land.[161] I am one who sees the

---

159 An allusion to the dismembered Osiris.
160 The chief religious center of each of the forty-two *nomes,* or districts, of Egypt was said to possess a single relic of the body of Osiris.
161 I.e., when land first emerged from the primordial flood.

secrets of Rosetau. I am one who recites the ritual book for the *ba* in Busiris. I am a *sem*-priest in his duties. I am the master craftsman (on) the day of placing the *henu*-boat on its sledge. I am one who took the hoe (on) the day of hacking up the earth in Herakleopolis.

O (you) who induct the faultless *bas* into the house of Osiris, may you induct my *ba* together with you (so that) it may see like you see, it may hear like you hear, it may stand like you stand, it may sit like you sit. O (you) who give bread (and) beer to the faultless *bas* in the house of Osiris, may you give bread (and) beer at all times to my *ba* together with you in the house of Osiris.

O (you) who open the paths (and) who open up the roads for efficacious *bas* in the house of Osiris, open indeed, open indeed the roads for my *ba* together with you in the house of Osiris. It enters in anger (and) comes forth appeased from the house of Osiris without anyone turning it away, without anyone turning it back. It has entered as one who is favored (and) it comes forth as one who is loved (and) who is vindicated. Its orders are done in the house of Osiris. This Goldworker of Amun Sobekmose, justified, has set out here. No fault of his was found therein. The balance-scale is free of his faults.

CHAPTER 80

The mention of the power to bring on sunlight and darkness draws attention to the lunar themes of this chapter, which are amplified in turn by references to the "filling of the eye" and the Mansion of the Moon that follow shortly. The idea of darkness shining bright has solar associations as well. The sun-god was believed to have the power to illuminate each hourly section of the Netherworld as he passed through it and to offer regenerative power to the deceased who were located there.

CONNECTING THREADS: *The lunar theme of this chapter will be continued in the next. The references to the "Eye" allude to the moon and its waxing and waning cycles.*

Chapter 80 (Col. 9; ll. 20–25)

TAKING ON THE FORM OF A GOD (AND) MAKING DARKNESS SHINE BRIGHT by this Goldworker of Amun Sobekmose, justified.

To me belongs the fringed cloth of the Nun, the whiteness that shines bright (for) the one before it. The darkness shines bright, united with the Two Companions who are in my belly by means of the great magic spell which is upon my mouth.

I will raise up the one who has fallen. The one who comes fallen, I will be placed with him in the valley of Abydos (when) I have been appeased. I am one who remembers him. I seized authority in my city when I found him in it. I have brought darkness by means of my power. I filled the Eye when it had nothing before the fifteenth-day festival[162] had come. I judged Seth in the upper houses in addition to the elder who was with him. I equipped Thoth in the Mansion of the Moon when I took the crown of Upper Egypt.[163]

Maat is in my belly with the turquoise (and) faience of its monthly festival. This field of mine is lapis lazuli in his[164] festival. I am the Nun who makes the darkness shine bright. I have made the *akhmy*-demons fall. Those who were in the darkness worship me. I have made the mourners stand whose faces were hidden (and) who were weary.

Look at me, you. I am the Nun. I will not let you hear about it (or) the place of water(s) would be destroyed.

---

162 Celebrated on the day or night of the full moon.

163 The White Crown, the crown of Upper Egypt, was thought of as the (damaged)

Eye of Horus, a clear allusion to the moon and its waxing and waning cycle.

164 I.e., the festival of Thoth, the god associated with the lunar cycle.

Chapter 132

The text of this chapter focuses on the Eye of Horus and its lunar association, although its title seems to have little to do with the text as it stands. The statement at the end of the chapter—"The Eye of Horus has passed through this period of time"—is likely an allusion to the full cycle of the moon, a potent symbol of regeneration and rebirth. The Eye of Horus may also allude to a funerary offering, as the Eye of Horus was connected with certain funerary offerings in the Pyramid Texts. If so, the reference to the house mentioned here may be to the tomb of the deceased.

Connecting Threads: *The lunar theme continues through the allusions to the Eye of Horus.*

Chapter 132 (Col. 9; ll. 25–26)

Spell for allowing him to turn around (namely) this Goldworker of Amun Sobekmose, justified, to see his house.[165] Words to be recited by this Goldworker of Amun Sobekmose, justified.

I am the lion who went forth with the bow. I have shot with it. I have netted. Repeat again. I have reached the shore. The Eye of Horus belongs to me. The Eye of Horus has passed through this period of time. I have reached the bank. Come in peace.

165 A possible reference to the tomb of the deceased.

CHAPTER 94

The identification of the deceased with scribal activity alludes to the knowledge he possesses. The most powerful knowledge was secret knowledge that was always written down in order to ensure its permanent and enduring effectiveness. The scribal theme also connects the deceased with Thoth, a god with strong lunar associations, and the lunar theme has run through many of the chapters in the previous section of the verso texts.

CONNECTING THREADS: *The lunar theme continues through the allusions to Thoth.*

Chapter 94 (Col. 9; l. 26–Col. 10; l. 2)

SPELL FOR REQUISITIONING A WATER BOWL (AND) PALETTE IN THE NECROPOLIS by this Goldworker of Amun Sobekmose, justified.

(O) keeper of the book of Thoth. See, I am come. I am an *akh*. I am a *ba*. I am mighty. I am one equipped with my writing(s). Bring to me the courier of Aker who is with Seth. Bring a water pot to me. Bring a palette to me with these writing materials of Thoth, the secrets which are in them (belonging to) the gods. See, I am a scribe. Bring to me the putrefaction of Osiris (so that) I may write with it (and) I may do what the great (and) perfect god says every day, namely the good things which you order for me, Horakhty. I shall do what is right (so that) I may go to Re every day.

CHAPTER 63B

As we saw in Chapter 63A, above, both chapters numbered 63 have to do with the ability of the deceased to move through water whose true nature seems to be fire. The paradoxical nature of such water is typical of what is encountered in the Netherworld. Again, the focus seems to be on the deceased's ability to move freely, regardless of the obstacles presented him, here, once again, a dehydrating fire threatening him or through which he must move.

Chapter 63B (Col. 10; ll. 2–3)

Spell for not being burned in water by this Goldworker of Amun Sobekmose, justified. He says:

I am this equipped paddle (with which) Re is rowed (and) the aged one is rowed. The effluxes of Osiris are raised to the Island of Flames. He who is not, he is rowed (though) he is boat-less. He who is not, he is roasted. I have climbed up the sunlight of Khnum, foremost one of the sail-lines. Come (and) cut away the net from the one traveling behind me [on] this path on which I have gone forth.

Chapter 64B

This chapter focuses on the specialized knowledge the deceased claims to have and on his ability to go forth, two common themes found in the chapters of the verso. Although the title alludes to the theme of "Going forth by day," many of the details of the text emphasize its Osirian and Netherworld connections. The mention of the Inundation and the god Khepri at the end of the chapter strongly suggests themes of rebirth and regeneration as well. It should be noted that in the myths of the solar cycle, it is in the Netherworld that the regeneration and eventual rebirth of the sun-god take place.
Connecting Threads: *The theme of "entering and going forth."*

Chapter 64B (Col. 10; ll. 3–17)

Spell for knowing the spells for going forth as one (spell). To be recited by this Goldworker of Amun Sobekmose, justified. Yesterday (and) tomorrow morning (are) in charge of each successive moment of his being (re)born.

The secret *ba* who made the gods (and who) gives offerings to those whom the west of the sky conceals, the steering-oar of the east, possessor of two faces, whose rays are seen, lord of supports who goes forth at twilight. (O you) two falcons of his in charge of their court, who hear matters by opening the mouth,[166] the foreleg is tied upon the neck, the buttocks upon the head of the West. Give to me what is in the two birds. Do not make me weep at what I have seen. I know the deep more than my name. You deal with the needs of the *akhs*—they are four million, four hundred thousand, (and) twelve hundred of more than twelve cubits, when passing by joined together,[167] by one giving (to) another from them.[168] It is one-sixth of what is required therein, being foremost in the Duat at the hour of overthrowing the rebels, returning from there justified. It is these then who are at the opening of the Duat. (His) steps are seven when he goes forth. My protection is the protection of his magical spells—cold blood (and) new wounds. I separated the two horns when I joined with the crocodile[169] (who was) against me.

(O you) whose natures are secret, do not turn me back. Those (of you) who are on their bellies,[170] do not let the eye swallow its tears. (O) silent one, open for me what is sealed. Give a good path to me (so that) I may pass.

Who, pray, is the one who bites in the place of concealment? I am one who enters in his name, who goes forth as the one who seeks, lord of millions [on] earth who makes his name. The one who has conceived puts down her load.

166 The reference seems to be to legal cases presented orally.
167 The reference is to the twelve hours of the day or those of the night.
168 I.e., one hour in turn yields to the next.
169 I.e., engaged in battle.
170 I.e., snakes.

The door in the wall that is overturned is sealed. It is *djaret*-fruit that is fallen upon the back of the *benu*-bird (and) upon the two companions. Horus is given his Eye (so that) his face will become bright at dawn. His name is my name. I have not vomited. I become a lion. The affairs of Shu are with me. I am green jasper. How good it is to see the mooring of the weary-hearted one when he alights upon the marsh. See me go forth. I am lord of life. This is my arrival. I go forth from the opening of the great door of the city. Osiris, your protections are for the ones in need. I have embraced the sycamore. The two Sekh-snakes open the Duat for me. I have come (and) I have embraced the Wadjet-eye. Where are you, my *ba*, on the Pesdjet-festival[171] (when) the corpse is silent? I have come to see the one who is in his Mehen-snake, face to face, eye [to eye]. The breeze rises at his goings forth. Weariness stares in my face.

(O) lion who is in Wetnet, you are in me (and) I am in you. Your forms (are) my forms. I am the Inundation. Great Black Water is my name. My forms (are) the forms of Khepri, the foliage of Atum. Repeat. I entered as one who was ignorant; I have gone forth as an *akh*. I am this Goldworker of Amun Sobekmose, justified. [I] shall be seen in my form as a human forever.

A spell for coming forth by day and not keeping away this Goldworker of Amun Sobekmose, justified, from the road of the Duat when entering (or) going forth. It means taking on any form [he] wishes. It means a spell for not dying again by the soul of this Goldworker of Amun Sobekmose, justified. As for [one who] knows this spell, it means he is justified upon the earth (and in) the necropolis. He does everything which a man who is upon the earth does in everything. This spell was found in the foundation wall of the one who is in the *henu*-boat by the Overseer of the Builders of Walls in the time of the Majesty of the King of Upper (and) Lower Egypt Apep, justified. Secret procedures, not to be seen (and) not to be beheld. Recite this spell being pure (and) clean, not approaching women (and) not eating goats (or) fish.

171 Festival held on the day
of the new moon.

CHAPTER 81A

This transformation text focuses on the lotus, a flower whose parts were used to repair the damaged Eye of Horus, the god mentioned at the end of the text. Thus, the themes of this lunar chapter hint once again at regeneration and rebirth.
CONNECTING THREADS: *The thematic material related to the Eye of Horus is further developed here.*

Chapter 81A (Col. 10; ll. 17–18)
TAKING ON THE FORM OF A LOTUS by this Goldworker of Amun Sobekmose, justified.

I am the pure lotus that goes forth through the sunshine (and) belongs at the nose of Re. I act, I descend. I seek it for Horus. I am the pure one in the field.

CHAPTERS 2-3

These two short texts are also spells for "Going forth by day." Their focus appears to be lunar, not solar, and emphasizes the connections of the deceased with Osiris and the sun-god after he has set. That said, the lunar and solar cycles were inextricably connected and even seen as two parts of one cycle. By the Nineteenth Dynasty, the Book of the Dead scribes had removed the lunar allusions found in these two chapters and replaced them with solar ones.
CONNECTING THREADS: *The lunar theme continues its development.*

Chapter 2 (Col. 10; ll. 18–20)
SPELL FOR GOING FORTH BY DAY (AND) LIVING AFTER DYING by this Goldworker of Amun Sobekmose, justified.

The sole one rises (as) the moon. The sole one shines as the moon. This Goldworker of Amun Sobekmose, justified, shall go forth with this multitude of yours to the outside. (O) one who releases those who are in the sunlight. Open the Duat. Lo, this Goldworker of Amun Sobekmose, justified, goes forth by day to do everything that he wishes upon earth among the living.

Chapter 3 (Col. 10; ll. 20–23)
ANOTHER SPELL LIKE IT [by] this Goldworker of Amun Sobekmose, justified.

(O) Atum who goes forth as the great one of the watery surge, magically empowered as Ruty, speak your words to those who came before (you).[172] This Goldworker of Amun Sobekmose, justified, comes into their midst. He gives orders to the crew of Re in the evening. Let this Goldworker of Amun Sobekmose, justified, live after his death like Re every day. Assuredly, the one who gave birth to Re yesterday gave birth to this Goldworker of Amun Sobekmose, justified. Every god rejoices since this Goldworker of Amun Sobekmose, justified, is living just as they rejoiced when Ptah was living, as he went forth from the palace of the prince which is in Heliopolis.

172 I.e., the ancestors.

CHAPTER 152-75-78

These final three chapters have largely solar allusions and as a group bring the theme of "Going forth by day" to its logical conclusion.

In Chapter 152, the deceased is described as both "allowed to turn himself around to see his house on earth" and as "passing over [Geb]," the personification of the earth. The text then moves on to describe the deceased as building a house that has specific ties to a number of shrines, all of which have connections with Osiris. The ability of the deceased to build a house in the next life underscores his continued existence as a social being now integrated into the world of the akhs *and highlights his powers as an* akh. *But the textual references to Heliopolis, a place that dated to very ancient times and was the center of the solar cult in Egypt, also locate the deceased outside of the Netherworld, again pointing to his freedom of movement.*

Chapter 75 begins with the deceased leaving the Netherworld and traveling to Heliopolis. After ingratiating himself with certain divinities in the Netherworld, he finds himself in the eastern sky from which he rises with the sun-god.

Chapter 78 is a transformation text, through which the deceased takes on the form of a divine falcon, a probable allusion to the god Horus, who is mentioned in the text. A theme that runs through the text is the desire on the part of the deceased to instill fear in the gods of the Netherworld as well as their gates. He asks the "Eldest" to empower him so that he may accomplish this wish. The mention of the gates of the Duat hints once again that the deceased yearns to have access to any place he wishes, and the power to leave it as well. As we read through the text of the chapter, we see that the places and beings mentioned are located in both the Netherworld and the sky. Thus, the total freedom of movement that the chapter demands for the deceased extends to the entire cosmos with the exception of earth. A text whose scope has such a broad range forms a fitting conclusion to the chapters of the verso and to the funerary papyrus text as a whole.

CONNECTING THREADS: *Chapter 132 in the previous column of the papyrus had a similar heading and thematic material that is somewhat related to the first chapter of this group. The theme of "Going forth" in Chapter 75 and the claim on what rightfully belongs to the deceased as well as the words "houses" and "house" also tie it to the preceding chapter.*

Chapter 152 (Col. 10; l. 23–Col. 11; l. 2)
SPELL FOR ALLOWING this Goldworker of Amun Sobekmose, justified TO TURN HIMSELF AROUND TO SEE HIS HOUSE ON EARTH. This Goldworker of Amun Sobekmose, justified, he says:

O Geb rejoices (when) this Goldworker of Amun Sobekmose, justified, passes over him, (namely) his body. The followers turn around. Men, gods, children, (and) their fathers give praise to me (when) they have seen what Seshat has brought to Geb. Anubis summons the Osiris,[173] this Goldworker of Amun Sobekmose, justified, to Osiris to build a mansion that is in the earth, its foundation in Heliopolis, its circuit in Kheraha, while the foremost one of Letopolis in the sanctuary is the scribe for renewing what belongs to it. Men bring its water bowls for (its) gangs.

Then Osiris said to the gods who are in his following: Go, see the building of this house of an *akh* who is provisioned. He has come today, appearing among you. Make (him) feared (and) give to him the praise (of) one honored there. You will see what I have done myself. Then Osiris said [of] this god: He has come today appearing among you. So said Osiris. Bring for him herds by the south wind; bring for him barley by the north wind; bring for him *emmer* that the earth brings to completion.

The mouth of Osiris who has perished announces me. He has turned himself from his left side; he places himself on his right side. Men, gods, the *akhs*, the dead have seen you. May they pass their time praising the one who is honored there.

Chapter 75 (Col. 11; ll. 3–5)

Spell for going to Heliopolis (and) taking a seat there by this Goldworker of Amun Sobekmose, justified. He says:

I have come forth from the Duat. I have come from the ends of the earth. Take this linen wrapping of mine as the entrails of a baboon. I have run through the pure houses which were in Djebau; I break into the houses of Remrem.[174] I have arrived at the house of Ikhsesef. I have entered the sacred Senshu. I have passed by the house of Kemkem. Tyet has placed her two arms on me. She has entrusted me to her sister Khebnet (and) to her mother Sekket. She puts me on the eastern side of the sky where Re appears in glory (and) where Re rises high. I appear in glory. I am conducted within. I am ennobled as a god. She places me on this sacred path on which Thoth traveled when he pacified the Two Fighters.[175] He shall travel to Pe (so that) he may come to Sepa.[176]

Chapter 78 (Col. 11; l. 5–Col. 12; l. 18, the end of the verso)

Spell for taking on the form of a divine falcon by this Goldworker of Amun Sobekmose, justified, in that land of eternity. He says:

O Eldest (god), come indeed to Busiris. May you clear the paths for me. May you encircle my thrones for me. May you see me (and) may you raise me up.

---

173 Not the god, but the deceased Sobekmose as Osiris.
174 Name of a deity.

175 I.e., Horus and Seth.
176 Sepa is the name of a locale in the vicinity of Heliopolis, possibly

associated with one of the relics of Osiris (or all of them collectively).

Then may you cause fear of me. May you create awe of me. May the gods of the Duat fear me. Their gates, may they beware of me. You shall not do harm, when there is physical decay in the house of darkness (and) he reveals (my) weariness that was hidden. Act accordingly, they say, the gods who hear the voices of the leaders who are in the following of Osiris.

Be silent, gods. A god speaks with a god (so that) he may hear the truth which I am saying to him. Speak to me, Osiris. May you grant that what has come forth from your mouth against me be redirected. I see your own forms which your power has built. May you grant that I go forth (and) that I may have power over my feet (and) that I may exist there like the Lord of All. May the gods of the Duat fear [me]. Their gates, may they beware of me. May you grant my movement there to me together with those who have movement. May this Goldworker of Amun Sobekmose, justified, [be] upon my standard like the lord of eternity (and) unite with Isis, the divine one. May they unite themselves for me over the one who would harm me. He shall not come (and) see my weariness. I shall proceed (and) I shall come to the limits of the sky. I consult with Geb. I beg for authority from the Lord of All. May the gods of the Duat fear me. Their gates, may they beware of me. Let them see that your catch of fish and fowl is for me. I am one of those *akhs* who are in the sunlight. I have made my forms from his forms. He comes (and) he goes forth to Busiris, clothed with my *ba*, (so that) he may tell you my affairs. Then he will cause fear of me. He will create awe of me. May the gods of the Duat fear me. May their gates beware of me. I am, for certain, an *akh* who is in the sunlight, whom Atum himself created, who came into being from the bloom of his eye, one whom he brought into being, whom he made an *akh*, whose face he lifted when they were together with him, he being alone in the Nun. They announce him (when) he goes forth from the Duat. They place fear of him in the gods (and) the *akhs* who came into being with him. I am one of those snakes that the eye of the sole lord created before Isis came into being (and) gave birth to Horus. I am made strong. I rejuvenate myself. I am raised higher than those who are in the sunshine, the *akhs* who came into being with him. I appear in glory as a divine falcon. Horus has clothed me in his *ba* to take his affairs[177] to Osiris in the Duat.

Ruty speaks to me, the chief keeper of the House of the *nemes*-cloth, he who is in his cavern: How will you return to the region of the sky being clothed in the forms of Horus? You have no *nemes*-cloth. Will you speak then to the region of the sky? I am the one in charge of taking the affairs of Horus to Osiris in the Duat. Horus has repeated to me what his father Osiris said to him of the years,

177 I.e., news of what Horus has been doing.

of the days of burial. To me belongs the *nemes*-cloth, said Ruty to me, so that you shall proceed and come upon the path of the sky. Those who are in the region of the horizon will see you. The gods of the Duat will fear you (and) their gates, they will beware of you. O attacker, then there will be destruction at the words of the gods, the great lords of all, the keepers of the shrines of the sole lord. Then the one who is high upon his float said: Take the *nemes*-cloth to him. Thus Ruty spoke concerning me. O attacker, make a path for me. I am one who is high upon my float. Ruty has brought a *nemes*-cloth for me. My wings are given to me. He has fastened my heart for me to its back—repeat—on its great neck (so that) I cannot fall through Shu.[178]

I am one who appeases his beautiful twin, the lord of the two honored cobras. I am one, for sure, who knows the paths of the Nun. There is breath in my belly. The raging bull cannot turn me away. I proceed to the place which holds the sleeper, the boat-less one, the foremost one of the field of eternity who guides me to the darkness of the ill ones of the West, (including) Osiris. I have come today from the house of Ruty. I have gone forth from it to the house of Isis, the divine one. I have seen the secret sacred places; I was guided to the hidden sacred places; likewise, she allows me to have seen the birth of the great god who clothed me in his *ba*. I have seen what is in it. If I say, ... Shu is great, (then) they turn back the attack.

I am the one in charge of taking the affairs of Horus to his father Osiris in the Duat. I am, for sure, Horus who is in the sunlight who has power [over] his [fillet] (and) I have power over his sunlight. I proceed (and) I arrive at the limits of the sky. Horus is in his place. Horus is on his throne. My face is that of a divine falcon. My buttocks are those of a divine falcon. I am one whom his lord equips. I go forth to Busiris to see Osiris. I have tousled my hair before him. Nut tousles her hair when she sees me. I see the gods. The Eye of Horus Mekhenty-irty burns against those who stretch out their arms against me. The powerful one stands, turning back the needy one. They open the paths of the sacred place for me (when) they see my forms (and) they hear what I have said. Upon your faces, gods of the Duat, whose faces are turned back, who approach the powers, who drag the Unwearying Stars, who make the paths of the salt region passable because of the lord, the *ba* great of majesty. Horus has ordered: [Lift] your faces. I have beheld you. I have appeared in glory as a divine falcon. Horus clothes me in his *ba* to take (news of) his affairs to his father Osiris in the Duat. I have seized for myself the grey-haired ones. The guardians at their gates have gone forward for me.

---

178 I.e., the air.

(O you) who are before me, make paths for me (so that) I may move forward (and so that) I may reach the ones who are the foremost ones of their caverns, the keepers of the House of Osiris. I shall tell them of his powers. I shall inform them that they[179] are like him whose terrors are great, whose horns are sharper than Seth's. I shall inform them that he has seized Hu and that he has acquired the power(s) of Atum. Pass by, goodly one, they say—the gods of the Duat— to me. They are distinct from those who are the foremost ones of their caverns (and) the keepers of the House of Osiris. See, I am come to you. I have seized the grey-haired ones. I have assembled the powers of those defiant gods who are in your under-sky, defiant men who are in the under-sky. Clear the way for me, powers who guard the path of the horizon, keepers of the horizon (and) the *hemty*-region in the sky. I have set in order the gates on behalf of Osiris (and) I have cleared the way on his behalf. I have acted in accordance with what was commanded. I go forth to Busiris (so that) I may see Osiris. I tell him the affairs of this eldest son of his whom he loved, who hacked on the heart of Seth. I have seen the lord of weariness. Then I shall inform them of the plans of the gods which Horus carried out in the absence of his father, Osiris.

O lord *ba*, great of majesty, see, I am come. You have seen me; I am exalted. I open the Duat. The paths which belong to the sky (and those) which belong to the earth are open for me. No one holds himself back from me, high upon your seat, Osiris. You hear well, Osiris. Your backside is sound, Osiris. Your head is joined to you, Osiris. Your neck is set in place for you, Osiris. Your heart rejoices, Osiris. Your plea endures. The hearts of your courtiers are in joy, as you endure as the Bull of the West (and) your son Horus appears in glory upon your throne, all life being with him (who is) your *ba*. Millions serve him (and) millions fear him. The Ennead serves him (and) the Ennead fears him. Atum, the Powerful One, sole one of the gods for whom there is no reversal, has said what Hu had said to him: Horus is the one who is endowed, passing by the faces (that) his father [was wary of]. Horus is the one who rescues (and) who impedes. Horus is his father. Horus is [his] mother. Horus is this [brother]. Horus is this friend. Horus came from the seed of his father when he[180] was decaying. He rules Egypt (and) the gods serve him. Nursing millions, he causes millions to live through his Eye, sole one of her lord, the Mistress of All.[181]

---

179 The "powers" just mentioned.
180 I.e., his father, Osiris.
181 I.e., the "Eye."

Translation of
the Offering Formulae

Beginning at the damaged right-hand edge of the texts of the recto, there are two horizontal lines of text, one above and the other below the main text field. These lines each comprise a sequence of offering formulae—a fixed text or prayer that accompanied an offering ritual in a temple or a tomb. The beginning of each of these offering formulae is also lost; again, it is unclear how much of the beginning of the papyrus may be missing.

Text on the Upper Margin of the Recto

... placed in the land (as) one justified in the great broad hall (where) the ruler of the place of eternity rests, joined with the *akhs* who exist there, (their) heads with them in the following of the great god, Lord of the West.

That he may give an offering from (that which) comes forth upon the altar of Osiris consisting of everything good, pure from the offerings of Hapi [...] everything upon the [...] everything, bread, beer, cattle, poultry, alabaster, incense, breathing the sweet breath of the north wind, drinking water at the watering place of the river, entering (and) going forth as he desires, not [...] at the gate of the Duat, for the *ka* of this Goldworker of Amun Sobekmose, justified, in the presence of Osiris, great god, ruler of eternity, chief of all of the gods of the necropolis.

Text on the Lower Margin of the Recto

... the following of the town god in all of his festivals like one of those of the *akhs* at the side of the great god, that he may give an offering of bread, beer, cattle, poultry, alabaster, incense, *henket*-offering, everything good, pure (that) a god lives on to the *ka* of this Goldworker of Amun Sobekmose, justified, before the great god.

Second Text on the Lower Margin of the Recto

An offering which the king gives, Imsety, Hapi, Duamutef, Qebusenef, the gods, goddesses who are in the necropolis, (that) they may give an offering consisting of everything that exists, namely everything good, pure that Re has created, that they come into being for (?) you, a god among the *akhs*, [...] gods, goddesses, the *akhs*, the things made [by] the great god [...] ...

Notes on the Translation

*Works cited here in abbreviated form
can be found in full in the Reference List.*

CHAPTER 105

[...] [in]cense (so that) I may purify
you with them: Given the damage
to the papyrus at its right-hand side,
it is uncertain if this was originally
the first spell of the papyrus. Also
note that a number of textual problems
obtain here.

(and that) [I may purify] your fluids:
The writing is extremely garbled here.
The scribe wrote only the first sign of the
phrase *sw⁽b=i* ("I may purify") and then
wrote *ntnt* ("fluids").

this evil wrong which I have done will
[not] be put on me: The negative particle
n has been omitted.

(O) balance-scale: Some early texts have
"You who weigh with the balance-scale."

may truth be joyful: Other texts have
"rise up to." *ḥ⁽* is written clearly
in place of *k₃* found in other texts.

Are there no invocation offerings from
me for those in charge?: The translation
given here sees this line as a continuation
of the preceding phrases. It is possible that
the final sentence means: "There will not
be an invocation offering from me to those
above," reading this line as a threat that
states what will happen if the wishes of the
deceased are not fulfilled. The word "those
above" has the determinative 𓀀, a seated
god, whose presence offers a visual link
to the thematic material of the three texts
that follow.

CHAPTER 103

Given its similar content, Chapter 103
may be seen simply as a continuation
of Chapter 47, although it has an
introductory heading written in red. Such
an arrangement seems to be somewhat
common in Books of the Dead of this
time period.

BEING IN THE ENTOURAGE: Some
contemporaneous texts instead have *r-gs*
("at the side of") here.

[To be recited]: The earlier chapters
in the papyrus lack the heading *r₃ n* ("A
spell for") followed by the name of the
deceased introduced by *in* ("by"). Some
of these earlier chapters have *ḏd mdw in*
("To be recited by"), while others omit the
phrase *ḏd mdw*. For the sake of uniformity

in the translations, I have added *ḏd mdw*
("To be recited") in brackets where it has
been omitted.

CHAPTER 104

the cicada bringing me: *b₃.t*; often
translated as "*b₃.t*-bird" despite the
presence of the insect determinative
(as in *Book of the Dead of Nebseni*, British
Museum EA 9900; see Lapp 2004, pl. 23;
the exemplar Coffin Text 639 has the
bird determinative and also has the
construction *in b₃.t in.t tw N pn* ("It is by
the *b₃.t* that this *N* is brought").

CHAPTER 76

I pass by the house of the king:
Whether the proper transcription and
reading is "house of the king" or "house
of the chantress" is uncertain, since the
words "king" and "chantress" are written
somewhat similarly, at least in hieratic; for
the idea that the text was already corrupted
in the Coffin Text tradition, see Lucarelli
2006, p. 93.

CHAPTER 10

In later texts, Chapter 10 is found at
the end of a longer sequence to which
Chapters 105-47-103-104 belong.

I have traveled through the earth (to)
its edges: The text is confusedly written
here. The Brooklyn text has *tnm.wt=f*, which
means "its furrows" or "its wanderers."
Other texts have *r nmt.f* ("to its footsteps").
See Lucarelli 2006, p. 152 and n. 1074 for
the translation "through the earth to its
outermost bounds."

one who is equipped with his millions:
For "his," understand "my"; such pronoun
shifts are common in Egyptian texts.

I was given these things fixed that make
the Goldworker of Amun Sobekmose,
justified, prosper: Contemporaneous
manuscripts show a variety of writings
here.

CHAPTER 22

born of the Mistress of the House Sa(t)-
Montu: The mother's name appears to
be 𓊃𓏏𓐍𓅓𓏏𓏤 [*s₃(.t) mntw*], for which see
Ranke 1935–52, vol. 1, p. 289, 9.

I have arisen from my egg which is
in the lands of the secrets: The book-
roll determinative and plural strokes
may reflect a botched writing of *sšt₃.w*
("secret").

this one who is at the top of the dais:
The correct reading and meaning of *ḥty* is
uncertain here. *Book of the Dead of Nebseni*
has a similarly unclear writing.

CHAPTER 86

The text of this chapter as given is the
short form that corresponds to Coffin
Text 283; this chapter occurs again on the
verso in its long form that follows Coffin
Texts 283 and 296.

On transformations into non-human
forms, see Hollis 2008, p. 185.

I am that scorpion: *ḥḏḏ.t*; a word
for "scorpion" as well as the name of a
goddess in scorpion form.

CHAPTER 87

Note that in the writing of this text the
scribe has slipped into writing some words
and signs in hieratic.

I am sound every day: The scribe
has written an abbreviated form of the
verb *wḏ₃* ("be safe (and) sound"). Other
contemporaneous texts have "I am
renewed, I am rejuvenated every day."

CHAPTER 88

MAKING THE FORMS OF A CROCODILE:
Contemporaneous texts have the name of
the god Sobek in place of the generic term
"crocodile" that occurs in this chapter.
Sobek was the divine personification of
the crocodile, whose most important cult
center was in the Faiyum region in Middle
Egypt. The change of the divine name
to the generic one may have been due to
the fact that Sobek was an element in the
name of the owner of the papyrus.

I am in truth the one in the middle
of his waters: *nnw/nw* ("water") is written
here without the water determinative,
𓈖. Other texts have *nrw* ("terror"), giving
something like "immersed in dread";
the exemplar Coffin Text 969 has *dšrw*
("blood"); Twenty-first Dynasty texts
have *ntt* or *ntnt* ("sweat; fluids"). On the
variations that are found in different Book
of the Dead texts and between Book of

the Dead texts and Coffin Texts, see the Introduction to this volume.

I am the crocodile who seizes: For the writing *smtw*, read *sꜣm* ("grasp; seize").

I am one who takes by robbing: The word *ꜥwꜣ* conveys the notions of plundering and deprivation as well.

CHAPTER 56

I am the one who occupies this great seat which is in the middle of Wenu: The text is somewhat confused here, reading *st hry-ib wr imy wnw*, instead of the expected *st wr.t hry-ib wnw*.

CHAPTER 5

Some scholars have understood the allusion to labor in the Netherworld not as manual labor that the deceased must undergo but rather as an obligation for which he is somehow responsible. Hence, the inclusion of *shabtis* in a burial provided a labor force from which the deceased could draw in order to participate in the obligatory labor of the next life. See Assmann 2005, pp. 110–12.

I am the glutton: The text as written follows that of Coffin Text 431 exactly. Contemporaneous Book of the Dead copies have the word *wḏꜥ* ("judge") here.

I am in truth a *ba*: Possibly, "A *ba* belongs to me"; compare Coffin Text 431, where the text has *nnk bꜣ nb* ("Every *ba* belongs to me").

CHAPTER 96/97

MAKING A MAN BECOME AN *AKH*: Written *rḏi.t ꜣh n s* with an apparently superfluous *n*. Or meaning, "giving an *akh* to a man."

To be recited: Marks the original beginning of Chapter 97. The phrase *ḏd mdw* ("To be recited") is written oddly here.

These four *akhs* who are in the entourage of the lord of offerings are pleased with me: An alternative translation is "I have appeased these four *akhs*."

The field is mine by their commands: The text has *ink sht* whereas contemporaneous texts have *ink nb sht* ("I am the lord/possessor of the field").

this opposition that comes forth from your mouths: Lit., "obstacle."

I will not cause injury to myself: The text has the somewhat garbled *n rḏi꞊i nkn rꜣ꞊i*; other texts have *imi rḏi nkn r꞊i* ("Do not cause injury to me").

CHAPTER 117

The upper path: Reading uncertain. *Book of the Dead of Nebseni* has the same writing. See Lapp 2004, pl. 33.

this path of mine, make it (so): The papyrus is damaged here; the text seems to conform to that of *Book of the Dead of Nebseni*, which is damaged in exactly the same place. See *ibid*.

CHAPTER 118

Although Chapter 118 is a separate chapter from Chapter 117, it is not introduced with a heading or with rubrics here. In Twenty-first Dynasty texts, a title is commonly given to Chapter 118, "Spell for reaching Rosetau," but the *Book of the Dead of Gatseshen*, in Cairo, from that time period, for example, similarly lacks the title. See Lucarelli, 2006, p. 56.

CHAPTER 17₁

The tripartite partitioning of Chapter 17 found here occurs as well in *Book of the Dead of Nebseni*, another Eighteenth Dynasty Book of the Dead from Saqqara. For *Book of the Dead of Nebseni*, see Lapp 2004, pl. 33.

among the gods in the presence of the Lord of All: The text is confusedly written here, as if the scribe were trying to write "in the presence of Re."

to whom the Lord of All has given magical powers: *ꜣh.w* ("*akh*-powers").

CHAPTER 20

Chapter 20 is rare in New Kingdom Books of the Dead, found only here and in *Book of the Dead of Nebseni* among Books of the Dead earlier than the Late Period, and forms a pair with Chapter 13. In the Coffin Texts, the exemplars of Chapter 20—Coffin Texts 337-339—immediately precede Coffin Text 340, the exemplar of Chapter 13. Chapter 13 occurs without its own heading, following the pattern found in most of the Coffin Text exemplars

for this chapter. The text of Chapter 13 is repeated as Chapter 121 and a section of Chapter 122 in the Book of the Dead corpus.

Of the three exemplars of Chapter 20, Coffin Texts 337-339, the text of Chapter 20 given here follows that of Chapter 338 most closely but not exactly.

O Thoth, who vindicated Osiris against his enemies: The word translated as "vindication" is the compound term *mꜣꜥ-ḫrw* (lit., "true of voice").

Snare [the enemies] of the Osiris: An evident omission, perhaps a haplographic error—the accidental writing of one sign where there should be two—due to the fact that the last signs of the word *sht* ("snare") are the same as several signs used in the writing of *ḫft.yw* ("enemies"). Such "visual" errors are not uncommon in Egyptian texts and may reflect the difficulties inherent in the task of copying. On becoming "the Osiris," see Smith 2006, pp. 325–37.

in the presence of the council that is in Djedet: The other texts have *ḏdw* (Busiris). *ḏd.t* is the name of the necropolis in Heliopolis. The choice of the writing here immediately following a reference to Heliopolis may be intentional and not just due to scribal error. The problem is that Chapter 20 is a very rare text, found only here and in *Book of the Dead of Nebseni* among New Kingdom Books of the Dead; the two texts show variant writings in a number of places in this chapter. For comparison, see Lapp 2004, pls. 33, 34.

the council that is in Letopolis: The word *sḥm* is written without the town-sign determinative and has the house-sign determinative instead, a writing more typical for the word "sanctuary." The Coffin Text exemplars that are legible all have the writing "Letopolis." *Book of the Dead of Nebseni* has a very fancy shrine determinative twice in this chapter.

the council that is in Seshty: The place name Seshty (*sꜣty*) has been explained in a variety of ways: "Two Banks; Bird-Pond; Washerman's Shores."

(on) that night (when) Isis made mourning behind her brother Osiris: *m-sꜣ* ("behind; following after"). The preposition refers either to the traditional position of Isis at the head of the coffin or to Isis walking behind the coffin in the funerary procession, perhaps as part of the *Trauer*-entourage (procession of mourners).

the ones who have nothing: The debate continues over whether the phrase *iwty sw* means "those who have nothing" or "those who are no one," i.e., the translation "nobodies" that one often encounters.

the council that is in the "great hacking up of the earth": This obscure "place" name has been equally translated with a positive connotation, like fertilization, or a negative one, like destruction. The exemplar Coffin Text 337 has "great hacking up of the earth in Herakleopolis."

(O) Thoth, vindicate the Osiris, the Goldworker of Amun Sobekmose: Written without the tag *mꜣꜥ-ḫrw* ("justified"), probably because the similarly written phrase *smꜣꜥ-ḫrw* immediately precedes.

CHAPTER 13

The text of Chapter 13 is essentially that of Coffin Text 340.

[I have entered as a falcon; I have gone forth]: The papyrus is damaged here. The restoration here is based on the traces of signs and on contemporaneous versions of the text.

CHAPTER 17₂

The text of this section is difficult and somewhat problematic, diverging from that of most contemporaneous Books of the Dead.

I was conceived by Isis, I was begotten by Nephthys: Alternatively, "I conceive through Isis, I beget through Nephthys."

The [odors] which offerings create are provided for me: The text is difficult and perhaps confused here. The translation offered is based on the text and on the readings of contemporaneous Books of the Dead. The word *bꜣ.w* shows the same writing found in *Book of the Dead of Nebseni* with the plant determinative. Such a word is not attested in the lexica. Later texts have *bnr* instead. The translation "odors" given here is a conjecture based on the context.

I cause offerings to be made for Kheraha which is in very great fear of me: Both here and in *Book of the Dead of Nebseni*, the word "fear" is written with the single sign of the *atef*-crown. The meaning "fear" is thus metonymic, as the *atef*-crown is known from a number of myths in which its wearer terrorizes other divinities.

CHAPTER 44

SPELL FOR NOT DYING AGAIN: This is the first time in the papyrus that a chapter heading has been introduced by the term *rꜣ* ("spell; chapter," lit., "utterance").

I sanctify the Eye of Horus: The text may have been slightly miswritten with one sign omitted; if that is the case, the text reads "The Eye of Horus sanctifies me."

Imperishable Stars: *iḥmw-sk.*

Its neck is (that of) Re: The text seems somewhat confused here.

I live for you, my father, son of Isis: It is uncertain whether the epithet "son of Isis" refers to "father" or to "I."

CHAPTER 50

SPELL FOR NOT ENTERING THE SLAUGHTERING PLACE OF THE GOD: Note that the rubric ends with the word *nmt* ("slaughtering place"), avoiding writing the word *nṯr* ("god") in red.

To be recited by the Goldworker of Amun Sobekmose: Note the absence of the tag *mꜣꜥ-ḫrw* ("justified").

A knot is tied around me in the sky where it connects to earth by Re every day: Reading uncertain, as the text deviates significantly from contemporaneous examples.

first activity: For *sp* meaning "activity," see Bickel 1994, p. 16.

I am Penty: Written *npty*, which is meaningless. *Book of the Dead of Nebseni* has *ink pty*, as do a number of other early texts; on the various spellings of this divine name, see Lucarelli 2006, p. 132 and nn. 893ff. The meaning of the name may be something like "the one who (is)." It may be that the scribe has actually written *spty*, possibly a writing of the divinity *spꜣ*. It may also be an allusion to the "first activity," mentioned earlier in this chapter.

CHAPTER 38A

This chapter is somewhat rare, best known from Books of the Dead of the Eighteenth Dynasty.

watery region of the sky: Based on its determinative, the word *ḥnḥnyt* refers to a celestial region. The same writing occurs in *Book of the Dead of Nebseni*. Several texts have this word written with the boat determinative, and it has been interpreted as the name of the divine boat of Khepri. The word *ḥnḥn* ("jubilation") occurs later in the chapter; it is likely that some form of wordplay is involved here.

CHAPTER 153

The text of this chapter is very difficult and is closer in places to that of its predecessors Coffin Texts 473–481, especially Coffin Text 474, than to the parallels found in other early Eighteenth Dynasty Books of the Dead. The correct reading of a number of phrases here has been established from the Coffin Text passages.

fishers who go around in the canals of waters: *mn.w* (Wb. II, 72, 1–2). The scribe is following the text of Coffin Text 473 here, using *mn.w* ("canals") in place of *wdꜥ.w* ("artificial channels"), the term found in the Book of the Dead exemplars.

You shall not catch me in these nets: The demonstrative pronoun *twy* is oddly written as *wi tw.*

the earth wanderers: *ḥty.w-tꜣ* ("those who wander the earth"); note that the writing of *tꜣ* ("earth") has been omitted.

the bag of its net: *ib*; undetermined part of a fish or bird net. Here it is written with the wood determinative; in Coffin Text 474 the same word is written with the bag determinative, suggesting the body of the net proper. See Faulkner 1973–78, vol. 2, p. 115, n. 5.

fish-catcher: The word *ḥnw* here replaces *ḥꜣm* found elsewhere.

I have gone forth from its hands: *ḥr* for the expected *m.*

I have made offerings against you: This sentence is found essentially the same in *Book of the Dead of Nebseni* but not elsewhere to my knowledge. See Lapp 2004, pls. 35–37.

shinbone of Shesmu: The word "shin" is written *skbḥ* instead of *sbḫ*, but it does have the correct determinative.

My knife: Written *ꜥšꜥ* instead of *šꜥt*, but again with the correct determinative.

it is this cutter of Isis with which the navel-cord of Horus was cut: *im⸗s* is written seemingly out of place.

Akhby-gods: *ꜣḫby*-gods; see Leitz 2002, vol. 1, pp. 60–61.

The arms of its washings: The writing of *ꜥ.wy* is odd.

Mansion of the Moon: *ḥw.t-iʿḥ.t*, whose location is uncertain.

the brander: The word *sȝb* written here seems not found elsewhere. It resonates with the word *ȝb.t* ("branding-knife") that follows soon after.

he is the branding-knife with the tail: Other contemporaneous texts show *ds* for *sd* (" jar(s)") except *Book of the Dead of Nebseni*, once again. This variant is typical of those found in this section of the papyrus where two words written with similar letters show a confused metathesis.

The path on which he places it: *sw* ("it") referring to the fish; alternatively, "him" referring to the guard.

this table of Horus: *ṭ* for *ṭt* ("table").

he is this Horus who sits alone in darkness, who is not seen, the one whom those fear who have not praised him: The sense is clear here, but the writing seems very confused.

I appear in glory as the great god: It is uncertain whether the writing here is to be read *wr* ("great god") or *ḥr* ("Horus").

Its wooden plug: Uncertain part of a net.

it is the hand of Osiris: Other contemporaneous texts have "of Isis."

They are the earth-gods: Written with 𓀀, the seated man determinative instead of 𓀭, the divine determinative.

who are in the presence of Re, the ones who have ceased who are in the presence of Geb: The sense in both epithets here may be temporal, not spatial, the translation then being "who proceeded" in both cases.

You have swallowed (and) I have swallowed what Geb (and) Osiris have swallowed: Or, "have swallowed Geb and Osiris." Contemporaneous texts give different readings.

violent one: Alternative translation: "one who has power over his heart."

I shall live, its weights: The writing of this sentence is problematic. See the note following.

Look at me: The text is problematic here: *dns mk.wi* is followed by the sign *ḥt*, the determinative of the word *ḏbȝ* ("floats"). I am reading that sign as a logogram for *ḏbȝ*. The words following *mk.wi* should be *m ḏrt⸗i*, or perhaps that phrase has been omitted because of apparent dittography.

slicing-knife: Technical term found in the parallel Coffin Text passages.

I have come (so that) I may net him (and) I may put him, I may put him

in (his) place: The repetition here may be due to the fact that in the last line, the scribe began to write *di⸗i sw* ("I place him") and finished it at the top of the next column. He then repeated it, a common error of dittography when moving from one column to the next.

shin: Again written *sḳbḥ*, instead of *sbḳ*.

I act for them who praise my *ka* thereby: Possibly a pronoun error here and the text should begin "I do what they do." The gods' praise for the *ka* of the deceased is a good example of the *do ut des* formula. This Latin phrase describes the reciprocal relationship existing between men and gods. Each group gives to the other in order to receive the benefits it requires.

Chapter 124

I have plowed my field(s) (as) they are (normally) done: The writing of *m ir.w* looks as if its meaning is "by means of (my) manifestations."

(My) *dom*-palm is (that which) Min is upon: Wordplay on *mȝmȝ* ("*dom*-palm") and the name of the god Min.

I eat by my pool (and) under (its) branches: Lit., "under my pool (and its) branches."

I am powerful in the sky, guarding against that which is evil to me: The reading of the text here is not shared by any of the other early exemplars; the translation is, thus, provisional, based on what appears to be written here.

is assigned to the ancestors of the light: Unclear whether this reference is temporal (i.e., "ancestors of the light") or spatial (i.e., "those preceding the light").

I have come forth because of Ihy: Other texts have *rḥ.wy* ("the Two Comrades") in place of *iḥy*.

Fear of me (is) in the twilight within Mehet-weret at the side of his forehead: The phrase *dhn⸗f* ("his forehead") is written *hdf*, a senseless writing that seems born, again, of metathesis. The restoration is based on contemporaneous versions of this chapter.

Chapter 119

Often found as an individual text, Chapter 119 comes originally from two of the texts that belong to the Book of Two Ways, a collection of texts found in the Coffin Texts corpus.

I am the Great One: Possibly "the eldest god."

I have come before you, Osiris, (so that) I may worship you, (so that) I may be purified [by] the efflux that pours from you: The text reads "the effluxes that I pour from you." The Egyptian word *stȝ* ("pour") offers some wordplay on the Egyptian place name "Rosetau."

Sole one, Re indeed circles with you: Possibly "Re encircles you," but the text would have to be somewhat emended.

I say to you, Osiris: To me belongs the dignity of a god: The word *sʿḥ* conveys the notions of nobility and dignity that are bestowed on the deceased through the act of mummification.

Chapter 102

O Great One who is in his sacred boat, bring me to your sacred boat (so that) [I] may draw near your staircase, (so that) I may govern for you your sailing voyages in these duties of yours allotted to the Unwearying Stars: *ḥrp⸗k n⸗i* ("so that you may govern for me") is what is written here, an error for *ḥrp⸗i n⸗k* ("so that I may govern for you"). *iḫm-wrḏ* ("the Unwearying Stars") are those stars that rise above and set below the horizon in seasonal patterns, as compared with the circumpolar stars that never set.

"Descend (and) sail," Re commands: *h* for *hȝ*. The text actually reads "when I command Re," a probable corruption of the text.

Chapter 7

Spell for passing by the vertebrae of Apophis: The name of *ʿȝpp* is written in red with knives in black ink drawn over it.

Your poison shall not enter my limbs: The writing of *ʿ.wt* ("limbs") is odd here.

My protection is that of the gods, lords of eternity: The word eternity *ḏt* is written *ḏd* ("to say").

Chapter 136A

I will sail in it with the ape: Written as a singular noun.

CHAPTER 136B

SPELL FOR SAILING IN THE GREAT SACRED BOAT OF RE TO PASS BY THE RING OF FIRE: Or, "pass over."

This fire is bright behind Re, bound together—to be recited—behind him: As written, the text appears to be "interrupted" throughout by the rubric *ḏd mdw* ("to be recited"). In *Book of the Dead of Nebseni*, the rubric *ḏd mdw* ("to be recited") is written at the top of each column, in a way familiar from the layout of the Pyramid Texts and Coffin Texts, where the phrase *ḏd mdw* is repeated at the top of each column of writing. In all likelihood, the exemplar from which *Book of the Dead of the Goldworker of Amun Sobekmose* was copied had a layout similar to these texts, but the scribe who copied the Brooklyn papyrus seems to have misunderstood the function of that rubric at the top of each column and simply copied it wherever it occurred, and the layout of his text ended up with *ḏd mdw* now appearing wherever it occurred in his running text.

I have seen the ones who have attained truth as well as the Double Lions who belong there: Reading *ḥft* in place of the text's *ḥrf*.

being the ones who are in coffins: Several other texts have "O those in their coffins."

more numerous than (those in) the Field of Reeds (whom) I have seen there: The text is problematic here. Most versions of the Book of the Dead and of the Coffin Texts show a variety of writings here.

their greater gods: Or, "older gods."
their smaller ones: Or, "younger gods."
Who—to be recited—is the underling?: Text problematic.

Replacement: Marks an alternative reading or text to be read here, like *ky ḏd* ("variant").

he shall say: Possibly, "his father"; the text seems confused here.

the Lord of Greatness: So the text reads. Other contemporaneous texts have *nb tm* ("Lord of All"), but the Brooklyn text does not support such a reading.

the jaws of Rosetau: Written *ṯsr.t*, not *ʿrt* as elsewhere, but perhaps an attempt to write *ṯs.t ʿrt* ("teeth of the jaws").

To be recited—Come, pass by for the Lord of Perception: Reading uncertain as the text is corrupt here.

Extinguish—to be recited—the fire: Written *kt*, an abbreviation for *ḳdr.t*.

("incense; smoke offering") in place of *ḥt* ("fire").

Make a path for me, fathers (and) their offspring: *bn.w*; passive participle of *bnn* ("beget").

The *fentu*-snakes grant it to me that I may pass by: *fnṯ.w*-snakes; it looks as if the scribe was trying to write *ḥfꜣ.w fnṯ* ("snakes {and} serpents"). The writing of the text is confusing here.

The protections of Re [are my protections]: The scribe's omission of the word *mk.wt* ("protections") is due to the similarity in writing of the word *mk* ("behold") that immediately follows here.

CHAPTER 149

Take off your head-cloths when I approach: Compare the different writing and translation in a parallel phrase at col. 168, below.

Set my head in place for me, Nehebkau: Nehebkau is preceded by the preposition *r*, which yields no sense; the writing of the name Nehebkau is odd as well. The context seems to require a vocative here and that is what is found in other contemporaneous versions.

Fill and make the balance-beam firm: Note that *bḳs.w*, written with the balance-scale determinative, may be a pun on the word *bḳs.w* ("spine"), given that the passage here is focused on reestablishing the various parts of the body of the deceased.

It is *akhs*, nine cubits tall thereof, who cut it down at the side of Re-Horakhty: Many texts have seven cubits here.

I know these twin sycamores of turquoise from which Re goes forth, going through the two props of Shu: Written with a single hieroglyph that reads *sṯs* ("supports; props") or possibly *st.wt* ("rays of the sun"), both of which make sense in a context with the god Shu. The four supports or props of Shu hold the sky up above the earth.

her flame is a flame of fire: *ꜣḫ nt bs* could also be translated "the power of fire."

He lives by beheading the *akhs* (and) the dead in the necropolis: These two terms comprise all of those who have died; *akh* refers to those dead who have passed judgment and have thus attained a transfigured state; the "dead" refers to those who failed to pass judgment and who thus wander in the necropolis and on earth as disenfranchised beings. They were

particularly feared by the Egyptians as powerful, malignant forces.

As for any of the gods (or) any dead man who licks his mouth in my presence on this day, [he] shall fall to the deep: The writing here may be *in* instead of *ir*, in which case the translation would be: "It is any of the gods (or) any dead man who licks his mouth in my presence on this day who shall fall to the deep."

O you cavern: *imḥ.t* is used as the name of various necropoleis and of a locale near the source of the Nile.

O you, Ises, too far to be seen, whose hot breath is fire in whom there is a snake—Rerek is its name—who is six cubits in length in his backbone [who lives on] the *akhs* (and) is equipped with their power: The text is problematic and has been restored based on contemporaneous versions.

His ka falls because of a *sedeh*-snake and vice versa: *sḏḥ*-snake; some texts have "A bull falls to a *sḏḥ*-snake and vice versa," the writing of *ka* and "bull" being virtually identical.

the height of its roaring: Firebrand determinative from association with the word *hm* ("burn").

I am that *nur*-bird: *nwr*-bird; offers wordplay with the word *nrw* ("terror") that follows.

on the day of the great doings: The sign *ʿꜣ* was added as a vertical stroke, seemingly as an afterthought.

O you city of Qahu who seize the *akhs*, who have power over the shadows, who eat what is fresh (and) gulp down what is corruption because of what their eyes see, whose guarding the land does not exist: The root *kꜣḥ* means mud of the Nile, and the writing of the word *kꜣḥ.w* as a plural word with the divine determinative may allude to personifications of the mud of the Nile, hence an entity that has primordial associations. The text is corrupt here, but the sense is clear and supported by other contemporaneous texts.

[No one shall seize] my akh (or) have power over my shade: Both *akh* and "shade" are written as plural nouns.

whose body is concealed: Cursorily written.

O you Idu-town: *idw*-town; reading uncertain. The word may be connected to a generic word meaning "youngster(s)."

I have passed the waters of heaven: The word "heaven" is cursorily written.

O you mound Wenet: Written here like the verb "to hurry."

It is he who guards it because of fear that the gods will drink her waters while it is keeping (them) afar [from the *akhs*]: The papyrus is damaged here, and a number of signs are missing. The restoration is based on other Eighteenth Dynasty versions.

CHAPTER 150

Some of these vignette captions read right to left while others are written in retrograde.

The Pool Whose River Burns with Fire: The text is corrupt and difficult in other versions as well.

CHAPTER 64

lord of the elevations who goes forth at twilight, manifestations [...]: The latter thought has been left incomplete; other texts read "manifestations of the house of death."

O (you) [two] falcons: Contemporaneous texts have *bik.wy* ("two falcons"). Note that the verbal forms used here with the singular noun "falcon" are often written as plurals.

who drag Re: Written *st3.w n s*; probably *st3.w=sn* was meant, the plural pronoun *=sn* referring to the "two falcons."

the seat of the shrine that is above [the sky], [lord]: The restoration is based on contemporaneous versions and the traces of the text.

Enter from the under-sky: The writing here can be read *nn.t* ("under-sky") or *ḥmn.t* ("Hermopolis").

O you, great one whose island does not exist, summon those: "Summon" is written *is* instead of *nis*.

Your arm is your tent: As written, *ḥnt* means "tent." Other texts have "skin," similarly spelled but with a different determinative.

[that sniffs at the shrine]: The papyrus is damaged here; restoration is based on contemporaneous versions.

Anubis has arrived at (the place called) No Limit. [...]: The papyrus is damaged here, making restoration difficult.

I am the distraught one: If the reading is *psḫ.ty*, the meaning is as given; if the reading is *sph.ty*, then the meaning is "deliverer."

I have come from Letopolis: Or "from the sanctuary."

CHAPTER 125

I have not known that which is not (to be known): Possibly meaning "that which I should not know."

I have not [spoken ill of] the god: *s3.w*, meaning uncertain.

I have not deprived the orphan: The text is corrupt here.

I have not committed rape: *nk*.

I have not acted lasciviously: *d3d3*.

I have not decreased [an *aroura*]: The text is damaged but the traces indicate the reading of *st3.t* ("*aroura*").

There is no evil that can happen to me [in this land, in this hall of]: Text missing in part. Restoration and translation is based on contemporaneous versions.

O one whose eyes are flint who came forth from Letopolis: Or, "from the sanctuary."

wammty-snake: *w3mmty*-snake; found in the Amduat as well.

Weryt: Not known.

I have not had sexual relations, I have not committed rape, I have not copulated: The three verbs *nwḥ*, *nk*, and *nkk* are synonyms, but their specific differences are not known.

Nedjfeti: The text has the phonemes *df*, but determinatives suggest *ndfti*, one of two similarly named places in Upper Egypt.

Tem-sep: Lit., "he who does not [allow] what is left over."

one who brings his portion: The literal translation of the phrase *in ʿ=f*.

You will tell the truth about me in the presence of the register: So also *Book of the Dead of Nebseni*.

who swallow from their excesses: The text is corrupt. Contemporaneous texts have "who swallow truth."

You will not report against me in the presence of [the great god]: Contemporaneous texts have *nṭr ʿ3*, following *m-b3ḥ; m-b3ḥ* by itself as it is written here means "like before."

He gives forth [cries]: Text problematic; restoration based on contemporaneous texts.

within the silent places: "among (?)"

calming the hearts of the gods after they pass through it by night [or by day]: Text problematic; restoration based on contemporaneous texts.

a town north of the *moringa*-tree: Lit., "*moringa*-tree town." The name of the town is a pun on the Egyptian word for *moringa*-tree.

I buried them on the shore of Maak: *mʿ3k*; so written, but see spelling in next column.

What did you find there on the shore of Maak?: *mʿ3t*; see preceding note.

Toe-of-Iunmutef: Texts more typically have "toe of your mother." The name Iunmutef means "pillar of his mother."

Wenpet-of-Nephthys is the name of my left foot: *wnp.t*; substantive of uncertain meaning: "leg," "sidelock," and "root" have been suggested.

TEXT X

The text of this chapter is highly problematic due to a number of uncertain readings; the known parallels are excerpts from sections of a number of texts from both the Book of the Dead corpus and from that of the Coffin Texts. A number of sections have no apparent parallels. The title given here is that of Chapter 146, although the text that follows is not from the text of that chapter. There are identifiable excerpts from Coffin Text 404-405 and Book of the Dead Chapters 58, 72, and 99.

I am transformed to an *akh*: Lit., "become an *akh*."

(O) Thoth, I know the Two Combatants of the *akh* who falls in the doorway of the slaughterer: Translation provisional.

The doorkeeper of Shu is his name. He exists [...] whose name is foremost of the valley which he is in: The text is problematic here.

I have come, a possessor of *akhs*: I.e., as one who has power; an alternative translation is "come to me, (o) lord of *akhs*."

Tekem: This god is known from Coffin Text 404 and Book of the Dead Chapters 72 and 99, where he is described as the "opener of the West," among other things.

The name of the ferryman is "the one who finds faces, who uplifts faces." The name of the ferry (is) "the one who finds faces, who uplifts faces": "The name of the ferryman" is written without a personal determinative. The epithet *gm ḥrw* "the one who finds faces" is found in Book of the Dead Chapter 58. The repeated text here may be a dittographic error made by the scribe as he moved from one column to the next.

"pool of wounds": The text shows *š nsp.w*.

The name of the bailer (is) "report that its excellence has spread": The text seems hopelessly corrupt.

The name of the river is "(he) who sees *snš*": The text is problematic as written; two possible readings are "those who see the (divine) sea," and "he who sees the lotus god." In the case of the latter, *snš* is seen as a miswriting of *sšn*.

COFFIN TEXT 901

First gate: Beginning here, the text is a conflation of headings from Chapter 146 and text from Coffin Text 901. Both of these texts deal with the Field of Reeds and its various gateways.

Chamber of Sebtef: *sbtf*; the reading is uncertain; the text of the Coffin Text exemplars is problematic as well.

those upon their bellies: Snakes, as the determinative shows.

Chamber of the district: The text is problematic here.

Chamber of the concealed one, mistress of the paths, who guides Horus (and) Seth when she passes by: The Coffin Text version has "when the sacred boat passes by."

TEXT Y

whose flood waters raise you up as one who is made divine: Text uncertain.

Save him from everything done to him: Or, "from everything which he has done."

Asha-khet: Known only from two New Kingdom sources.

CHAPTER 119

Chapter 119 is identical to the beginning section of text with which the deceased addresses the first gate in Book of the Dead Chapter 147.

I am the Eldest (god): Written with the divine determinative.

its name made in Rosetau: "in," or "as"(?).

Your might, your power (are) in Rosetau: Or, "you are mighty (and) you are powerful."

you are rowed at the time when Re (is): Or, "you are rowed before Re."

CHAPTER 18

the great council that is in Pe: The scribe has inadvertently omitted "and Dep."

Seshty: *sšty*, variously translated as "Two Banks," "Bird-Pond," and "Washerman's Shores."

Then it was given by [...] to those in Busiris: Text problematic; the word *ib* can be read but it has no determinative.

I have seen it happen often: Lit., "greatly."

CHAPTER 17₃

when the props of Shu had not (yet) come into existence: The scribe has omitted the negative marker *n* and has written 𓀐, the seated man determinative, in its place, creating a writing that makes little sense.

he was not turned away by the gods: Some contemporaneous texts have: "I am one who is not turned away from the gods."

Then he fought him on account of it: The writing is confused here. The sentence seems to allude to a cosmic conflict in which the solar deity fought against his enemy.

Iahesy: Some contemporaneous texts have "Min"; *Book of the Dead of Nebseni* has the same reading as the Brooklyn text.

I set out upon [a road I know]: Scribal omission after the preposition *tp*; restoration based on contemporaneous texts.

(O you) who were before (me): Or "you who are in (my) presence."

It means Shu and Sia: Other texts have the pairing "Hu and Sia."

I say that which his lord loves: The word "lord" is written as a plural noun.

Hail to you: Written *n* not *tn*.

it means Sobek: Written as a plural.

Then I Saw My Father: The text may read "the one who saw my father."

As for these seven *akhs*, Nedhedhu, Qedqed, the Bull To Whom the Flame from His Heat was Given, the One Who Enters with the One Who Is in His Hour: Note that only four or perhaps five names are given here.

the red West: Or "sacred West."

Now as for that day of "Come then to me": Note that in the text above the day was called "Come then from there."

"Come then from there (so that I) may see you": Possibly, "so that you may be seen."

Then (they) became the two *bas*: The verb *hpr* is subjectless here and in other texts as well. The idea is that from the embrace of Osiris and Re the "two *bas*" came into being.

who rises from his horizon, who swims: Oddly written with three land signs and not three water signs.

(on) that night of reckoning with the "robber": A day of "reckoning with the robber" occurs in Book of the Dead Chapter 71.

who causes the lassoing of sinners for his slaughtering-block for *bas*: Other contemporaneous texts add *dnd* ("slaughter"); what is written here looks simply like *nt*.

It means Horus; he exists with [two] heads: The text has "with my head." What follows indicates that the reading should be "with two heads."

The one is in possession of truths: Written as "one man."

who is foremost in Letopolis: Or, "the sanctuary."

I am one who was prosperous on earth with Re, who died along with Osiris: I.e., died with.

I fly as a falcon; I honk as a *semen-goose*: "honk" is oddly written.

Back, lion, whose mouth is white, whose head is stamped flat: Some contemporaneous texts have "whose head shines."

(O you) who make guard while he is unseen guarding: Or, "he is unseen while guarding."

I am Wadjet, mistress of those who are in the flame: Elsewhere, "Mistress of the devouring flame."

CHAPTER 23

My mouth is split open by Ptah with the metal harpoon [of his]: Restoration based on contemporaneous texts.

I am Sakhmet, Great of Magic: Odd writing after the spelling of *sḫt* that is not a determinative. The translation here is a conjecture based on what can be read. *Book of the Dead of Nebseni* has "I am Sakhmet, Wadjet."

I sit at the western side in the sky: The text is confusingly written here.

I am Orion: The writing is odd here with *sꜣy.t* in place of *sꜣḥ*.

CHAPTER 24

hounds: Written *bḫsrw*, not *bḫsw*.

Now, assemble for yourself: Or, "Now, you have assembled."

Variant: swifter than Shu. The *nur*-bird was created, the gods were held silent; the *nur*-bird was made to cry out, submission to the gods: There are a number of words in this sentence whose writings are very odd; as written, their meanings have not yet been determined by the lexica. Roughly contemporaneous manuscripts show great variation here.

Now, this magic of mine is given to you: Or, "Now, you have given."

CHAPTER 26

I will not eat the cakes given (to) Osiris on that eastern side of the narrows: The word *gȝy.w* is sometimes determined with the pool sign; here we have the plant determinative and plural strokes. This word appears to be a toponym indicating a pool or perhaps a swampy, marshy realm. See *pChester Beatty VII*, rt. 1, 1, for which see Gardiner 1935.

when you sail downstream or (you) sail upstream (or) descending (to) the boat which you are in: Other texts read: "I will not descend to the boat which you are in."

CHAPTER 28

O lion. I am Re: Some other texts have "*weneb*-blossom."

Your temple: Some other texts have "slaughterhouse."

(O you) (bone) breakers of Osiris when he saw Seth: Or, "O crushers of Osiris (who) has seen Seth."

You have not advanced his seat: Some other texts have "I am the one whose seat you have advanced."

CHAPTER 31

Messenger: Written *pw*, not *wpw*.
Badty: *bȝdty*: Not known to Leitz 2002.
My teeth are flint: Or, "knives."

CHAPTER 34

the standard of the divine years: *rnp.w* ("years") with the divine determinative

means the divinized forms of the years. Note that many contemporaneous texts have *dnp.w*, a writing that seems meaningless.

CHAPTER 35

zekzek-**snake:** Known from as early as the Pyramid Texts and the Coffin Texts in connection with the *sema*-plant.

cleared: Lit., "washed."

Truth apportions (when) assessing what has accumulated: The confusion here goes back to the Coffin Text exemplars. Nonetheless, it is clear that the reference is to judgment.

CHAPTER 74

Senek, Senek: The reading here is challenging. The word *snk* (lit., "darkness; obscurity") is a designation of the sun-god; thus, its occurrence is not surprising given the number of solar references found here. The writing of what appears to be *snk* may reflect a misunderstanding of the hieratic sign *sti* used in the writing of a verb meaning "to shine" and a noun meaning "sunlight." Comparison with contemporaneous texts does not help, as they all have "Sokar." It is possible that what is written here is an error for the writing *skr* ("Sokar"). The Coffin Text exemplar does not have any sections in which the difficulty found here occurs.

CHAPTER 93

The text of this chapter more closely resembles that of its exemplar Coffin Text 548 than it does the text of contemporaneous or even later Books of the Dead.

the phallus of Re will swallow the head of Osiris: The translation of the text as it is written. The Coffin Text text has "I will swallow the phallus of Re (and) the head of Osiris."

Now, I am led to the fields of the one whom the gods have beheaded where they give answer: The text is problematic here.

CHAPTER 41

I lead Imyadjwer: *imy-ʿd-wr*; this epithet is found only in this chapter of the Book of

the Dead. A number of translations have been offered, all conjectures.

O one who brings offerings: Many of the epithets that follow here refer to Thoth.

CHAPTER 61

(so that) he may have power over [it] as Hapi (does): Or, "have power over it as the Nile," i.e., have power over it as a source of water.

CHAPTER 42

The land belongs to the staff. The White Crown belongs to the images of the standards of Min: Or, "(O) land of the staff; White Crown of the images of the standards of Min."

Ibu-weret: *ibw-wr.t*. A number of translations of the name of this deity have been offered, such as "great calf; calf of the eldest; great thirsty one," but none convincingly so.

you have said today: The word "today" is oddly written as if it were "today of Re."

How (much) more beautiful today is than yesterday: Reading uncertain. The writings found in other texts seem confused here as well.

(If) I prosper, one prospers, this day prospers: Text corrupt.

My hair is the Nun: Each of the statements in this list can be translated as, for example, either "My hair is the Nun" or "My hair is that of the Nun."

My flesh: Oddly written with a mixture of elements from the words *iwf* and *ȝf*.

My feet are Ptah: The writing of *rd.wy* is odd.

I am yesterday. The one who sees millions of years is my name. Go, go upon the path of the Chief Examiner: An alternative translation for this last section is "I am yesterday who sees millions of years. My name is 'He who goes upon the path of the Chief Examiner.'"

I am the lord of eternity: Possibly also "I am the possessor of eternity."

I have allowed them to live: Reading uncertain. An alternative translation is "grant to me that they live."

I sit in my structure before it: The reading of the text is uncertain here.

My throne has been assigned to me (so that) I may rule from it with a mouth that speaks (and) is silent: The text is confusedly written *ḥkꜣ st m* instead of *ḥkꜣ=i m st m*. The translation given is based on the text as it is written.

[I am one who] opens a gate in the sky. I rule (from my) throne, judging those born on this day. There is no child who treads upon the road of yesterday. This day belongs to me, man as man: It is difficult to decide whether the phrase *rmṯ m rmṯ* goes with what precedes or what follows.

I do not die again: The text is written *n mwt=i m wḥm* where one would expect *nn mwt=i*.

Children of misfortune are united: Other texts typically have "cannot be united" or "are buried," the reading there being *smꜣ tꜣ*.

With words I speak [to] you: Written as "to us." The text is confusedly written here, likely due to haplographic errors.

No day is free of its responsibilities: Lit., "the things that pertain to it."

I am the blossom that came forth from the Nun—that means my mother: I.e., "the Nun." Contemporaneous texts have "Nut is my mother."

the great commander: Alternatively "binder," though the determinatives present argue for the translation as given.

I am Horus who is foremost over men, (my) scorching heat against your faces whose hearts would be sick against me: Contemporaneous texts have "foremost of/over millions." The text is evidently corrupt here reading *ꜣšy.w ib.w=sn ḏr.t* for *šmm ib.w=sn r=i*. The problem seems to lie in the hieratic text.

the foremost one of Memphis: Mistakenly written *ḥw.t ptḥ*, not *ḥw.t kꜣ ptḥ*.

Say this word: May you illuminate the one you are driving away: The writing of *ꜥbꜣ* with the eye determinative seems to be unattested. The *Book of the Dead of Nu*, in London, has *ꜥbꜣbꜣ*, which also seems unattested; see Lapp 1997, pl. 17; Quirke 2013, p. 120, gives for *pNu*: "When you clear your eyes (?), you repel." Allen, T. G., 1974, p. 49, offers "look kindly upon." I am taking what is here as a writing of the verb *ꜥbꜣ* ("funkeln; leuchten"); Hannig 1997, p. 135b.

Chapter 14

The god unites with Truth: What is written is apparently the verb *smꜣ*. Other texts have *smꜣ.w* ("companions").

Drive away all the anger which is in your heart against [me]: The text seems garbled, having "Drive away the anger of all which is in the heart against you."

Chapter 68

The mouth of the pelican is revealed to me: *sš*; translation provisional. "Opened" remains a possibility.

The mouth of the pelican grants to me that I go forth by day to any place my heart desires: The sense is clear but the writing *mry=i ib=i im* shows a superfluous subject pronoun *=i*.

I again have power over my invocation offerings: Text has *wḥm=i sḫm pr.t* ... Possibly: "I repeat the power of my invocation offerings."

I swallow red-wheat beer of Hapi: *nt ḥꜥpi* ("of Hapi") is given in a supra-linear writing.

the writings of the god's words: *mdw-nṯr*, i.e., "hieroglyphs."

Raise me from my left side to my right side: *ṯs wi* is written as an imperative in this section while other texts have *ṯs=i wi* ("I raise myself").

Chapter 69

Their bonds were placed: Possibly "Put their bonds on."

I am Anubis, the centipede: This phrase has been interpreted elsewhere to mean "I am Anubis (on the day of) the Centipede"; or "I am Anubis (of) Sepa," the latter a location in the neighborhood of Heliopolis.

It is I who am the Lord of All: Or, possibly, "I am Lord Atum."

(O) eldest who has entered, [say] to the collector of writings: The text here reads *ꜥḳ=f n ꜥb sš.w* ("he enters to the collector of writings").

I have protected my body: The text has *nḏ.n=i* instead of the prospective *nḏ=i* ("so that I may protect") found in other texts.

I wrap these knees of mine (and) the lower part of Osiris: The text seems to have *knm* ("wrap") where the other exemplars have *kfꜣ* ("unwrap"). Reading uncertain.

I make a presentation to Thoth, a slaughtering for the one who is chief of Teryt: *try.t*, reading uncertain.

Chapter 70

[I grasp] the mouth of the south wind by its plaits: The scribe has omitted *nḏr=i*; the same error is found in other texts as well.

Chapter 92

Opening the tomb for the *ba* and the shadow: "*ba*" is written as a plural; "shadow" is written *ḥp.wy*, the name of a somewhat obscure divinity that is written with the *šw.t*-sign.

(my) flesh is made fast: Reading uncertain. *dꜣy* is written here, possibly for *dꜣr*.

Open the ways: Oddly written as *wn wi wꜣ.ty n* ...

you keepers of the limbs of Osiris: The text has "eaters of the limbs of Osiris."

who would do evil against me, (and) those who have done evil against me: Reading uncertain in tense and mood.

your *ka* is with my *ba*: "my" is probably an error for "your."

Are you held by the sky?: The text reads *in ḏr=k in pt* for *in nḏr=k in pt*.

Chapter 63A

I have prevented another from living on me: The word *ky* ("another") is written in retrograde here as 𓇌𓎡 instead of 𓎡𓇌; a similar writing is found in several other contemporaneous papyri.

Chapter 105

I am healthy: The writing is confused here; it appears that the scribe began to write *inn* ("bring"), the verb of the clause immediately following. Realizing that he had omitted *snb=kwi*, he attempted to correct his error but mistakenly wrote *sb* for *snb*. Other papyri show much variation here, but the text of *Book of the Dead of Nebseni* conforms closely to that of the Brooklyn text.

(so that) I may purify you: The scribe has mistakenly written "so that I may purify myself."

Chapter 72

The excess of my hands is in the temple: The reading of the hieratic here is uncertain. The text of *Book of the Dead of Nebseni* is damaged here.

Chapter 71

I penetrate to the one who makes the fringed garment: Reading uncertain. The other texts have *wbꜣ=i ntt ḥr sdb* ("I penetrate to what is at the fringe").

O [...] who is in his egg: Same writing in *Book of the Dead of Nebseni*.

I know you, I know your names: Written *rḫ.n=i* in both cases.

May you know me: Written *rḫ.n=tn*.

many days upon days of life, many nights upon nights of life until I go forth: "go forth (to the horizon)," i.e., "die."

Chapter 83

I am the fruit: The text has *dḳnw* (unattested word) instead of *dḳrw* ("fruit").

the cobras that came into being in the West: The hieratic writing here looks more like *ꜥpr.t* than *imn.t.t*.

I am Khonsu, the rage of the lords: Or, "who slaughters everyone"; other texts have "the anger of the lords."

Chapter 84

The text of this chapter is difficult with insertions from several chapters from the Coffin Texts. It is problematic as well in other contemporaneous Book of the Dead texts.

making the wideness of my strides (stretch) to my city (and) settlements: A conjectured attempt to make sense of this difficult part of the passage.

Chapter 85

I think about truth: The text has *n ḳꜣ=i* ("I have not thought").

I cross the firmament which they have made: Reading uncertain.

Commended to me are the [...] upon the western mounds of the ibis: Reading uncertain as the text seems garbled here.

Chapter 82

drinking: Other texts have "drinking beer."

I have flown: Other texts have "flown as a falcon."

The four suns, the gifts of the land of Re: Reading uncertain.

I remember the words of Atum for my father with my mouth (when) he destroyed the servant of the wife of Geb, fire upon him: Reading uncertain. Other texts have "whose head was broken."

Chapter 86

I have examined what is in Letopolis: Or, "What is in Letopolis has been assigned to me."

I have bent my arms to Osiris: Written with an apparently intrusive *ib*.

Chapter 99

who make necks firm when wounds come forth: Reading uncertain.

they raise themselves up: *ṯs=sn st*; other texts have *n gm ṯs=sn st* ("they cannot raise themselves up").

Nebgu: The other texts have *mngb* (Mengeb).

whose face is red: *ḥr=f*; the reading of other texts is *ḥr tp dšrw* ("chief of the red one[s])").

the place which you know: Or, "the place where you are known."

Tell me my name, says the steering-post ... Tell me my name, says the mast-step: The words "mast-step" and "steering-post" are both spelled *ḥtp*. The determinative used here suggests the latter but the word "steering-post" that immediately precedes argues for the former.

oar-loop: This word has also been interpreted to mean something like "strap of the sail."

oar-handle: Likely the handle of the steering oar.

This Goldworker of Amun Sobekmose, justified, penetrates [to you] (so that) you may give to me funerary offerings at his side (so that) I may eat from it: Reading uncertain.

the *sheser*-cake that Nephthys baked in the broad hall in the presence of hands: *šsr*-cake. The text is somewhat suspect here.

Chapter 38A

My words are commanded to the *akhs* whose seats are hidden (and) more

powerful with [...]: Text uncertain.

I associate with Horus (and) Seth: Possibly, "make Horus and Seth fraternize with each other."

Chapter 39

your father [ordered] that your slaughter be done: the bracketed word is *r bw ... wd*.

O leave the desert margins: *rwi ꜥd.w*

he is one who licks his heart: A direct translation of *nsb ib=f pw*. Other texts have *nbd ib=f pw* (he is the one who twists his heart); *nkn ib=f pw* (he who offends his heart).

Turn back the Bristler: The text is difficult here; there may be a miswriting of the preceding noun *nsb*.

Take your paths: *wꜣ.w* ("paths"); other texts have *ꜥḥꜣ.w* ("weapons").

Chapter 65

What Allen, T. G., 1974, p. 60, calls "Spell Naville 65." Chapter 65 designated by Lepsius 1842 is a later variant of Chapter 2.

He has united the Ennead, namely those whose faces are secret: The text is oddly written here.

Chapter 8B

He does not exist in it. I do not exist in it: "It" seems to refer to the West, the idea being that knowledge of this chapter keeps the deceased from being confined to the West; rather, he may move freely in and out of it.

Chapter 8A

Hermopolis is open: Wordplay in the original Egyptian: *wn wnw*.

Chapter 80

the place of water(s) would be destroyed: A possible alternative is: "the place of waters will not be trampled." The text seems extremely corrupt here.

CHAPTER 63B

He who is not, he is rowed (though) he is boat-less: The text seems somewhat confused here.

CHAPTER 64B

What Allen, T. G., 1974, p. 58, calls Spell 64 Variant.

each successive moment of his being (re)born: Text has *m sp ky* in place of *m ky*.

they are four million, four hundred thousand, (and) twelve hundred of more than twelve cubits: The word "thousand" is oddly written *ḥfn*. The text is corrupt here. The restoration is based on contemporaneous sources.

Those (of you) who are on their bellies: The reference is to snakes as the determinative makes clear.

It is *djaret*-fruit that is fallen upon the back of the *benu*-bird: *ḏꜣr.t*-fruit. Either a New Egyptian writing of *psd* ("back") or *pꜣ sd* ("the tail").

It means a spell for not dying again: What Assmann 2005, pp. 74–74, calls the "second death."

the King of Upper (and) Lower Egypt Apep: Other texts have (King) Khasty or Semty.

CHAPTER 152

SPELL FOR ALLOWING THIS GOLDWORKER OF AMUN SOBEKMOSE, JUSTIFIED TO TURN HIMSELF AROUND TO SEE HIS HOUSE ON EARTH: In other texts this chapter has the title "Spell for building a house that is on the earth," i.e., a tomb, which is where the deceased will also pass eternity.

The followers turn around. Men, gods, children, (and) their fathers give praise to me (when) they have seen what Seshat has brought to Geb: Text differs here from other papyri.

Anubis summons: The text seems confusedly written here.

Then Osiris said to the gods who are in his following: Go, see: Perhaps, "oversee."

He has come today, appearing: Written as a form of the verb "see" (*mꜣꜣ*) and not with the root for "new" (*mꜣꜥ*) that the other texts have.

Bring for him: The dative that follows the imperative *in* ("Bring") is written *n=s* ("for her").

Men, gods, the *akhs*, the dead have seen you: One expects "have seen me."

May they pass their time praising the one who is honored there: Or, "me as one who is honored there."

CHAPTER 75

Kemkem: Uncertain.

I am conducted within: The verb *bs* has connotations of initiation.

I am ennobled as a god: Text damaged. Restoration based on contemporaneous texts.

He shall travel to Pe (so that) he may come to Sepa: Instead of Sepa, the other texts have Dep, the name of a city that occurs commonly in tandem with Pe.

CHAPTER 78

You shall not do harm, when there is physical decay: Text damaged but traces of the determinative ⌇ and plural strokes are visible.

If I say, ... Shu is great, (then) they turn back the attack: The text here follows a Coffin Text exemplar whose text is also confusing.

I see the gods: Other texts have "the gods see me."

I shall tell them of his powers: For "his," some texts have "my."

Horus is [his] mother: Reading uncertain.

Reproduction
of the Papyrus

Overview
of the Papyrus

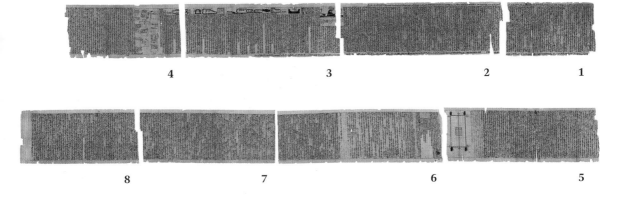

4	3	2	1

8	7	6	5

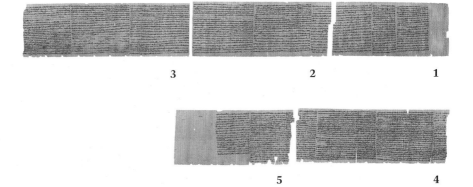

3	2	1

5	4

Recto

1

2

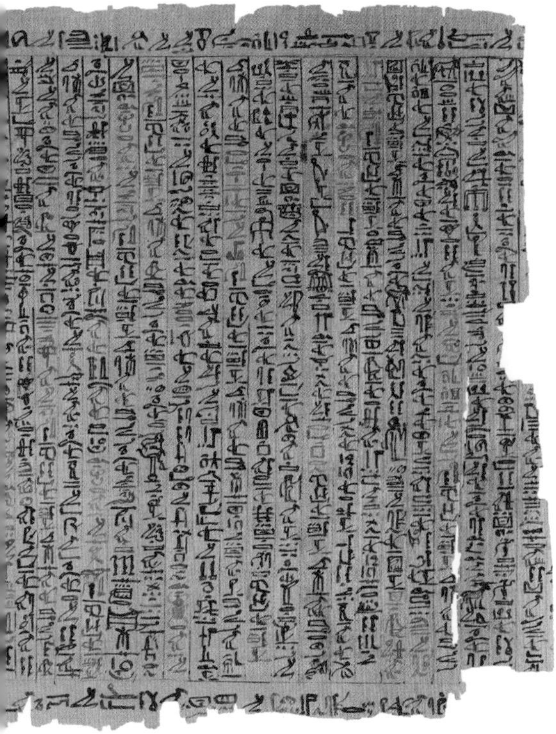

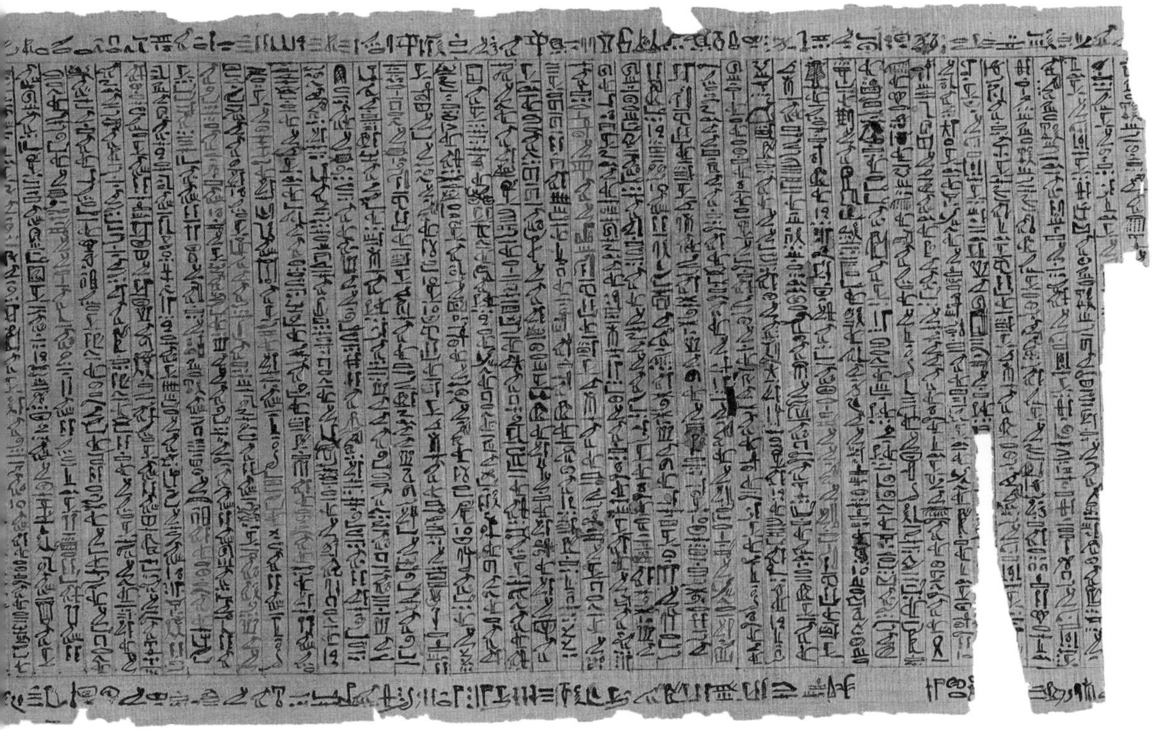

Recto

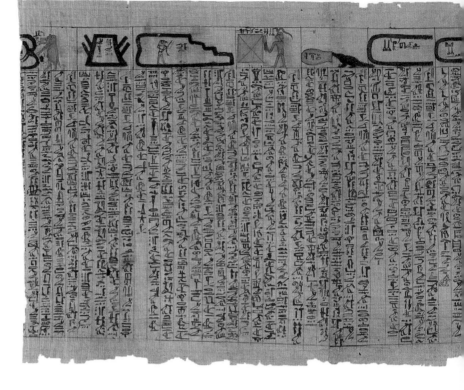

3

4

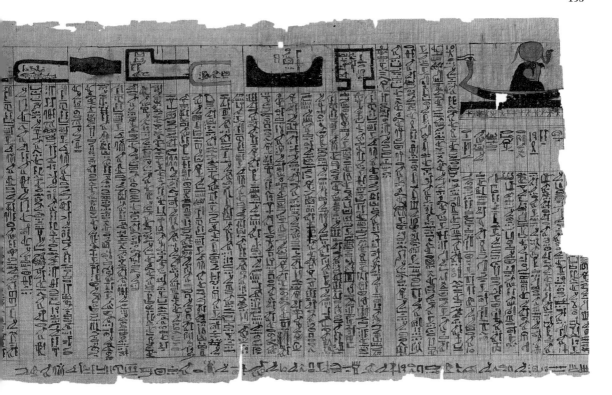

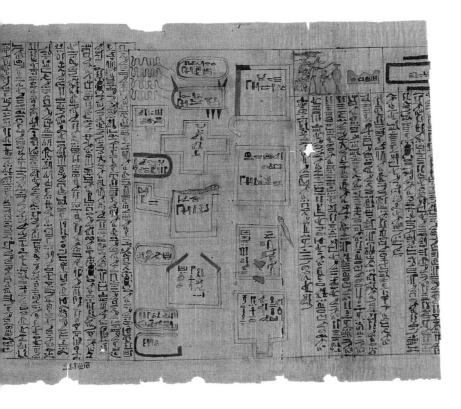

194

Recto

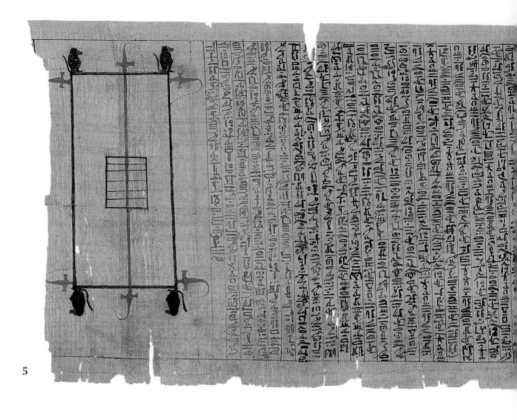

5

6

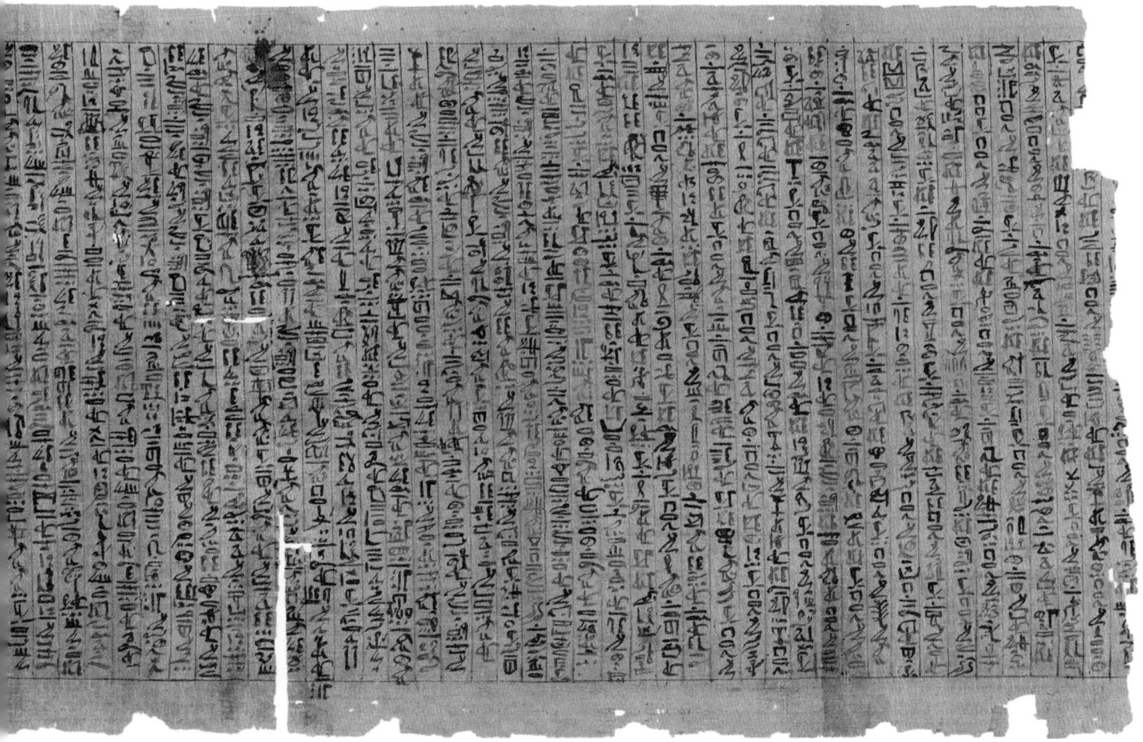

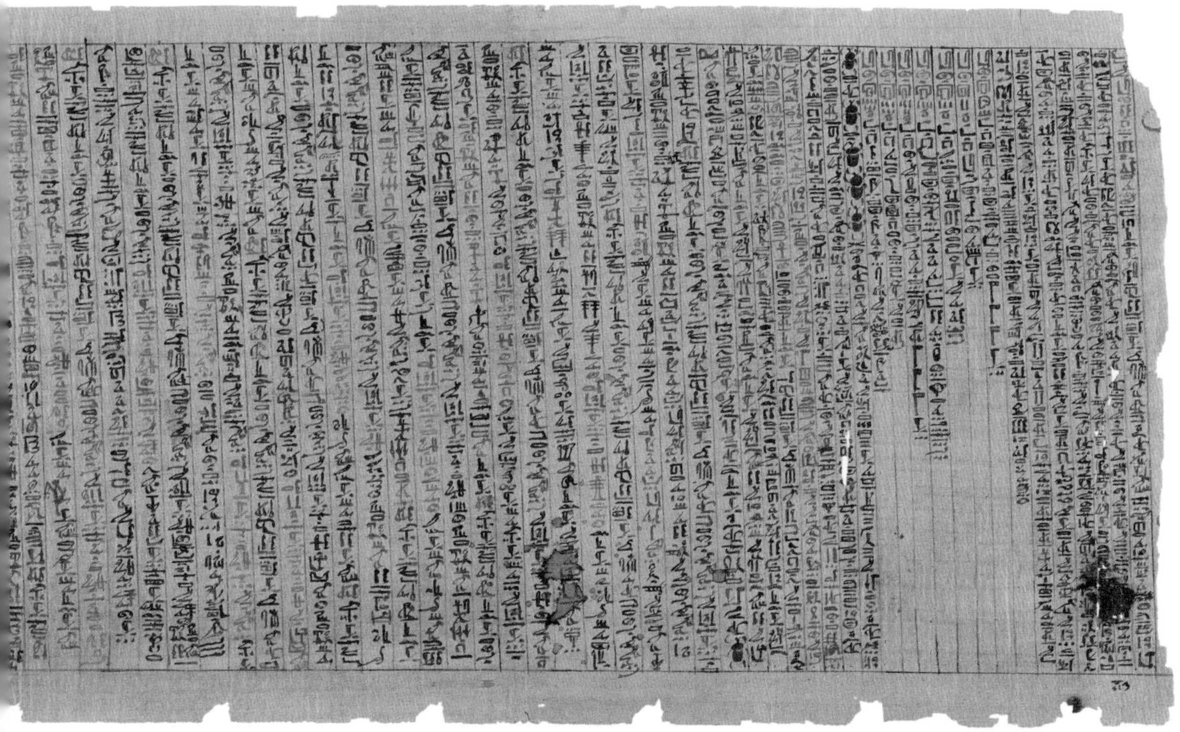

Recto

7

8

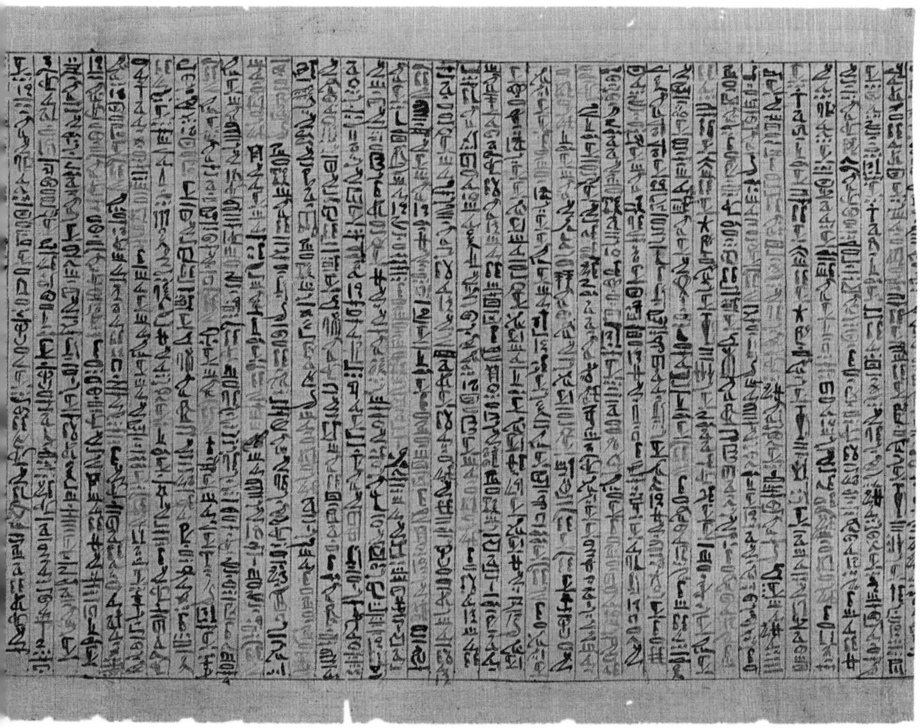

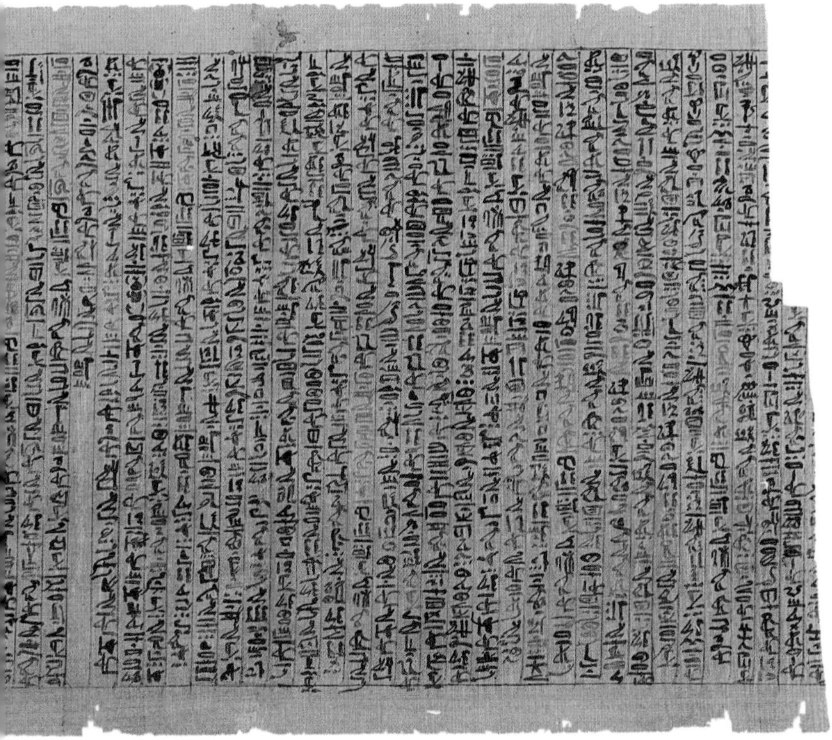

Verso

1

2

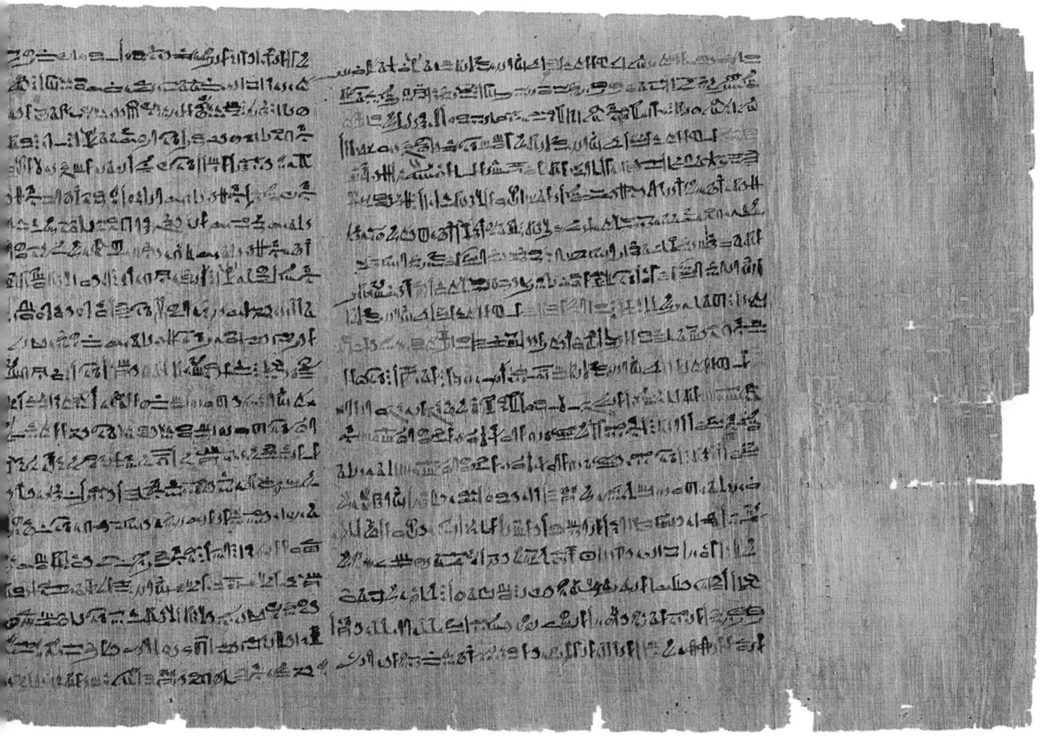

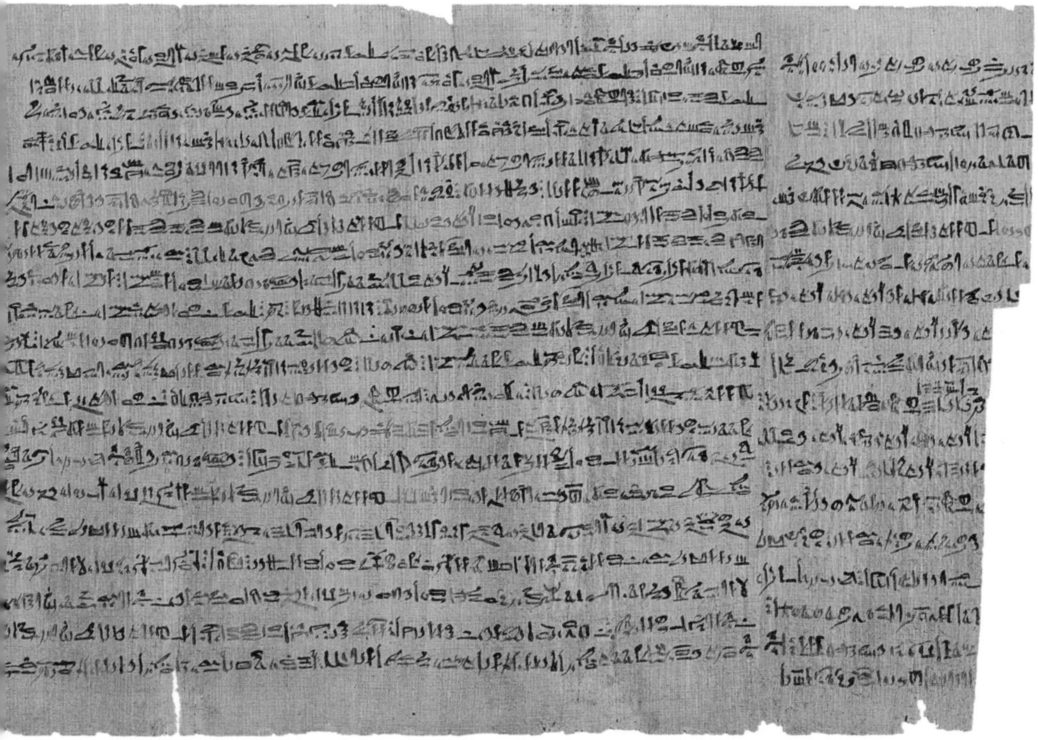

3

4

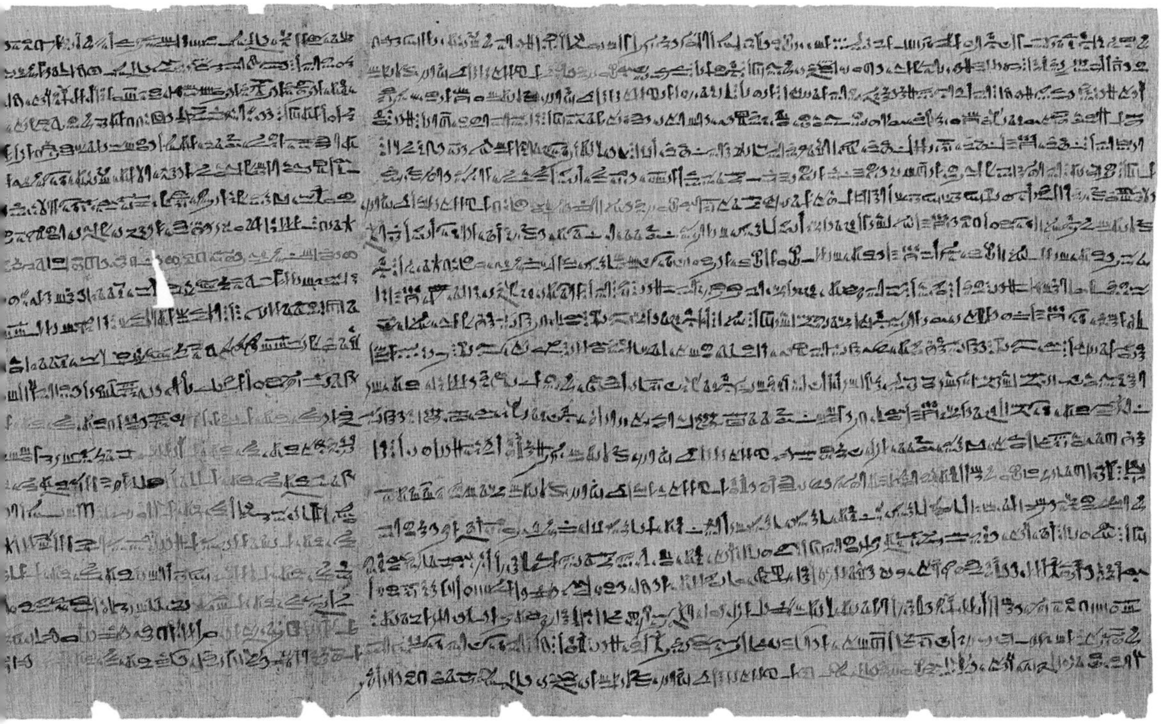

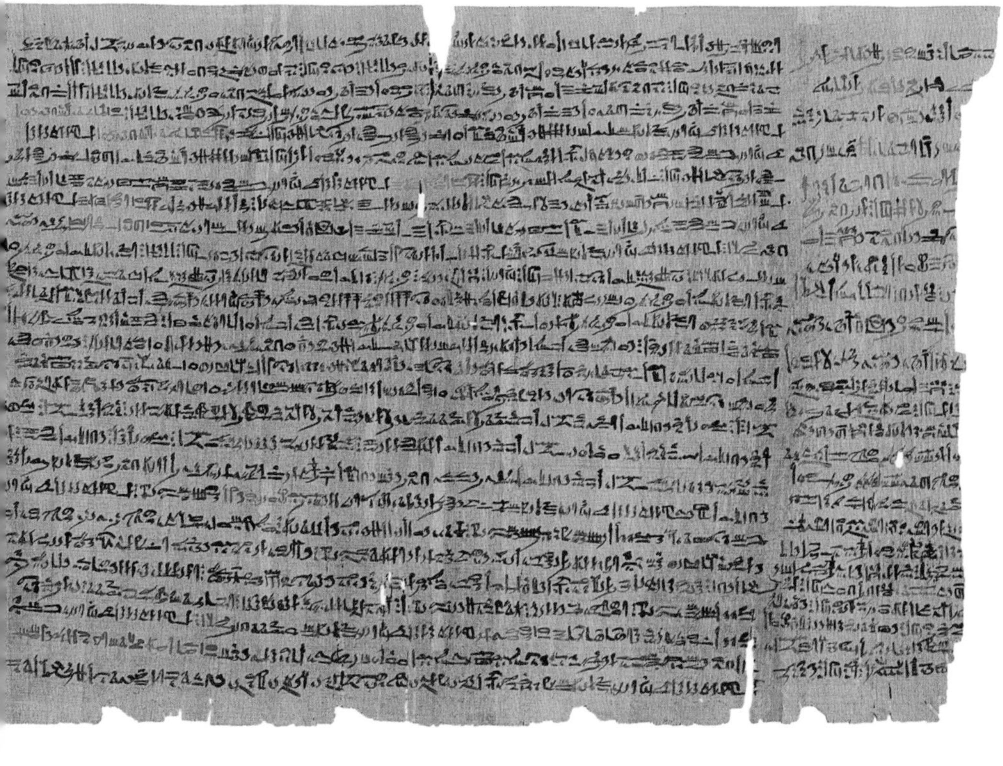

Verso

5

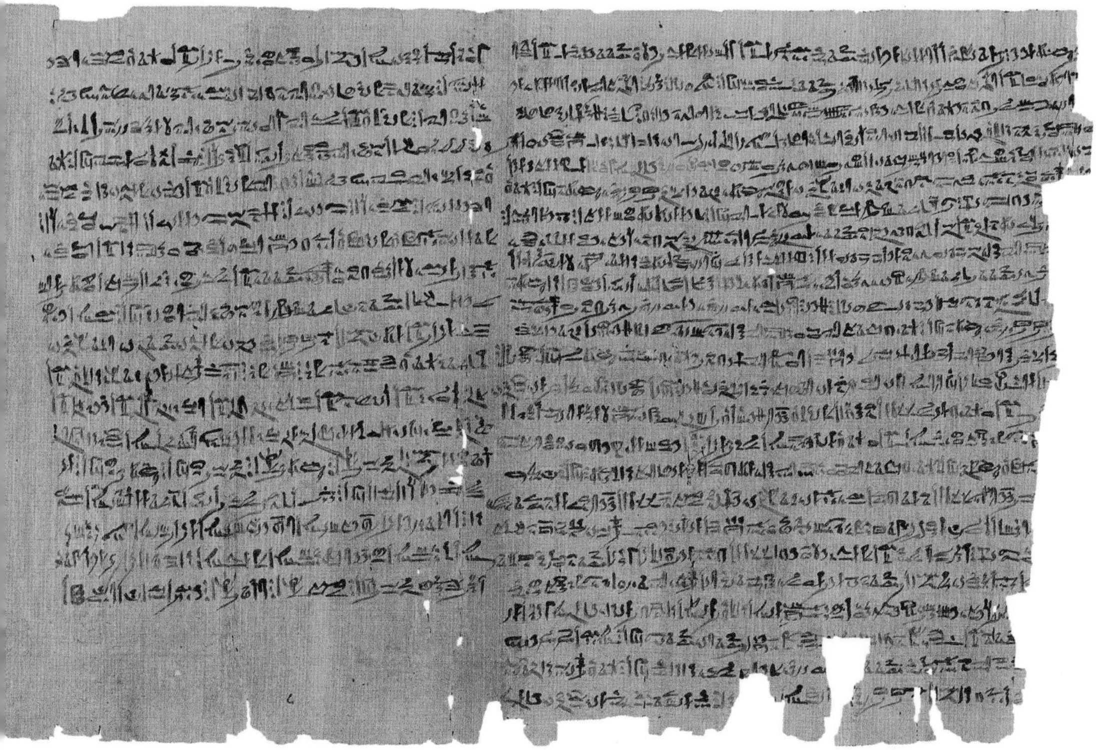

Reference List

⋆ ⋆ ⋆

**Glossary of Egyptian
Terms and Names**

⋆ ⋆ ⋆

**A Brief Chronology
of Ancient Egypt**

⋆ ⋆ ⋆

Picture Information

Reference List

Allen, T.G. 1974
Allen, Thomas George. *The Book of the Dead or Going Forth by Day: Ideas of the Ancient Egyptians Concerning the Hereafter as Expressed in Their Own Terms.* Studies in Ancient Oriental Civilization, 37. Chicago: Oriental Institute of the University of Chicago, 1974.

Allen, J.P. 2000
Allen, James P. *Middle Egyptian: An Introduction to the Language and Culture of Hieroglyphs.* New York: Cambridge University Press, 2000.

Allen, J.P. 2005
Allen, James.P. *The Ancient Egyptian Pyramid Texts.* Atlanta: Society of Biblical Literature, 2005.

Assmann 1995
Assmann, Jan. *Egyptian Solar Religion in the New Kingdom: Re, Amun, and the Crisis of Polytheism.* Translated from the German by Anthony Alcock. Studies in Egyptology 25. London and New York: Kegan Paul, distributed by Columbia University Press, 1995.

Assmann 2005
Assmann, Jan. *Death and Salvation in Ancient Egypt.* Translated from the German by David Lorton. Ithaca, N.Y.: Cornell University Press, 2005.

Backes 2009
Backes, Burkhard. "Was zu sagen ist—zum Gesamttitel des Totenbuchs." In Burkhard Backes, Marcus Müller-Roth, and Simone Stöhr, eds, *Ausgestattet mit den Schriften des Thoth. Festschrift für Irmtraut Munro zu ihrem 65. Geburtstag,* Studien zum Altägyptischen Totenbuch 14. Wiesbaden: Harrassowitz, 2009, pp. 5–27.

Barbash 2011
Barbash, Yekaterina. *The Mortuary Papyrus of Padikakem: Walters Art Museum 551.* Yale Egyptological Studies, 8. New Haven, Conn.: Yale Egyptological Seminar, 2011.

Bickel 1994
Bickel, Susanne. *La cosmogonie égyptienne avant le Nouvel Empire.* Orbis Biblicus et Orientalis 134. Fribourg: Editions Universitaires Fribourg, 1994.

Blackman 1972
Blackman, Aylward M. *Middle-Egyptian Stories.* Bibliotheca Aegyptiaca, 2. Brussels: Fondation Égyptologique Reine Élisabeth, 1972 (reprint of the 1932 edition).

Bleiberg 2008
Bleiberg, Edward. *To Live Forever: Egyptian Treasures from the Brooklyn Museum.* Brooklyn, N.Y.: Brooklyn Museum; London: D. Giles Ltd, 2008.

Borghouts 2010
Borghouts, J.F. *Egyptian: An Introduction to the Writing and Language of the Middle Kingdom.* 2 vols. Leiden: Nederlands Instituut voor het Nabije Oosten; Leuven: Peeters, 2010.

Buck 1935–61
Buck, Adriaan De. *The Egyptian Coffin Texts.* 7 vols. Chicago: Oriental Institute, 1935–61.

Campbell 1967
Campbell, David A. *Greek Lyric Poetry: A Selection of Early Greek Lyric, Elegiac and Iambic Poetry.* New York: St. Martin's Press, 1967.

Černý 1952
Černý, Jaroslav. *Paper and Books in Ancient Egypt: An Inaugural Lecture Delivered at University College, London.* London: H.K. Lewis & Co., 1952. [Publication of a lecture delivered in 1947.]

Clère 1967–68
Clère, J.J. "The Collection of 'Book of the Dead' Papyri in The Brooklyn Museum." *The Brooklyn Museum Annual,* 9 (1967–68), pp. 88–93.

Daumas 1958
Daumas, François. *Les mammisis d'Egypte et de Nubie.* Paris: Société d'édition "Les Belles Lettres," 1958.

de Meulenaere 1977
de Meulenaere, Herman. "Derechef Arensnouphis." *Chronique d'Égypte,* 52 (1977), pp. 245–51.

Dodsen and Ikram 2008
Dodsen, Aidan, and Salima Ikram. *The Tomb in Ancient Egypt: Royal and Private Sepulchres from the Early Dynastic Period to the Romans.* London and New York: Thames & Hudson, 2008.

Dorman 2014
Dorman, Peter A. "Innovation at the Dawn of the New Kingdom." In José M. Galán, Betsy M. Bryan, and Peter F. Dorman, eds, *Creativity and Innovation in the Reign of Hatshepsut.* Studies in Ancient Oriental Civilization, 69. Chicago: Oriental Institute of the University of Chicago, 2014, pp. 1–6.

Englund 1978
Englund, Gertie. *Akh—une notion religieuse dans l'Égypte pharaonique.* Uppsala, Sweden: University of Uppsala, 1978.

Faulkner 1973–78
Faulkner, R.O. *The Ancient Egyptian Coffin Texts.* 3 vols. Warminster: Aris & Phillips Ltd., 1973–78.

Fox 1977
Fox, Michael V. "A Study of Antef." *Orientalia,* 46 (1977), pp. 393–423.

Gaballa 1977
Gaballa, Gaballa A. "Three Acephalous Statues." *Journal of Egyptian Archaeology,* 63 (1977), pp. 122–26.

Gaballa 1979
Gaballa, Gaballa A. "Three Funerary Stelae from the New Kingdom." *Mitteilungen des Deutschen Archäologischen Instituts Kairo,* 35 (1979), pp. 65–83.

Gardiner 1916
Gardiner, Alan H. *Notes on the Story of Sinuhe.* Paris: Librairie Honoré Champion, 1916.

Gardiner 1935
Gardiner, Alan H., ed. *Hieratic Papyri in the British Museum. Third series: Chester Beatty Gift.* 2 vols. London: British Museum, 1935.

Gee 2010
Gee, John. "The Book of the Dead as Canon." *British Museum Studies in Ancient Egypt and Sudan,* 15 (2010), pp. 23–33.

Geisen 2004
Geisen, Christina. *Die Totentexte des verschollenen Sarges der Königin Mentuhotep*

aus der 13. Dynastie: Ein Textzeuge aus der Übergangzeit von den Sargtexten zum Totenbuch. Studien zum Altägyptischen Totenbuch 8. Wiesbaden: Harrassowitz Verlag, 2004.

Gourlay 1979
Gourlay, J.-L., "Trois stèles memphites au musée de Grenoble." *Bulletin de l'Institut Français d'Archéologie Orientale,* 79 (1979), pp. 87–101.

Goyon 1985
Goyon, Jean-Claude. *Les dieux-gardiens et la genèse des temples (d'après les textes égyptiens de l'époque gréco-romaine): les soixante d'Edfou et les soixante-dix-sept dieux de Pharbaethos.* Bibliothèque d'Étude, 93. Cairo: Institut Français d'Archéologie Orientale, 1985.

Hannig 1997
Hannig, Rainer. *Großes Handwörterbuch Ägyptisch-Deutsch: Die Sprache der Pharaonen (2800–950 v. Chr.).* Kulturgeschichte der antiken Welt, 64. 2nd ed., Mainz: Philipp von Zabern, 1997.

Hollis 2008
Hollis, S.T. *The Ancient Egyptian "Tale of Two Brothers": A Mythological, Religious, Literary, and Historico-Political Study.* Oakville, Conn.: Bannerstone, 2008.

Hornung 1983
Hornung, Erik. "Fisch und Vogel: zur altägyptischen Sicht des Menschen." *Eranos Jahrbuch,* 52 (1983), pp. 455–96.

Lapp 1997
Lapp, Günther. *The Papyrus of Nu (BM EA 10477): Catalogue of the Books of the Dead in the British Museum,* vol. 1. London: British Museum Press, 1997.

Lapp 2004
Lapp, Günther. *The Papyrus of Nebseni (BM EA 9900): Catalogue of the Books of the Dead in the British Museum,* vol. 3. London: British Museum Press, 2004.

Leitz 2002
Leitz, Christian, *et al. Lexikon der ägyptischen Götter und Götterbezeichnungen.* 8 vols. Orientalia Louvaniensia Analecta, 110–16, 129. Dudley, Mass.: Peeters, 2002.

Lepsius 1842
Lepsius, Richard. *Das Totenbuch der Ägypter nach dem hieroglyphischen Papyrus in Turin.* Leipzig: G. Wigand, 1842. Reprinted, Osnabrück: Otto Zeller Verlag, 1969.

Lesko 2001
Lesko, Leonard H. "Coffin Texts." In Donald B. Redford, ed., *Oxford Encyclopedia of Ancient Egypt.* New York: Oxford University Press, 2001.

Lucarelli 2006
Lucarelli, Rita. *The Book of the Dead of Gatseshen: Ancient Egyptian Funerary Religion in the 10th Century BC.* Egyptologische Uitgaven, 21. Leiden: Nederlands Instituut voor het Nabije Oosten, 2006.

Lucarelli 2010
Lucarelli, Rita. "Making the Book of the Dead." In John H. Taylor, ed., *Journey Through the Afterlife: Ancient Egyptian Book of the Dead.* Cambridge, Mass.: Harvard University Press; London: British Museum Press, 2010.

Martin and Ryholt 2006
Martin, C.J., and Kim Ryholt. "Put My Funerary Papyrus in My Mummy, Please." *Journal of Egyptian Archaeology,* 92 (2006), pp. 270–74.

McDowell 1999
McDowell, Andrea G. *Village Life in Ancient Egypt: Laundry Lists and Love Songs.* New York: Oxford University Press, 1999.

Meskell 2002
Meskell, Lynn. *Private Life in New Kingdom Egypt.* Princeton, N.J.: Princeton University Press, 2002.

Milde 1991
Milde, Henk. *The Vignettes in the Book of the Dead of Neferrenpet.* Egyptologische Uitgaven, 7. Leiden: Nederlands Instituut voor het Nabije Oosten, 1991.

Mosher 1992
Mosher, Malcolm. "Theban and Memphite Book of the Dead Traditions in the Late Period," *Journal of the American Research Center in Cairo* 29 (1992), pp. 143–72.

Mosher 2001
Mosher, Malcolm. *The Papyrus of Hor: Catalogue of the Books of the Dead in the British Museum,* vol. 2. London: British Museum Press, 2001.

Munro 1988
Munro, Irmtraut. *Untersuchungen zu den Totenbuch-Papyri der 18. Dynastie: Kriterien ihrer Datierung.* London: Kegan Paul, 1988.

Munro 1994
Munro, Irmtraut. *Die Totenbuch-Handschriften der 18. Dynastie im Ägyptischen Museum Cairo.* Wiesbaden: Harrassowitz, 1994.

Munro 1995a
Munro, Irmtraut. *Das Totenbuch des Bak-su (pKM 1970.37/pBrocklehurst) aus der Zeit Amenophis' II.* Wiesbaden: Harrassowitz, 1995.

Munro 1995b
Munro, Irmtraut. *Das Totenbuch des Jah-mes (pLouvre E. 11085) aus der frühen 18. Dynastie.* Wiesbaden: Harrassowitz, 1995.

Munro 2010
Munro, Irmtraut. "The Evolution of the Book of the Dead." In John H. Taylor, ed., *Journey Through the Afterlife: Ancient Egyptian Book of the Dead.* Cambridge, Mass.: Harvard University Press; London: British Museum Press, 2010.

Nunn 1996
Nunn, John F. *Ancient Egyptian Medicine.* Norman, Okla.: University of Oklahoma Press, 1996.

O'Rourke 2014
O'Rourke, Paul F. "The Book of the Dead of Ankhefenkhonsu in Brooklyn." *Studien zur Altägyptischen Kultur,* 43 (2014), pp. 277–314.

O'Rourke 2015
O'Rourke, Paul F. *A Royal Book of Protection of the Late Period.* Yale Egyptological Studies, 9. New Haven, Conn.: Yale Egyptological Institute, 2014.

Quack 2009
Quack, J.F. "Redaktion und Kodifizierung im spätzeitlichen Ägypten. Der Fall des Totenbuches," in J. Schaper (ed.), *Die Textualisierung der Religion.* Forschung zum Alten Testament 62. Tübingen: Mohr Siebeck, 2009, pp. 11–34.

Quirke 2013
Quirke, Stephen. *Going out in Daylight—prt m hrw: The Ancient Egyptian Book of the Dead: Translation, Sources, Meaning.* GHP

Egyptology, 20. London: Golden House Publications, 2013.

Ranke 1935–52
Ranke, Hermann. *Die ägyptischen Personennamen.* 2 vols. Glückstadt: Augustin, 1935–52.

Raver 1997
Raver, Wendy. "The Sad Egyptological Career of Dr Henry Abbott, M.D." *Bulletin of the Egyptological Seminar,* 13 (1997), pp. 39–45.

Robins 1994–95
Robins, Gay. "Women and Children in Peril: Pregnancy, Birth and Infant Mortality in Ancient Egypt." *Kmt: A Modern Journal of Ancient Egypt,* 5, no. 4 (Winter 1994–95), pp. 24–35.

Robinson 2014
Robinson, James T. "Samuel Ibn Tibbon." *The Stanford Encyclopedia of Philosophy* (Summer 2014 Edition), Edward N. Zalta, ed., http://plato.stanford.edu/archives/sum2014/entries/tibbon/

Saleh 1984
Saleh, Mohamed. *Das Totenbuch in den thebanischen Beamtengräbern des Neuen-Reiches: Text und Vignetten.* Mainz am Rhein: von Zabern, 1984.

Sayed 1977
Sayed, A.M.A.H. "Discovery of the Site of the 12th Dynasty Port at Wadi Gawasis on the Red Sea Shore." *Revue d'Égyptologie,* 29 (1977), pp. 138–78.

Schott 1978
Schott, Erika. "Das Goldhaus im Grab des Nefer-Renpet." *Göttinger Miszellen,* 29 (1978), pp. 127–32.

Sethe 1908–22
Sethe, Kurt. *Die altägyptischen Pyramidentexte nach den Papierabdrücken und Photographien des Berliner Museums: Neu herausgegeben und erläutert.* 4 vols. Leipzig: J.C. Hinrichs, 1908–22.

Shafer 1991
Shafer, Byron E., ed. *Religion in Ancient Egypt: Gods, Myths, and Personal Practice.* Contributions by John Baines, Leonard H. Lesko, David P. Silverman. Ithaca, N.Y.: Cornell University Press, 1991.

Simpson 1979
Simpson, W.K. "Two Stelae of the Overseer of the Goldworkers of Amun, Amunemhab, at Yale and the Oriental Institute." *Bulletin of the Egyptological Seminar,* 1 (1979), pp. 47–54.

Smith 2006
Smith, Mark. "Osiris NN or Osiris of NN?" In Burkhard Backes, Irmtraut Munro, and Simone Stöhr, eds, *Totenbuch-Forschungen: Gesammelte Beiträge des 2. Internationalen Totenbuch-Symposiums 2005.* Studien zum Altägyptischen Totenbuch 11. Wiesbaden: Harrassowitz Verlag, 2006, pp. 325–37.

Svenbro 1993
Svenbro, Jesper. *Phrasikleia: An Anthropology of Reading in Ancient Greece.* Ithaca, N.Y.: Cornell University Press, 1993.

Taylor 2001
Taylor, John H. *Death and the Afterlife in Ancient Egypt.* Chicago: University of Chicago Press, 2001.

Taylor 2010
Taylor, John H., ed. *Journey Through the Afterlife: Ancient Egyptian Book of the Dead.* Cambridge, Mass.: Harvard University Press; London: British Museum Press, 2010.

Thompson 1992
Thompson, Jason. *Sir Gardner Wilkinson and His Circle.* Austin: University of Texas Press, 1992.

Turner 1980
Turner, E.G. *Greek Papyri: An Introduction.* 2nd ed., Oxford: Clarendon Press, 1980.

Vercoutter 1959
Vercoutter, Jacques. "The Gold of Kush: Two Gold-washing Stations at Faras East." *Kush,* 7 (1959), pp. 120–53.

Von Dassow 1994
Von Dassow, Eva, ed. *The Egyptian Book of the Dead: The Book of Going Forth by Day; The Complete Papyrus of Ani Featuring Integrated Text and Full-Color Images.* Translated by Raymond O. Faulkner. Preface by Carol Andrews. Introduction by Ogden Goelet. San Francisco: Chronicle Books, 1994.

Wb
Erman, Adolf, and Herman Grapow. *Wörterbuch der ägyptische Sprache.* 7 vols. Berlin: Akademie-Verlag, 1926–31.

Žába 1956
Žába, Zbyněk. *Les maximes de Ptahhotep.* Prague: Editions de l'Academie Tchécoslovaque des Sciences, 1956.

Zandee 1992
Zandee, Jan. *Der Amunhymnus des Papyrus Leiden I 344, verso 1-3: Collections of the National Museum of Antiquities at Leiden,* vol. 7. Leiden: Rijksmuseum van Oudheden, 1992.

Glossary of Egyptian
Terms and Names

In this book, specialized terms are generally defined at first use. This list includes a selection of key technical terms, divine symbols, divine epithets, place names, and the names of gods.

Abydos. Al-Araba al-Madfuna in Middle Egypt. Principal cult place of Osiris, and thought to be the site of his burial. Important temples were built there by Seti I and Ramesses II (1306–1224 BCE).

Aker. Divine personification of the earth; supported and carried the solar boat through the night. Often depicted as a large snake.

akh. The spiritualized, transfigured being that the deceased becomes after reintegration through the process of mummification and the proper carrying out of funerary rites and successful passing of judgment.

akh-iqer. A particularly efficacious form of an *akh* for whom no obstacles are impassable.

Akhby-gods. A name of primordial gods found in both the Coffin Texts and the Book of the Dead. Their name means, literally, the "Gulpers."

Amarna Period (*c.* 1353–1335 BCE). A designation of the reign of the pharaoh Akhenaten (Amenhotep IV) of the late New Kingdom, during which period the traditional religious practices of Egypt were replaced by a new one emphasizing the supremacy of the solar-disk to the exclusion of all other deities.

Amduat. A funerary text whose title means "That Which Is in the Netherworld." The scenes and texts of the Amduat record the journey of the sun through the Netherworld during the twelve hours of the night.

amulet. Any object believed to be endowed with magically protective power. Egyptian amulets range from scarabs to images of animals, deities, or human body parts. For example, a roll of papyrus, like a Book of the Dead, was believed to play an amuletic role.

Anedjti. Local god of Busiris connected with rulership and fertility; closely associated with Osiris from early on.

Anedjty. The 9th *nome* (or district) of Lower Egypt; its capital was Busiris.

Anu. The 8th *nome* (or district) of Lower Egypt.

Anubis. A god portrayed with the head of a jackal. Associated with the embalming rituals and the cemetery. Responsible for the embalming of Osiris and, in tandem with Isis, responsible for the revivification of that god as well.

Apophis. The archenemy of the sun-god in the form of a giant serpent who attempts to swallow the solar-disk as it makes its journey through the night sky.

Asiut. Capital of 13th *nome* (or district) of Upper Egypt; site of important tombs dating to the First Intermediate Period–Middle Kingdom (2134–1640 BCE), a number of which had coffins inscribed with Coffin Texts.

atef-crown. Feathered crown worn by gods and particularly associated with Osiris. It endowed its wearer with the power to terrorize those he encountered.

Aten. The divine personification of the solar-disk. In the Amarna Period (*c.* 1353–1335 BCE), the designation of the sole god of Akhenaten's solar religion, or "religion of light."

Atum. A divine name meaning the "Complete(d) One." Used as one of the names of the creator-god and also to designate the solar-disk at its setting.

ba. One of the physical constituent elements of a person or animal. It continued to live after death, when the *ba* and the corpse were partners in a cycle of regeneration much like the solar cycle to which they were also linked. Commonly portrayed as a human-headed bird.

Baba. Called the "elder son" of Osiris; found in contexts of diminished virility and vital strength and often in the company of the Weary Ones.

Bah. A word for flood; often used as the personification of the Inundation, the annual flooding of the Nile.

Bastet. Chief goddess of the site of Tell Basta in the Delta. She was a lion-headed deity associated with the Eye of Re, the dangerous and protective *uraeus* on the brow of the sun-god.

Behbeit. Site of one of the most important temples to Isis, built and decorated by the kings of the Thirtieth Dynasty (380–

343 BCE) and the early Ptolemaic rulers (305–221 BCE).

Bekhu. A mythological region whose name means "mountains."

benu-stone. The triangular-shaped capstone atop a pyramid or obelisk.

Bull of the West. A mythical being associated with the Seven Hathors, the goddesses connected with the fates of each individual. He was represented as a bull in the sky and called "Lord of Eternity."

buri-fish. A fish believed to swim at the prow of the solar boat as a guide and protector.

Busiris. Capital of the 9th *nome* (or district) of Lower Egypt; cult site of Osiris, Isis, and Horus Khenty-irty.

Buto. The ancient Greek name of a place in the Delta now known as Tell al-Fara'in. Made up of the two towns of Pe and Dep, the site came to be called Per-Wadjet after these merged.

canopic chests/jars. The containers in which were stored the various organs removed during the process of mummification.

coda. The closing section of an Egyptian text. Like a text heading, it is often written in red (rubrics).

Coptic. The final stage of written and spoken Egyptian (*c.* third through eighth centuries CE), when texts were written in the borrowed letters of the Greek alphabet and several additional signs. The term Coptic Egypt is sometimes used to refer to Christian Egypt before the Islamic conquest.

cursive hieroglyphs. A specialized hieroglyphic writing used first in the Coffin Texts and then in the Books of the Dead of the New Kingdom. Essentially, it was used only in the writing of these kinds of texts.

demotic. The penultimate stage of the ancient Egyptian language (seventh century BCE to third–fourth centuries CE). Also, the cursive form of writing used for non-religious texts during that period.

Dep. Tell al-Fara'in in the Delta. Part of the ancient town of Buto; cult site of the goddess Wadjet, chief goddess of Lower

Egypt. Commonly appears paired with the place name Pe.

determinative. An Egyptian sign that has no sound value in the writing of a word but gives a visual reference. It helps associate a written word with a class of words that share features indicated by the sign.

djed-**pillar.** A hieroglyph depicting a pillar with horizontal cross-bars at the top. It is commonly used in the writing of the word *djed* (which means "stability"). As a symbol it has close associations with the god Osiris and is believed to represent his backbone.

Djedet. Tell el-Rub'a and Tell el-Timai in the northern Delta. Site of ancient Mendes.

Djedu. Abusir in the northern Delta. The principal cult center of Osiris in Lower Egypt.

dom-**palm.** A tree that grows only in Upper Egypt. Its fruit has often been found in ancient Egyptian tombs.

Double Crown. A composite crown consisting of the White Crown of Upper Egypt surmounting the Red Crown of Lower Egypt. The Egyptian name for this crown is *sekhemty*, a word that has clear connections with the Egyptian word *sekhem* which means "power."

Duat. The most widely used name for the Egyptian Netherworld.

Elders. A term often encountered in funerary texts. Used to describe the ancestral dead.

Elephantine. Capital of the 1st *nome* (or district) of Upper Egypt. Cult site of Khnum, Satis, and Anukis, deities associated with the annual Inundation, among other things.

emmer-**wheat.** A hulled wheat whose wild form was widespread in the ancient Near East. It became domesticated early, evidence for which reaches back almost to ten thousand BCE in Syria. It was common in Egypt and is usually paired in texts with barley.

Ennead. A word meaning "nine." Used to designate groups of gods collectively, usually those of a given cult site. As the number nine is three times three, the word also designated an immeasurable number; "three threes" essentially means "the plural of plurals" in Egyptian thought. Thus, in certain contexts it means "all of the gods."

exemplar. An individual manuscript that belongs to a certain textual genre.

Eye of Horus. The god's eye that was damaged in his battle with Seth and magically restored by Thoth. As such, it came to represent the moon and its lunar cycle. In the New Kingdom it becomes closely associated with the Eye of Re.

Eye of Re. A divine power associated with Hathor and other lion-headed goddesses, such as Sakhmet and Bastet. Hathor was the destructive power of the sun-god manifest in the fiery heat of late spring and early summer; in her appeased form she is the protective *uraeus* on the brow of Re.

Fenkhu-people. Certain inhabitants of Syria and Palestine, erroneously connected to the Phoenicians. The word may also designate woodworkers who were either carpenters or shipbuilders.

Field of Reeds. A mythical realm whose name designates one of the goals of the deceased, as it seems to have been considered one of the important places in the Netherworld that allowed the deceased to "enter and go forth."

Four Sons of Horus. Four protective deities associated with the cardinal geographical points. As early as the Pyramid Texts, they served to protect and guide the king in the hereafter; by the New Kingdom, their role was largely protection. They are often represented on the sides of coffins. Canopic jars containing the mummified viscera of the deceased begin to be topped with their heads in the New Kingdom.

Geb. Personification of the earth who received the dead but also played roles like the "earth-shaker." In later mythology, he became the champion of Horus, who rightfully installed him on the throne of his father Osiris.

Great God. An epithet commonly used of Osiris.

Great of Magic. *Heka* ("magic") was considered a primal force and played an important role in creation. The epithet Great of Magic was commonly assigned to Sakhmet and other lion-headed goddesses.

Guey. An important religious site in the central Delta.

Haker-festival. A festival associated with planting that took place in the fall, after the Inundation had receded.

Hapi. Personification of the annual Nile flood who brings life-giving water and new land with each Inundation.

Hathor. A name that means "House of Horus," a reference either to the womb of the goddess, in which she carried the unborn Horus, or more likely, the sky in which Horus in falcon form flew. In early mythology, Hathor is the mother of Horus, a role taken over later by Isis; she is also a daughter of the sun-god and plays the important role of the *Eye of Re* (see above). She was also associated with fertility and the divine gift of drunkenness.

Hedjedjet. An Egyptian goddess whose manifestation was typically a scorpion. Texts describe her as the daughter of Re.

Heqa-andju. Capital of the Heliopolitan *nome* (or district).

Heliopolis. Located northeast of modern Cairo, it was the most important cult site of the sun-god Re.

hem-netjer **priest.** Lit., "servant of the god." The term designates a large class of priests in ancient Egypt.

heqat-**measure.** A unit of dry measure; about 4.5 liters.

Herakleopolis. Capital of the 20th *nome* (or district) of Lower Egypt whose ancient name was Hut-nen-nesu ("Mansion of the Royal Child"). Cult center of the god Heryshef.

Hermopolis. Tuna el-Gebel in Middle Egypt. An important cult site of the god Thoth.

hieratic. A cursive form of writing that developed from hieroglyphic writing during the Old Kingdom. Hieratic quickly underwent its own development, and by the Middle Kingdom (2040–1786 BCE) its signs bore little resemblance to the hieroglyphs from which they derived. Developed for and used in administrative texts, hieratic became the script of choice for literary texts beginning in the Middle Kingdom. It was also used for writing Coffin Texts.

Horakhty. Horus of the Two Horizons, an epithet of the sun-god Re in his aspect of the solar deity who rises at dawn from the eastern horizon and sets in the western one.

Horus. In early thought, a solar deity, as his name (the "One Above") indicates. Also the son of Isis and Osiris and subsequently the adversary of Seth, his uncle (or, in some texts, brother), in the struggle for the rightful claim to the throne of Osiris. The kings of Egypt were believed to be human incarnations of this god.

Horus Khenty-irty/Horus Mekhenty-irty. An aspect of Horus as both a god who can see and a god who is blind. His dual aspect stems from his role of solar deity, his sight and blindness referring to the sun and moon, respectively; thus his dual nature has a benign as well as a malign aspect. His cult center was Letopolis.

Hut-Iahut (*ḥwt-iˁḥt*): Lit., "Mansion of the Moon"; geographical location unknown.

ias (*iꜣs*) **priest.** A priest of Hathor often depicted with a shaved head and at times as a squatting beggar.

Ibka. A divine name or epithet that has been variously interpreted. Some think that it designated Seth in his manifestation as a boar.

Igeret. An ancient name of the Netherworld.

Ihy. The son of Hathor (in some traditions, the son of Isis or Nephthys or Sakhmet).

*ima***-tree.** The Egyptian name of the tree *Zizyphus vulgaris* or *Zizyphus sativa*, all of whose parts have medicinal uses.

Imhet. Another name for the Netherworld. Originally the name of a necropolis situated between modern Helwan and Cairo.

Imperishable Stars. The circumpolar stars that never set below the horizon (see *Unwearying Stars).*

Imsety. One of the four sons of Horus (see *Four Sons of Horus*).

Imu. Kom el-Hisn, in the western Delta.

Inert One. An epithet of both Osiris and the solar deity in their nighttime manifestations.

Inundation. The annual flood of the Nile that historically began in late June and continued through September, when the flood waters began to recede, a process that lasted until mid-November. The modern High Dam built at Aswan in southern Egypt now prevents an annual flood as the ancient Egyptians knew it.

Isdes. A deity usually identified as the "Lord of the West"; portrayed as a dog-headed divinity and associated with Thoth as the messenger of the gods.

*ished***-tree.** A sacred tree located in or associated with Heliopolis. It had particular connections with kingship as the name of each king was written on its leaves.

Isis. Consort of Osiris and mother of Horus. With Anubis, she was responsible for the revivification of the murdered Osiris.

Island of Fire (Island of Flames). A location in the Netherworld situated presumably near the eastern horizon, the general area of the activity of the rising sun. It also had associations with the cosmic battle that took place before dawn.

Iunmutef. Lit., "Pillar of His Mother." A manifestation of Horus as the son who initiates his deceased father into the social community of the *akhs*, the transfigured ancestral spirits. The son carries out certain funerary rituals daily after the burial and is responsible as well for the memorial chapel of his father.

ka. A non-physical, spiritual constituent element of a human created at the same time as the physical self. The symbiotic relationship between the *ka* and the body was broken at death and needed to be restored again, in a different form, through ritual. (In the Egyptian worldview, life is integration, community, and interaction, while death is not only decay but also isolation and the dissolution of social bonds.) The restored *ka* returns to the original social sphere, that of the dead ancestors; one's *ka* is one's individual identity as well as one's identity as a member of a family or specialized group, such as kings.

Kem-wer. The name of three places in ancient Egypt: Lake Timsah in the Delta; the 10th *nome* (or district) of Lower Egypt; and Athribis (Tell Atrib), an important site in the Delta.

Khenty-imentyu. Lit., "Foremost One of the Westerners." An ancient name or epithet of Osiris.

Khenty-khas. Lit., "Foremost One of Xoïs."

Khepri. Lit., the "One Coming into Being." He had solar connections as the sun at its rising and, thus, strong ties to the theme of resurrection and regeneration.

Kheraha. The name of a district of modern-day Old Cairo. It was the site of a cosmic conflict in ancient Egyptian religious and mythological thought.

Khnum. A god whose main center of worship was Elephantine Island, thought by the Egyptians to be the source of the Inundation. Khnum was also a creator-god most closely associated with the act of physically creating from matter; thus, he is commonly shown creating humans, most typically the king, on a potter's wheel.

Khonsu. A deity with lunar associations; often shown as a child god—the son of Amun and Mut or Ptah and Sakhmet. A potentially dangerous god like his mother Sakhmet, he also played the role of protector against dangerous animals, such as scorpions, snakes, and crocodiles.

*lector***-priest.** The priest who oversees the carrying out of sacred rituals. In representations, he is often depicted reading from a papyrus roll.

Letopolis. Another cult site associated with Osiris, especially as the site of the reliquary of the left shoulder of the god. Capital of the 2nd *nome* of Lower Egypt.

Lord of All. An epithet of the creator-god Atum, whose name means the "Complete(d) One."

Maat. Personification of truth and cosmic order; later thought to be the daughter of the sun-god Re. Her name is often written with the hieroglyph, pronounced much like her name.

Mafdet. A goddess portrayed as a cat or mongoose who was the protector of the sun-god Re as early as the Old Kingdom. She is often found in texts dealing with protection from snakes.

Maxims of Ptahhotep. One of the earliest wisdom books known from ancient Egypt; it comprises several hundred aphorisms for Egyptian officials that address comportment in contexts like listening to petitioners, and proper behavior in the presence of superiors, peers, or inferiors.

Mehet-weret. Lit., "Great Flood." Another personification of the Inundation or the primeval waters from which the creator-god emerged. Portrayed as a large cow.

Memphis. Capital of ancient Egypt. In the Old Kingdom it was the site of the "ideal" necropolis with its tutelary god Sokar, who was associated with the fertility principles of the Netherworld. Also the site of the procession of the *henu*-bark, the sacred boat of Sokar that had the shape of a crescent moon.

Mesqet. An uncertain area of the night sky formerly thought to correspond to the Milky Way. It is the region of the east through which the celestial bodies pass in their risings. It is also one the areas of the heavens that the deceased is said to travel through.

Min. Local deity of Coptos in Middle Egypt. Portrayed as an ithyphallic mummiform figure holding a flail behind him. He had associations with fertility and vegetation.

*moringa***-oil.** An oil made from pressing the seeds of *Moringa oleifera*, a deciduous tree that grows in tropical and semitropical regions. Commonly found in Egyptian tombs, the oil was believed to reverse aging. It continues to be used today as a remedy for dry and wrinkled skin and as a food supplement.

Naref. Originally the name of a necropolis in the 20th *nome* (or district) of Upper Egypt.

Nedjefty. The name of two different sites in Upper Egypt.

Nefertem. Son of Ptah and Sakhmet. Portrayed as a lion, a lion-headed god, or a human with a lotus blossom on his head. He had particular connections with the New Year and New Year festivals.

Nehebkau. A deity associated with the Netherworld, believed to be a guardian of the entrance of the Duat. Portrayed as a snake with two heads who protected the sun-god during his nocturnal journey through the Netherworld.

nemes-**cloth.** A head-cloth that was a distinct sign of royalty. In representations it has alternating gold and dark blue stripes and lappets that hang down onto the upper part of the chest.

Nephthys. Daughter of Nut and Geb and sister of Isis, with whom she is often paired as protector and guide of her dead brother Osiris.

night-boat. The solar boat that the sun-god travels in during his nightly journey through the Netherworld.

nome. A Greek word used to describe each of the forty-two territorial divisions that collectively made up ancient Egypt.

Nun. The primeval waters of the pre-creation cosmos. It was the matrix in which and from which all creation took place. As a deity, Nun was considered to be the father of the gods and in texts is often called "the Eldest."

Nut. Personification and embodiment of the sky. Often portrayed as an outstretched female being held aloft by the god Shu, the embodiment of the land, and giving birth to the solar-disk. She had close associations with the goddess Hathor.

offering formula. A fixed text or prayer that accompanied an offering ritual in a temple or a tomb. Such a text, if used on a Book of the Dead, was usually inscribed on the verso.

Orion. The Egyptian constellation Sah (*s3ḥ*), closely associated with Osiris. In Egypt this constellation disappears from the night sky for seventy days each year, the same period of time during which the body of Osiris (and the deceased) was hidden in the House of Purification while it went through the embalming rituals.

Osiris. Son of Geb and Nut and one of the original kings of Egypt. He was murdered and dismembered by his brother Seth in an attempt to seize the kingship; he was subsequently magically revived by Isis with the aid of Anubis (and, in some texts, Thoth), who then mummified him in an act of reunification and transformation. He became the ruler of the Netherworld.

ostracon/ostraca: Fragment(s), as of pottery, containing an inscription.

Pe. Tell al-Fara'in in the Delta. Part of the ancient town of Buto; cult site of the deity Wadjet, chief goddess of Lower Egypt.

Penty. A little-known deity mentioned in Coffin Text 640.

Pesdjet-festival. A festival held on the day of the new moon.

phoenix. In Egyptian creation myths, the phoenix, or *benu*-bird, was the *ba* of Re, the god who created himself.

phyle. A Greek word denoting a tribe or group of people who share kinship connections. In Egyptian studies, it refers to groups of priests who share responsibilities in a religious association. Priests of a designated *phyle* performed the same services, and served in the temple on a rotating basis. A typical period of temple service for a member of a priestly *phyle* was fifteen consecutive days per year.

Ptah. Chief deity of the Memphite region. In certain traditions he was a creator-god who called the elements of the cosmos into being through the act of divine utterance.

Qebusenef. One of the sons of Horus (see *Four Sons of Horus*).

Re. Personification of the sun who crossed the sky each day in a solar boat and then traveled back through the night sky on his night-boat. During the nocturnal journey he was forced to defend himself against the attacks of Apophis, a huge snake who was his archenemy. In certain creation myths, he was the original creator-god who created himself in and from the Nun. He was also the original king on earth. In the New Kingdom he became closely associated with Osiris, and as a pair they represented a cycle of life, death, and rebirth.

Re-Horakhty. The name means "Re-Horus of the Two Horizons." As a merging of the two gods, Re-Horakhty became the embodiment of the daily solar cycle, the two horizons referring to the places of the rising and setting sun.

recto. The side of a sheet or roll of papyrus on which the fibers of the top layer lie horizontally. The recto was the preferred side of a papyrus roll on which to write a text.

Renennutet. A deity associated with the harvest and, thus, nourishment. She was one of four protective goddesses connected with birth and the safety of the newborn. Portrayed as a cobra or cobra-headed goddess.

Rerek. A snake who poses a threat to the deceased in the Netherworld and who is neutralized by the deity Mafdet.

retrograde writing. A form of writing used in some Books of the Dead in which the order of signs appears to read from right to left but the text itself reads from left to right.

Ring of Fire. One of the dangerous locations in the Netherworld that the deceased has to pass by.

Rosetau. A mysterious place in the Netherworld associated with the embalming of the god Osiris. Commonly used as a designation or even name of the Netherworld.

Ruty. Lit., the "Double Lions." Portrayed as two lions who sit back-to-back. Originally represented Tefnut and Shu; later became associated with the edges of the eastern and western deserts and, thus, with the two horizons.

Sais. Modern Sa el-Hagar in the western Delta. Capital of the 5th *nome* (or district) of Lower Egypt. Cult site of the goddess Neith.

Sakhmet. A lion-headed deity originally connected with the Memphite region. She came to be one of the goddesses known as the Eye of Re; as such she was the personification of the sun's potentially destructive power. She also had strong associations with magic, both as a force that threatened and one that had curative powers as well.

Saqqara. Name of the necropolis of the ancient Egyptian capital Memphis.

Sebeg. The Egyptian name of the planet Mercury.

sefet-**oil.** An oil used in rituals and commonly found in lists of offerings made to the deceased.

sem-**priest/***setem*-**priest.** A priest originally associated with the cult of Ptah in Memphis. In funerary rituals, this priest performs the ceremony of the "Opening of the Mouth" of the mummy, a rite that serves to revitalize the deceased. In depictions of this scene in tombs and on papyri, it is often the son of the deceased who performs this function.

Sepa. An Egyptian god, depicted as a centipede, whose cult center was located in Heliopolis. The word is also the name of a site near Heliopolis.

sequence. A group of texts in a Book of the Dead that appear together and in a set order.

Seshat. A goddess associated with writing and the transmission of knowledge and information.

Seshty. A site located near Heliopolis in Lower Egypt. It has been variously translated as "Two Banks," "Bird-Pond," and "Washerman's Shores."

Seth. One of the personifications of chaos within the system of cosmic order. He murdered his brother Osiris and fought with Horus, in battle and in court, over the claim to the earthly throne of the dead Osiris.

shabti. A small funerary figurine included in the burial and believed to aid the deceased in the performance of certain tasks, such as labor imposed on him in the Netherworld. The word appears also as *shawabti* and *ushabti.*

Shesmu. A deity associated with wine and oil, two liquids extracted by means of a press. He also functioned as a henchman of Osiris in his guise as judge of the dead.

Shetyt. The sanctuary of Sokar in Memphis.

Shu. The divinity who personified sunlight. He was also believed to lift the goddess Nut (the sky) apart from her consort Geb (the earth).

Sobek. A god associated with the Faiyum and typically portrayed as a crocodile or crocodile-headed deity. His obvious connections with the Nile led to his portrayal as a creator-god and one of fertility, particularly in his capacity of "greening" the fields.

Sokar. A fertility-god originally associated with the area of Memphis. He became associated early on with Osiris as a god of the Netherworld. Often portrayed as a falcon or as a falcon-headed deity.

solar boats. A number of different terms occur in Egyptian texts that refer to the boat in which the sun-god travels through the sky by day and the Netherworld by night. These terms have been thought to designate different boats, but it may be that they actually designate a single boat and are used individually to locate the boat in either the day or night sky.

Sound Eye. The damaged Eye of Horus magically restored by Thoth (see *Wadjet*).

stela. A carved or inscribed stone or wooden slab used for commemorative purposes.

Tale of Sinuhe. A literary story known from a number of copies in the Middle and New Kingdoms. It tells of a man who flees Egypt, becomes well established and successful in Syria, but who then longs to return to Egypt to receive a proper Egyptian burial.

Tayt. A goddess associated with weaving and thus the production of linen cloth used in the process of mummification.

Tefnut. The daughter of the sun-god Re who personified the night sky. She was the consort of Geb, the personification of the earth.

Tekem. A name of the manifestation of Osiris in the unified Re-Osiris; thus, he was associated with the two horizons.

Tenenet. A sanctuary in Memphis.

Teshtesh-figure. An allusion to the dismembered Osiris.

Thebes. An important religious center in southern Egypt. The temple of Karnak, the major sanctuary of the god Amun, rose to great eminence in the New Kingdom and retained its standing until late in Egyptian history.

Thoth. An Egyptian deity closely associated with knowledge and wisdom, particularly as conveyed in writing. It was believed that, at the time of creation, he wrote down all of the words uttered by the creator-god, an act that ensured their permanence. He had strong connections with the god Osiris and played a major role in bringing him back from the dead. Often depicted as a human figure with the head of an ibis: in the vignette that typically occurs with Chapter 125 of the Book of the Dead, he is shown in this form leading the deceased into the presence of Osiris.

Tjebet. Lit., "Sandal-Town." Antaeopolis, in the 13th *nome* (or district) of Upper Egypt.

Tjeni. The ancient Egyptian city also called This. An important political and religious center in early Egyptian history. Its geographical location is not known.

Two Lands. A common name for ancient Egypt, referring to the North (the Delta) and the South (the Nile Valley from the Delta to Elephantine in southern Egypt).

Unwearying Stars. Stars that rise above and set below the horizon in seasonal patterns, as compared with the circumpolar stars, which never set.

uraeus. The cobra portrayed on the brow of a deity or member of the royal family (see *werret*-crown).

verso. The side of a sheet or roll of papyrus on which the fibers of the top layer lie vertically. The verso was usually uninscribed and thus served as the outside of an inscribed roll of papyrus.

vignette. An illustration accompanying the texts on a papyrus roll.

wab-**priest.** A "purification" priest who was associated with the embalming ritual. Such priests also served in temples, where they played roles in purification rites in which water was used.

Wadjet. The personification of the damaged Eye of Horus made whole again, or the Right Eye of Re. As the latter, she is a protective goddess. The whole or complete eye, sometimes also called the Wadjet-eye, is associated with health, rejuvenation, and prosperity. Wadjet is often portrayed as a celestial cow. (See *Sound Eye*.)

wammty-**snake.** A snake associated with Apophis and fire in a number of texts. Found in the Amduat as well.

Weary Ones. A term used to designate the dead.

Wenet. Chief goddess of the 15th *nome* (or district) of Upper Egypt.

Wennefer. A name of Osiris or perhaps originally an epithet used of the god, particularly in his divinized form having triumphed over his enemies.

Wensy. Place name in the 19th *nome* (or district) of Upper Egypt.

Wenu. See *Hermopolis.*

Wepwawet. A jackal-headed god associated with the cemetery and, thus, the Netherworld. His name means "Opener of the Ways." In funerary literature he guides the deceased in the Netherworld by clearing paths for him upon which to travel.

werret-**crown.** A crown worn by gods including Osiris and by goddesses associated with the Eye of Re. A characteristic feature of the crown was a *uraeus* designed to induce fear in anyone who looked at it.

West. Eulogism for both the necropolis and the Netherworld; the realm of the Blessed Dead, i.e., those who have passed judgment.

Wetenet. A site in Nubia or possibly Punt.

White Crown. Crown of the king as ruler of Upper Egypt.

Xoïs. The Greek name of the ancient city of Khasut, located in the Nile Delta.

A Brief Chronology
of Ancient Egypt

This chronology is intended to help readers navigate the vast tract of time known as ancient Egyptian history. The chronology outlines the development of Egyptian civilization through its many periods and comments briefly on the historical features of each principal era. Egyptologists divide ancient Egyptian history into twelve major periods. Over the centuries, periods of strong central government, or kingdoms, alternate with "intermediate" eras of weaker central authority and reliance on local rule.

Prehistoric Period
Neolithic Period; Omari Culture, Maadi Culture
c. 5000–4400 BCE

People lived in farming settlements. Nearly nothing is known of the political system.

Predynastic Period
Badarian Period, Naqada Period, and Dynasty 0
c. 4400–3000 BCE

The Predynastic Period witnessed the earliest villages in Egypt in prehistoric times, and it stretched to the very beginnings of recorded history in Dynasty 0 about 1,400 years later. At first, Egyptians experienced numerous localized cultures. Archaeological evidence indicates the beginnings of international trade with the Near East and Nubia and the first writing in Dynasty 0.

Early Dynastic Period
Dynasties 1 and 2
c. 3000–2675 BCE

Upper and Lower Egypt (i.e., southern and northern Egypt) were unified during the First and Second Dynasties. Monumental architecture appeared in tombs, and King Narmer founded the national capital at Memphis.

Old Kingdom
Dynasties 3 through 6
c. 2675–2130 BCE

Often called the Age of the Pyramids, the Old Kingdom witnessed the centralization of political power in Memphis, the national capital. King Djoser completed construction of history's first stone buildings, at Saqqara. The peak of this centralized power came in the reigns of Khufu, Khafre, and Menkaure, Fourth Dynasty kings who built their pyramids at Giza. Fifth and Sixth Dynasty kings allowed power to devolve gradually to the provinces, resulting in a new period of localized political control.

First Intermediate Period
Dynasty 7 through first half of Dynasty 11
c. 2130–2008 BCE

The First Intermediate Period included the last years of the Memphis royal house and the rise of rival kings of the Ninth and Tenth Dynasties in Herakleopolis, southwest of modern Cairo, and of the Eleventh Dynasty in Thebes. Local control was stronger than central government influence.

Middle Kingdom
Latter half of Dynasty 11 through Dynasty 13
c. 2008–after 1630 BCE

The Middle Kingdom was a period of high achievement in the arts, architecture, and letters. In the Eleventh Dynasty, political power remained in Thebes, the home of the ruling dynasty. In the Twelfth Dynasty, the seat of power shifted northward to Lisht, located southwest of modern Cairo. The Twelfth Dynasty was the apex of centralized power in the Middle Kingdom. The Thirteenth Dynasty witnessed the gradual infiltration of West Semitic-speaking peoples into the eastern Delta of the Nile and increased local control.

Second Intermediate Period
Dynasties 14 through 17
1630–1539/1523 BCE

Northern Egypt was dominated by western Semites called Hyksos from the Egyptian words meaning "Rulers of Foreign Lands." Native Theban princes ruled the south. Most of these dynasties overlap with each other in time.

New Kingdom
Dynasties 18 through 20
c. 1539–1075 BCE

Theban princes reasserted control over Egypt, founding the Eighteenth Dynasty. Pursuit of the defeated Hyksos rulers into the Near East resulted in long-term Egyptian interest in dominating the area. Expansion of Egyptian borders also occurred to the south, into modern-day Sudan. Kings grew rich and patronized vast architectural and artistic projects. For seventeen years near the end of the dynasty, a religious revolutionary and king named Akhenaten, together with his wife Nefertiti, worshipped only the sun-disk, which they called the Aten (the Amarna Period). After restoration of religious traditions, the Eighteenth Dynasty family was replaced by the Nineteenth and Twentieth Dynasty family of kings called Ramesses (the Ramesside Period). These kings maintained foreign possessions until the invasion of foreigners known as Sea Peoples. Egypt might have then lost its foreign possessions. The priests of Amun ruled southern Egypt.

Third Intermediate Period
Dynasties 21 through 25
c. 1075–656 BCE

This period witnessed overlapping local dynasties and kings of
foreign origin from both Libya and Nubia. The arts flourished in
this era.

Late Period
Dynasties 26 through 31
664–332 BCE

Though foreigners ruled the country at this time, Egyptian culture
was more likely to conquer them than be conquered. Libyans and
Persians alternated rule with native Egyptians, but traditional
conventions continued in the arts.

Ptolemaic Period
332–30 BCE

Alexander the Great conquered Egypt in 332 BCE. Following
his death, his general Ptolemy established a family dynasty
that ruled for three centuries. Egypt maintained a dual culture
encompassing both native Egyptian and Greek elements.

Roman and Byzantine Periods
30 BCE–642 CE

The Romans took control of Egypt in 30 BCE with the defeat of
the Egyptian navy of Cleopatra VII and Marc Antony at the Battle
of Actium. During the early years of Roman rule the country was
directly administered as the property of the emperor.

In the fourth century CE the Roman Empire split into two
halves and Egypt was part of the Eastern Roman Empire, ruled
from Constantinople (modern Istanbul). Egyptians increasingly
converted to Christianity and created art that reflected the
influence of the new religion.

Islamic Period
642 CE to Present

Arab Muslims conquered Egypt in 642 CE and founded the city
of Cairo in 969 CE. Subsequently, the Arabic language gradually
replaced ancient Egyptian, which disappeared in the eighteenth
century. Egypt became an important center of Islamic scholarship
in the medieval period. Today, Islam is the majority religion of
Egypt.

Picture Information

Fig. 1 Ptolemais Euergetis, Egypt, Roman Period, 177 CE
Papyrus, ink, $4 \times 8\frac{7}{8}$ in. (10.2×22.5 cm)
Brooklyn Museum; Bequest of Theodora Wilbour from the collection of her father, Charles Edwin Wilbour, 47.218.20

Fig. 2 (Photo: Brooklyn Museum; Bernard V. Bothmer)

Fig. 3 Sumenu, Egypt, New Kingdom, Dynasty 18, probably the reign of Amenhotep III, *c.* 1390–1352 BCE
Limestone, paint, $16 \times 8\frac{5}{8} \times 8\frac{5}{8}$ in. ($40.6 \times 22 \times 22$ cm)
Brooklyn Museum; Charles Edwin Wilbour Fund, 40.523

Fig. 4 Probably Saqqara, Egypt, New Kingdom, latter half of Dynasty 18 or first half of Dynasty 19, *c.* 1350–1250 BCE
Limestone, $12\frac{3}{8} \times 5\frac{5}{8}$ in. (31.3×14.4 cm)
Brooklyn Museum; Charles Edwin Wilbour Fund, 47.120.1

Fig. 5 Saqqara, Egypt, New Kingdom, late Dynasty 18–first half of Dynasty 19, *c.* 1319–1204 BCE
Limestone, $29 \times 16\frac{1}{4}$ in. (74.5×41.7 cm)
Brooklyn Museum; Charles Edwin Wilbour Fund, 37.31E

Fig. 6 From Nigel Strudwick and John H. Taylor, eds, *The Theban Necropolis: Past, Present, and Future* (London: British Museum Press, 2003), p. 8. © Trustees of the British Museum

Fig. 7 Satellite image, captured December 24, 2009
(Photo: © Apollo Mapping, LLC, courtesy of DigitalGlobe and enhanced by Apollo Mapping)

Fig. 8 Saqqara, Mastaba D43, Egypt, Old Kingdom, end of Dynasty 5, *c.* 2415–2350 BCE
Limestone, 17×29 in. (43.6×74.5 cm)
Brooklyn Museum; Charles Edwin Wilbour Fund, 37.25E

Fig. 9
Probably Bubastis, Egypt, Late Period, late Dynasty 26–early Dynasty 27, *c.* 570–510 BCE
Basalt; height: $18\frac{7}{8}$ in. (47.9 cm); base: $3 \times 7\frac{1}{4} \times 11$ in. ($7.6 \times 18.4 \times 27.9$ cm)
Brooklyn Museum; Charles Edwin Wilbour Fund, 37.36E

Fig. 10 Thebes, Egypt, New Kingdom, Early Dynasty 18, reign of Thutmose III, *c.* 1479–1425 BCE
Wood, pigment, $8\frac{7}{8} \times 15\frac{1}{4}$ in. (22.5×38.8 cm)
Brooklyn Museum; Charles Edwin Wilbour Fund, 48.27

Fig. 11 Tomb of Yepu, Thebes, Egypt, New Kingdom, late Dynasty 18–early Dynasty 19, *c.* 1332–1250 BCE
Limestone, $10\frac{3}{4} \times 24 \times 2\frac{5}{8}$ in. ($27.3 \times 61 \times 6.7$ cm)
Brooklyn Museum; Charles Edwin Wilbour Fund, 37.1487E

Fig. 12 Saqqara, Egypt, Old Kingdom, late Dynasty 5, *c.* 2371–2350 BCE
(Photo: Werner Forman/Art Resource)

Fig. 13 Tomb of Gua, Deir el-Bersha, Egypt, Middle Kingdom, Dynasty 12, *c.* 1938–1759 BCE
Wood, paint; length of inner coffin: $88\frac{1}{2}$ in. (224.9 cm)
British Museum, London
(Photo: © The Trustees of the British Museum)

Fig. 14 Probably Thebes, Egypt, Third Intermediate Period, second half of Dynasty 21–early Dynasty 22, *c.* 997–924 BCE
Papyrus, ink, $7\frac{3}{16} \times 8\frac{3}{16}$ in. (18.3×20.8 cm)
Brooklyn Museum; Charles Edwin Wilbour Fund, 37.899E

Fig. 15 Egypt, Late Period–Ptolemaic Period, 664–30 BCE
Linen, ink, $3\frac{9}{16} \times 40\frac{9}{16}$ in. (9×103 cm)
Brooklyn Museum; Charles Edwin Wilbour Fund, 37.902E

Figs 16, 17 Probably Tôd, Egypt, New Kingdom, Dynasty 19, *c.* 1292–1190 BCE
Papyrus, ink, pigment, $20\frac{1}{16} \times \frac{15}{16} \times 51\frac{1}{8}$ in. ($51 \times 2.4 \times 129.8$ cm)
Brooklyn Museum; Gift of Theodora Wilbour, 35.1448

Fig. 18 Tomb of Inherkau, Deir el-Medina Tomb 359, Egypt, New Kingdom, Dynasty 20, reigns of Ramesses III and IV, *c.* 1187–1150 BCE
(Photo: © Picture Finders Ltd./eStock Photo. All rights reserved)

Fig. 19 Possibly Thebes, Egypt, Third Intermediate Period, *c.* 1075–945 BCE
Papyrus, ink, $24\frac{1}{2} \times 13\frac{15}{16}$ in. (62.2×35.4 cm)
Brooklyn Museum; Charles Edwin Wilbour Fund, 37.1699E

Fig. 20 Possibly Thebes, Egypt, Roman Period, *c.* 2nd century CE
Papyrus, ink, $3\frac{3}{4} \times 5\frac{3}{16}$ in. (9.5×14.8 cm)
Brooklyn Museum; Charles Edwin Wilbour Fund, 37.898E

Fig. 21 Saqqara, Egypt, Ptolemaic Period, *c.* 1st century BCE
Linen, pigment, $44\frac{11}{16} \times 41\frac{5}{16} \times 1\frac{3}{16}$ in. ($113.5 \times 105 \times 3$ cm)
Brooklyn Museum; Charles Edwin Wilbour Fund, 37.1811E

Fig. 22 Egypt, New Kingdom, early Dynasty 18, *c.* 1500–1450 BCE
Limestone, $16\frac{7}{8} \times 8\frac{5}{16} \times 1\frac{5}{8}$ in. ($42.9 \times 21.1 \times 4.2$ cm)
Brooklyn Museum; Museum Collection Fund, 07.420

Fig. 23 Deir el-Medina, Egypt, New Kingdom, Dynasty 20, reign of Ramesses III, *c.* 1187–1156 BCE
Limestone, $16\frac{7}{8} \times 11\frac{3}{4} \times 3\frac{15}{16}$ in. ($42.8 \times 30 \times 7.7$ cm)
Brooklyn Museum; Charles Edwin Wilbour Fund, 80.113

Fig. 26 Probably Tôd, Egypt, New Kingdom, Dynasty 19, *c.* 1292–1190 BCE
Papyrus, ink, pigment, $20\frac{15}{16} \times \frac{15}{16} \times 51\frac{1}{8}$ in. ($51 \times 2.4 \times 129.8$ cm)
Brooklyn Museum; Gift of Theodora Wilbour, 35.1448

Fig. 27 Spectra of C-14 results from carbon-14 dating performed at the University of Arizona AMS laboratory in August 2009

Fig. 28 Thomas Hicks (American, 1823–1890). Oil on canvas, $39\frac{3}{4} \times 50\frac{1}{4}$ in. (101×127.6 cm). Brooklyn Museum; Gift of The New-York Historical Society, 48.191